Vault Reports Guide to Mastering Accounting

VAULT REPORTS™

TEAM

DIRECTORS
H.S. Hamadeh Samer Hamadeh Mark Oldman

EXECUTIVE EDITOR
Marcy Lerner

MANAGING EDITOR
Edward Shen

SENIOR WRITERS
Doug Cantor
Hans Chen
Michael Hasday
Elizabeth Morgan
Mat Johnson
Nikki Scott

LAYOUT PRODUCTION
Hans Chen
Robert Schipano
Jake Wallace

RESEARCH ASSISTANTS
Faisal Anwar
Alex Apelbaum
Stacy Cowley
Abigail Jackson
Sylvia Kovac
Shirley Lin
Austin Shau
Angela Tong

MARKETING
Archana Chand
Noah Zucker

WEB SITE DESIGN
James Ford

ADVERTISING
Kirsten Fragodt

VAULT REPORTS, INC.
80 Fifth Avenue
11th Floor
New York, NY 10011
212 366-4212
www.vaultreports.com

Vault Reports Guide to Mastering Accounting

STACY BROWN

Houghton Mifflin Company
Boston • New York 1998

Copyright © 1998 by Vault Reports, Inc. All rights reserved.

All information in this book is subject to change without notice. Vault Reports makes no claims as to the accuracy and reliability of the information contained within and disclaims all warranties. No part of this book may be reproduced or transmitted in any form or by any means, electronic or mechanical, for any purpose, without the express written permission of Vault Reports, Inc.

Vault Reports, and the Open Vault logo are trademarks of Vault Reports, Inc.

For information about permission to reproduce selections from this book, write to Permissions, Houghton Mifflin Company, 215 Park Avenue South, New York, New York 10003 or contact Vault Reports Inc., P.O. Box 1772, New York, New York 10011-1772, (212) 366-4212.

Library of Congress CIP Data is available.

ISBN 0-395-86173-X

Printed in the United States of America

KPT 10 9 8 7 6 5 4 3 2 1

ACKNOWLEDGEMENTS

First, I would like to give thanks to God for giving me this medium by which to share my knowledge to help others. Writing a book is an arduous task and one that could not be completed without both the criticism and support of my colleagues and my family. I would like to thank Chris, my mother, and my family for all of their love and support. I would also like to thank the staff at Vault Reports for their confidence in me and their patience in putting this guide together. Special thanks to Professor Carley and Kent McGuire for their much needed advice and direction.

Finally, special thanks to Robin Robinson, CPA for her creative, challenging problems that put some of the finishing touches on the book. Currently.completeing her PhD in Accounting/Taxation at Drexel University, she has taught tax and accounting at Drexel since 1992. Her time and effort was invaluable to this book.

Vault Reports greatly appreciates the efforts of the following: Marnie Cochran, Jake Wallace, Ed Shen, Marcy Lerner, Rob Schipano, David Chalfant, Megan Sercomb, Mark Hernandez, Glenn Fischer, Ravi Mahtre, Jay Oyakawa, and Lee Black.

Vault Reports Guide to Mastering Accounting

Contents

Introduction	1
Chapter 1: An Introduction to Accounting	3
Chapter 2: Three Fundamental Rules of Accounting	29
Chapter 3: The Six Steps to Stardom	57
Chapter 4: Cash, Accounts Receivable, and Marketable Securities	107
Chapter 5: Inventory	147
Chapter 6: Long-term Assets and Depreciation	185
Chapter 7: Liabilities and the Time Value of Money	219
Chapter 8: Bonds Payable and Leases	247
Chapter 9: Alternative Revenue Recognition and Income Tax	279
Chapter 10: The Statement of Cash Flows	303

VAULT REPORTS GUIDE TO MASTERING ACCOUNTING

INTRODUCTION

The purpose of this study guide is two-fold:

- To assist students in the development of a foundation based on fundamental accounting concepts that will serve as a basis for the application of accounting principles to new and different economic situations.

- To identify the complex issues surrounding key financial statement accounts and provide an approach for analyzing and solving the most difficult transactions.

This book is designed for use by both students seeking a better understanding of key accounting concepts or students with a solid understanding who want additional practice and/or preparation for an exam. If you are preparing for an exam make, this book your last stop to serve as a checklist for ensuring that you have mastered the most important issues.

Chapters 1 - 3 provide an overview of the fundamentals necessary for developing a solid basis upon which to build your knowledge of accounting concepts. In Chapter 4-9, we identify and simplify the major complexities in key balance sheet and income statement accounts. The last chapter covers the Statement of Cash Flows and gives you a "T-account Approach" for solving cash flow problems. Each chapter identifies and briefly explains the concepts behind the account addressed. This is followed by several illustrations and comprehensive examples of multiple or linked concepts.

As you navigate through the guide, you will notice the strong emphasis on mastering the fundamentals and always having an approach. We like to think of accounting as similar to the road of life because you need an approach and some basic fundamentals to successfully make it through. Whatever you want to do in life, you have to know how you're going to get there. That's your approach. Part of "getting there" is having some foundation upon which to build, whether it is advanced education or a certain amount of work experience. These are your fundamentals. Thus, if you can master the fundamentals and have a consistent approach to every problem, then you can master accounting.

We hope you enjoy using this book as an additional learning tool as much as we enjoyed writing it. For those of you who decide to pursue accounting as a major or a career, you will

Vault Reports Guide to Mastering Accounting

find that all you needed to know about financial accounting you learned in your introductory course! Good Luck!

Organization

Each chapter of this Vault Reports Study Guide begins with a brief overview of the concepts to be covered. The chapter then outlines and explains the concepts that will be critical to your success. Note the Vault Reports icons designed to help you navigate your way through the text. At the conclusion of each chapter, you will have the chance to test your knowledge with a section of Thrills, Chills, & Drills.

Key Concept: This icon marks the main ideas of the chapter, explained and supported with examples. These concepts should not be skipped, since they usually form the building blocks for future chapters. If you still have trouble with a key concept after reading a chapter, you should refer back to your text or seek help from your professor.

Commonly Tested Subject: This icon flags important ideas that often appear on exams. Be prepared!

Brownie Points: Once you have a firm understanding of the basics, you can add the bells and whistles. This icon flags some slightly advanced concepts that will earn you a little extra notice on an exam.

Difficult Terrain! While most economics is surprisingly straightforward, some topics can get a bit slippery. This icon will alert you to concepts that are easily misunderstood or confused. As with any difficult terrain, take your time and you'll be fine.

Key Terms: The most important terms in every chapter are defined in the Key Terms section. They can also be found in the glossary at the back of the book.

Thrills, Chills, and Drills: So how are you doing so far? Test yourself with Thrills, Chills, and Drills at the end of each chapter. This section is designed to test the Key Concepts of each chapter with 20 True/False questions, 20 multiple choice questions, and at least five longer questions. Answers and explanations are provided at the end of each chapter. Good luck!

Chapter 1

An Introduction to Accounting

Chapter 1: An Introduction to Accounting

Overview

Accounting is the process of **recording, processing, summarizing, and reporting** a series of **economic events** that affect the operations of a company. Accounting enables us to evaluate the total impact of those economic events upon a company's net worth over either a specified period of time or at a given point in time. One way to think about accounting is that it is the process of transforming a tangled mess of economic events into an easily understood set of financial statements. The key to beginning the accounting process is in identifying of the economic events that give rise to transactions. The rest of the process involves a set of methodical procedures that you will have mastered by the end of Chapter 3 of this book.

After completing this chapter, you should:

- Be able to classify an economic event
- Understand why financial statements are prepared and how they are used
- Have a general understanding of the rules for completing the accounting process
- Know about the four basic financial statements:
    1. balance sheets
    2. income statements
    3. statements of retained
    4. statements of cash flows

The concepts that this chapter covers form the foundation for a course in accounting. Be sure that you have mastered them before you move on, or you may run into difficulty when we tackle trickier subjects later.

Chapter 1: An Introduction to Accounting

Concepts

Types of economic events

As we have discussed, accounting is the process of recording, processing, summarizing and reporting a series of transactions that affect the operations of a company. In order to begin and complete the accounting process, it is necessary to understand and be able to identify what types of transactions should be recorded. Transactions that require recording are based on **economic events**: events that occur during the course of the entity's operations that have a financial impact on a company. We determine whether something constitutes a full-fledged economic event by referring to the **full disclosure principle**, which we cover in more detail in Chapter 2. There are four types of economic events, with examples of each shown in th table below.

	Frequent	**Infrequent**
Usual	Sales of merchandise Purchase of inventory	Effects of a strike Write-downs of receivables or inventories
Unusual	Foreign currency translations Purchase/sale of equipment	Natural Disasters Expropriations

Usual and frequent transactions are those transactions that occur in the normal course of business. Consider an example: for a clothing retailer, the purchase of goods as inventory for resale to consumers would be considered a usual and frequent transaction. On the other end of the spectrum, **unusual and infrequent** transactions, which are considered extraordinary in nature because they are both "abnormal" in nature and rare in occurrence. The other two types of economic events – **usual and infrequent** and **unusual and frequent** – are considered to be "in-between" the more extreme categories. These "in-between" events do not occur on a regular basis, but they are not rare in occurrence, either.

While the identification of an economic event determines whether a transaction should be recorded, classifying the event into the proper category determines *how* it should be recorded. The same event, in fact, might be classified differently by two different companies, because their operating environments vary so widely. For example, the purchase of office furniture by a wholesaler for resale would be a part of the company's inventory and therefore, classified as a usual and frequent transaction. In contrast, the purchase of office

Chapter 1: An Introduction to Accounting

furniture by a professional service corporation (like an accounting firm) would be classified as a usual, infrequent transaction, because the purchase would be considered a fixed asset purchase. As you will learn going through this guide, inventory and fixed assets are treated quite differently by accountants. (Inventory is initially recorded as a current asset on the balance sheet; it is then removed from the balance sheet and becomes an expense when it is sold. Fixed assets are initially recorded as non-current assets and are amortized as an expense over the useful life of the asset.) The correct identification and classification of an economic event are the first steps to its being properly presented in the company's financial statements.

Why We Prepare Financial Statements

Financial statements have a variety of different uses, depending on who uses them. The types of people who commonly use financial statements are:

- managers
- current and future investors
- current and future creditors
- financial analysts

Financial statements allow these users to make important decisions about a company. Managers may use financial statements to assess the overall profitability of its business segments and to determine how to allocate resources to those different segments – or even whether to dispose of a certain business segment altogether. Current investors may use financial statements when making decisions about whether to maintain, increase, or sell their financial interest in a company. Future investors may look at a company's financial statements to assess the potential return that an investment would bring. Current and future creditors use financial statements to assess the liquidity of a company, analyze its future cash flow, and then determine a company's ability to repay loans in a timely manner. Finally, financial analysts use financial statements to evaluate the company's place within its industry and to learn about the industry as a whole.

Chapter 1: An Introduction to Accounting

A Basic Overview of GAAP: Where Do All These Rules Come From?

Many of those who will look at a company's financial statements are "outsiders," i.e. individuals external to the company such as creditors and investors. Therefore, it is important that financial statements properly reflect the company's financial position, results of operations, and cash flows. Companies accomplish this by employing a uniform set of standards. These standards are called the **Generally Accepted Accounting Principles (GAAP)**, which are accepted accounting practices developed by accountants and businesses to define the guidelines and procedures of reporting economic events. These guidelines and procedures are issued as Statements and Interpretations by the Financial Accounting Standards Board (FASB). In addition, the American Institute of Certified Public Accountants issues Statements on Auditing Standards, which are required standards that must be followed by independent CPAs (certified public accountants) who audit the financial statements of a company. Independent auditors provide assurance to financial statement users that a company is properly presenting its financial statements in accordance with GAAP. Without these rules and regulatory bodies, financial statement users would not be able to make important decisions about a company. Consider the problems that would arise without uniform rules and regulations.

- How could an investor decide in which company to invest if two companies in the same industry were using two different methods of calculating their income?

- How could a financial analyst examine the historical performance of a company if it were changing its method of recognizing revenue every year?

The application of GAAP when preparing financial statements ensures that all information relevant to financial statement users is reported and that the information is both understandable and reliable. By ensuring that the required guidelines and procedures used are applied on a consistent basis, GAAP also ensures that financial information from different periods and across companies can be compared. Consistency requires that once a particular accounting procedure is adopted by a company, it is used from one accounting period to the next unless users are notified of a change in the notes to the financial statements. All of these elements — relevance, reliability, comparability, and consistency — mean that financial statements can help those who use them understand both the shape a company is in and the direction in which it is going.

Chapter 1: An Introduction to Accounting

Basic Overview of Financial Statements

There are four basic financial statements that provide financial statement users with the information they need to evaluate a company:

- balance sheet
- income statements
- statements of retained earnings
- statements of cash flows

In addition, a company's annual report is almost always accompanied by notes to the financial statements. The notes to the financial statements provide additional information about the numbers provided in the four basic financial statements. The footnotes section of the report usually begins with a summary of the significant accounting policies employed by the company. These footnotes are followed by supplementary information to specific accounts presented in the four basic financial statements. The following accounts generally have supplementary information in the footnotes to financial statements:

1. property, plant, and equipment
2. long-term debt
3. income taxes

The next four sections provide an overview of the four basic financial statements.

The Balance Sheet

The **balance sheet** presents the financial position of a company at a given point in time. It is comprised of three parts: assets, liabilities, and equity. **Assets** are the economic resources of a company. They are the resources that the company uses to operate its business, including cash, inventory, and equipment. A company normally obtains the resources it uses to operate its business by incurring debt, obtaining new investors, or through operating earnings. The **liabilities** section of the balance sheet presents the debts of the company. Liabilities are the claims that creditors have on the company's resources. The **equity** section of the balance sheet presents the net worth of a company, which equals the assets that the

Chapter 1: An Introduction to Accounting

company owns less the debts they owe to creditors. Equity can also be defined as the claims that investors have on the company's resources.

The following example shows the basic format of a balance sheet:

MEDIA ENTERTAINMENT, INC
Balance Sheet
December 31, 19XX

Assets		Liabilities	
Cash	203,000	Accounts Payable	7,000
Accounts Receivable	26,000		
Building	19,000	**Equity**	
		Common Stock	10,000
		Retained Earnings	231,000
Total Assets	248,000	**Total Liabilities & Equity**	248,000

Because a company can obtain resources from both investors and creditors, one must be able to distinguish between the two and understand why one type is classified as a liability and the other type is classified as equity. Companies incur debt to obtain the economic resources necessary to operate their businesses and promise to pay the debt back over a specified period of time. This promise to pay is fixed and is not based upon the operating performance of the company. Companies also seek new investors to obtain economic resources. However, in contrast to their agreements with creditors, they make no promises to pay investors back a specified amount over a specified period of time. Instead, companies promise investors a return on their investment that is often contingent upon a certain level of operating performance. Since an equity holder's investment is not guaranteed, it is more risky in nature than a loan made by a creditor. But if a company performs well, the return to investors is often higher. **The "promise-to-pay" element makes loans made by creditors a liability.** Accountants would say these loans are more "senior" than equity holdings. To demonstrate this seniority and the difference between creditors and investors we will use an example.

Example: Suppose that the Morris Company has been in business for 25 years. Unfortunately, it has been operating at a loss for the past 3 years. The company therefore decides to liquidate (end its operations) with $100,000 in assets. Now suppose that you made a $45,000 investment in the Morris Company five years ago; at the same time, Loan International Bank loaned Morris Co. $75,000. Since you are the only investor, and Loan International is the only creditor, the total claims on the assets are $120,000.

Chapter 1: An Introduction to Accounting

In this example, Loan International Bank would receive the full $75,000 it is owed. You would receive $25,000, as there are only $100,000 in available assets. Moreover, if the Morris Company had assets only worth $50,000, Loan International Bank would receive the full $50,000 and you would receive nothing. The bank's loans are more "senior" than your equity.

Here are some tips on determining whether a transaction involving the receipt of economic resources should be classified as a liability or as an equity investment:

- If the transaction says someone "invested" or "issued stock," it is an equity investment
- If the transaction says someone "loaned" or "borrowed" or "issued debt," it is a liability

To summarize, the balance sheet represents the economic resources of a business, including the claims that creditors and equity holders have on those resources. Debts owed to creditors are more senior than the stake held by equity holders and are classified as liabilities. Equity investments are accounted for in the equity section of the balance sheet.

The Income Statement

We have discussed two of the three basic ways by which a company obtains the economic resources necessary to operate its business: by incurring debt and by seeking new investors. A third way in which a company can obtain resources is through its own operations. The **income statement** presents the results of operations of a business over a specified period of time (e.g. one year, one quarter, one month) and is composed of revenues, expenses, and net income. **Revenue** is a source of income that normally arises from the sale of goods or services that the company is in business to sell. For example, when a retailer of rollerblades makes a sale, the sale is considered revenue. However, income may also come from other sources. For example, selling a business segment or a piece of capital equipment generates a type of revenue for a company. This type of income is considered a **gain** on sale. **Gains** are sources of income from peripheral or incidental transactions (i.e. all economic events that are not usual and frequent).

Expenses are the costs incurred by a business over a specified period of time to generate the revenues earned during that same period. For example, in order for a manufacturing company to sell a product, it must purchase the materials with which to make the product. In addition, that same company must pay people to both make and sell the product. The company must also pay salaries to the individuals who operate the business. These are all

Chapter 1: An Introduction to Accounting

types of expenses that a company can incur during the normal operations of the business. When a company incurs an expense outside of its normal operations, it is considered a loss. **Losses** are expenses incurred as a result peripheral or incidental transactions. The destruction of office equipment in a fire, for example, is a loss.

Incurring expenses and acquiring assets both involve the use of economic resources (i.e. cash or debt). This raises a dilemma. When is a purchase considered an asset and when is it considered an expense?

A purchase is considered an asset if it provides future economic benefit to the company. Expenses only relate to the current period. For example, monthly salaries paid to employees are for services that they have already provided to the company during the month. These are considered expenses. On the other hand, the purchase of a piece of manufacturing equipment is classified as an asset, as it will probably be used to manufacture a product for more than one accounting period.

The revenue earned minus expenses incurred for a specified period of time equals **net income**. As we discussed earlier, a company normally obtains the economic resources with which to operate its business from investors and/or creditors. The company then uses those resources to generate revenues and pay for the expenses associated with the revenue generation process. Net income provides feedback to investors and creditors about how the company used its economic resources. A positive net income number indicates a profit, while a negative net income number indicates that a company suffered a loss (called a "net loss"). A positive net income number also indicates that a company now has additional economic resources. The tabulation is shown on an **income statement**.

Here is an example of an income statement:

MEDIA ENTERTAINMENT, INC
Income Statement
(For the year ended December 31, 19XX)

Revenues		
Services Billed		100,000
Expenses		
Salaries and Wages	(33,000)	
Rent Expense	(17,000)	
Utilities Expense	(7,000)	(57,000)
Net Income		43,000

Chapter 1: An Introduction to Accounting

Net income (or net loss) is reflected in the equity section of the balance sheet in a "retained earnings" account, because it represents an increase or decrease in capital. Technically, shareholders are entitled to income earned from the use of their resources after all other debts have been paid. These additional resources can either be paid out to shareholders in the form of dividends or retained in the business and used for future operations.

To summarize, the income statement measures the success of a company's operations; it provides investors and creditors with information to determine the profitability and creditworthiness of the enterprise. We say that a company has earned net income when its total revenues exceed its total expenses. A company has a net loss when total expenses exceed total revenues. Net income (or net loss) is reflected in both the income statement and in the equity section of the balance sheet as an indication to shareholders of a change in capital.

The Statement of Retained Earnings

The **statement of retained earnings** is a reconciliation of the retained earnings account from the beginning to the end of the year. When a company earns income or declares dividends, payments to shareholders representing a return on capital, this information is reflected in the statement of retained earnings. Net income increases retained earnings. Net losses and dividend payments decrease retained earnings.

Here is an example of a basic statement of retained earnings:

MEDIA ENTERTAINMENT, INC
Statement of Retained Earnings
(For the year ended December 31, 19XX)

Retained Earnings, January 1, 19XX	$200,000
Plus: Net income for the year	43,000
	243,000
Less: Dividends declared	(12,000)
Retained Earnings, December 31, 19XX	$ 231,000

Chapter 1: An Introduction to Accounting

KEY CONCEPT

As you can probably tell by looking at this example, the statement of retained earnings does not provide new information not already reflected in other financial statements. Yet it does provide additional information about what a company's management is doing with the company's earnings. Management may be "plowing back" the company's net income into the business by retaining part or all of its earnings, or it may be distributing current and accumulated income to shareholders. Investors use this information to align their investment strategy with the strategy of a company's management. An investor interested in growth and returns on capital may be more inclined to invest in a company that "plows back" its resources into the company for the purpose of generating additional resources. Conversely, an investor interested in receiving current income is more inclined to invest in a company that pays quarterly dividend distributions to shareholders.

To summarize, the statement of retained earnings is a reconciliation of the retained earnings account; it provides additional information to financial statement users about why net capital increased or decreased during the period.

The Statement of Cash Flows

Recall that the income statement provides information about the economic resources involved in the operation of a company. However, the income statement does not provide information about the actual source and use of cash generated during its operations. This is because obtaining and using economic resources does not always involve cash. For example, suppose you ordered and received a new mountain bike in July from a store catalog — but didn't pay the bill until August. Although the store did not receive cash in July, the sale would still be considered July revenue. The **statement of cash flows** presents a detailed summary of all of the cash inflows and outflows during the period and is divided into three sections based on three types of activity:

- **cash flows from operating activities:** includes the cash effects of transactions involved in the determination of net income.
- **cash flows from investing activities:** involves items classified as assets in the balance sheet and includes the purchase and sale of equipment and investments
- **cash flows from financing activities:** includes the payment of dividends as well as the issuance and payment of debt or equity

Chapter 1: An Introduction to Accounting

Here is an example of the basic format of the statement of cash flows:

MEDIA ENTERTAINMENT, INC
Statement of Cash Flows
For the year ended December 31, 19XX

Cash flows provided from operating activities		
Net Income		33,000
Depreciation Expense		10,000
Increase in Accounts Receivable	(26,000)	
Increase in Accounts Payable	7,000	(19,000)
Net cash provided by operating activities		24,000
Cash flows provided from investing activities		
Purchase of Building	(19,000)	
Sale of Long-Term Investment	35,000	
Net cash provided by investing activities		16,000
Cash flows provided from financing activities		
Payment of Dividends	(12,000)	
Issuance of Common Stock	10,000	
Net cash provided by financing activities		(2,000)
Net increase (decrease) in cash		38,000
Cash at the beginning of the year		165,000
Cash at the end of the year		203,000

KEY CONCEPT

Just as the statement of retained earnings is a reconciliation of the retained earnings account, the statement of cash flows is a reconciliation of the cash account and presents the details of the net increase or decrease in a company's cash. By presenting the net changes in cash, the statement of cash flows provides information about a company's liquidity, solvency, and financial flexibility. **Liquidity** refers to how "near to cash" (easily convertible into cash) a company's assets and liabilities are. **Solvency** refers to a company's ability to pay off its debts as they mature. Finally, **financial flexibitlity** refers to a company's ability to react to adverse or unexpected financial situations.

As you can tell by looking at the example above, the statement of cash flows is related to and relies upon information from all three of the other financial statements.

- Net income from the income statement is shown in the section devoted to cash flows from operating activities.

Chapter 1: An Introduction to Accounting

- Dividends from the statement of retained earnings are shown in the section dealing with cash flows from financing activities.

- Investments, accounts payable, and other asset and liability accounts from the balance sheet are shown in all three sections.

Because this statement is a compilation of information from the other three basic financial statements, we will cover the statement of cash flows last in Chapter 10. For now, it is sufficient to understand that the statement of cash flows presents information about the sources and uses of a company's cash. It is complex because it integrates all three of the other financial statements. At the same time, it is valuable because it provides information to financial statement users to help them analyze a company's liquidity, solvency, and financial flexibility.

Chapter 1: An Introduction to Accounting

Key Terms

accounting: the process of recording, processing, summarizing, and reporting a series of economic events that affect the operations of a company. Accounting evaluates the total effect of those economic events on a company's net worth over a specified period of time or at a given point in time.

assets: the economic resources of a company.

balance sheet: one of the four basic financial statements. The balance sheet presents the financial position of a company at a given point in time; it is comprised of three parts: assets, liabilities, and equity.

economic events: events that occur during the course of a company's operations that have a financial impact on it. There are four categories of economic events. The identification and classification of economic events determines both how and when a transaction is recorded.

equity: the claims that investors have on a company's resources.

expenses and losses: costs incurred by a business over a specified period of time to generate the revenues earned during that same period of time.

income statement: one of the four basic financial statements. The income statement presents the results of the operation of a business over a specified period of time (e.g. one year, one quarter, one month) and is composed of revenues, expenses, and net income.

liabilities: the claims that creditors have on the company's resources, including its assets.

liquidity: how "near to cash" a company's assets and liabilities are.

revenue and gains: income earned by the company over a specified period of time.

Chapter 1: An Introduction to Accounting

statement of cash flows: one of the four basic financial statements. The statements of cash flows presents a detailed summary of all of the cash inflows and outflows during a specified period and is divided into three sections: operating activities, investing activities, and financing activities.

statement of retained earnings: one of the four basic financial statements.

Chapter 1: An Introduction to Accounting

Thrills, Chills and Drills

True or False

1. Accounting is defined as the process of recognizing, processing, summarizing, and reporting a series of economic events that affect the operations of a company.

2. The primary purpose of the accounting process is to enable readers of financial statements to evaluate the individual effects of economic events on a company's net worth.

3. In order for an event to be classified as an economic event, it must occur during the course of the company's operations and have a financial impact upon it.

4. Economic events are categorized by how usual and frequent they occur during the normal course of business (for a specific industry and geographic location).

5. Transactions that occur during the normal course of business are classified as usual and infrequent transactions.

6. The same transaction may be classified differently by two different companies (and therefore receive a different accounting treatment), depending upon the companies' operating environments.

7. The treatment of a transaction in the accounting process is determined by the identification and classification of an economic event.

8. Financial statements provide those who use them with information about an entity's operations so they can make informed business decisions.

9. GAAP stands for Generally Accepted Accountant Principles.

10. The purpose of independent auditors is to provide assurance to financial statement users that a company's financial records are free of errors.

11. Consistency requires that once a company adopts a particular accounting procedure, it must be used from one accounting period to the next and can never be changed.

12. The four basic financial statements are the balance sheet, income statement, statement of related earnings, and statement of cash flows.

13. The balance sheet presents the financial position of a company over a specified period of time.

Chapter 1: An Introduction to Accounting

14. The income statement presents the results of operations of a business at a given point in time.

15. The terms "revenues" and "gains" (like "expenses" and "losses") are interchangeable.

16. The income statement provides information about the source and use of actual cash generated during a company's operations.

17. The statement of cash flows is divided into three sections — operations, investments, and financing — based on the type of activities being described.

18. A company's liquidity, solvency, and financial flexibility can be determined by analyzing the financial statements.

Multiple Choice

1. Choose the correct sequence of steps in the accounting process.
    a) recording, summarizing, processing, and reporting
    b) processing, summarizing, recording, and reporting
    c) recording, processing, summarizing, and reporting
    d) reporting, processing, summarizing, and recording
    e) none of the above
    f) all of the above

2. An economic event can be
    a) frequent and usual
    b) frequent and unusual
    c) infrequent and usual
    d) infrequent and unusual
    e) none of the above
    f) all of the above

3. An example of an infrequent and unusual economic event is
    a) the sale of merchandise
    b) the effects of a strike
    c) the purchase of equipment
    d) a natural disaster
    e) none of the above

Chapter 1: An Introduction to Accounting

4. An example of a frequent and usual economic event is
   a) the write-down of inventory
   b) expropriations
   c) foreign currency translations
   d) the purchase of inventory
   e) none of the above

5. Examples of frequent and unusual economic events and infrequent and usual economic events are
   a) sale of merchandise and natural disaster
   b) foreign currency translations and the effects of a strike
   c) write-down of inventory and sale of equipment
   d) expropriation and purchase of inventory
   e) none of the above

6. Identify the false statement.
   a) Management uses financial statements to assess the overall profitability of its business segments.
   b) Current investors use financial statements to manage their investment portfolios.
   c) Future investors use financial statements to assess potential returns.
   d) Creditors use financial statements to assess the liquidity of a company.
   e) Analysts use financial statements to compare companies to one another and to industry standards.
   f) All are true.

7. Which statement is not true?
   a) GAAP stands for Generally Accepted Accounting Principles.
   b) GAAP are accepted accounting practices developed by accountants and businesses that define the guidelines and procedures of reporting economic events.
   c) GAAP are issued as Statements and Interpretations of the FASB.
   d) Independent auditors provide assurance to financial statement users that a company properly presents its financial statements in accordance with GAAP.
   e) All are true.

Chapter 1: An Introduction to Accounting

For Questions 8-23, match the following terms with their definitions.

Terms

8. Assets
9. Liabilities
10. Equity
11. Revenue
12. Expenses
13. Gains/Losses
14. Cash flow from operations
15. Cash flow from investing
16. Cash flow from financing
17. Liquidity
18. Solvency
19. Financial flexibility
20. Balance sheet
21. Income statement
22. Statement of retained earnings
23. Statement of cash flows

Definitions

a) Costs incurred over a specified period of time to generate revenues earned during the same period.
b) Ability to pay debts as they mature.
c) Economic resources of a company.
d) Involves items classified as assets in the balance sheet.
e) How "near to cash" a company's assets and liabilities are.
f) Claims investors have on the company's resources.
g) Involves items classified as liabilities and owners' equity in the balance sheet.
h) Cash effects of transactions involved in determining net income.
i) Company's ability to react to adverse or unexpected financial situations.
j) Presents the financial position of a company at a given point in time.
k) Presents a detailed summary of all cash inflows and outflows during a given period.
l) Reconciliation of earnings from the beginning and the end of a year.
m) Source of income from sale of goods or services.
n) Claims creditors have on the company's resources.
o) Sources of income or expenses from peripheral or incidental transactions.
p) Presents the results of the operation of a business over a specified period of time.

Chapter 1: An Introduction to Accounting

Short Essays

1. Classify each of the following economic events as frequent and usual, frequent and unusual, infrequent and usual, or infrequent and unusual.

   a. natural disasters

   b. purchase of inventory

   c. purchase of equipment

   d. write-downs of receivables

   e. effects of a strike

   f. sale of equipment

   g. expropriations

   h. sale of merchandise

   i. foreign currency translations

   j. inventory write-downs

2. What is the difference between Statements and Interpretations by FASB and the AICPA's Statements on Auditing Standards?

3. Captain Cable Company owes its creditors $10,000. The company expects to receive $30,000 from its customers. During the last year, the company issued $20,000 in common stock. The cash account has a balance of $205,000 on 12/31/xx. The company had prior earnings of $300,000. The company's building originally cost $95,000. Prepare a balance sheet in good form.

4. Captain Cable Company billed its customers for $100,000 worth of services during the year. The company paid the following expenses during the year: utilities, $20,000; salaries and wages, $40,000; advertising, $10,000. Prepare an income statement in good form.

Chapter 1: An Introduction to Accounting

5. Captain Cable Company had net income for the year of $30,000. The company paid $20,000 in dividends. Prior earnings totaled $290,000. Prepare a statement of retained earnings in good form.

6. Captain Cable Company purchased a building for $38,000. The company had net income of $86,000. The value of common stock issued was $20,000. Accounts receivable increased by $52,000. The company sold $70,000 worth of long-term investments. Accounts payable increased by $14,000. The company paid $24,000 worth of dividends. Prepare a statement of cash flows.

7. Explain how the financial statements are interrelated.

Chapter 1: An Introduction to Accounting

Answers

True or False Answers

1. **False.** Although the key to beginning the accounting process is the identification of the economic events that give rise to transactions, the accounting process itself involves recording, processing, summarizing, and reporting.

2. **False.** The individual effects of economic events that impact the company's financial statements are the transactions that are recorded in the accounting records. The primary goal of accounting is to provide information about how a company has performed over a specified period of time, or about its performance at a given point in time.

3. **True.**

4. **True.**

5. **False.** Usual and infrequent transactions (along with unusual and frequent transactions) are the two types of economic events that are considered the "in-betweens." These events either do not occur on a regular basis even though they are common business events (strikes), or occur on a regular basis and are uncommon transactions (foreign currency translations). Usual and frequent transactions occur in the normal course of business (sale of inventory).

6. **True.**

7. **True.**

8. **True.**

9. **False.** GAAP stands for Generally Accepted Accounting Principles.

10. **False.** Independent auditors can assure only that a company is properly presenting its financial statements in accordance with GAAP. Independent auditors conduct tests on a sample of the company's records based on their impact on the financial statements.

11. **False.** Consistency allows for changes of accounting procedures that are justified, provided that they are described in the notes to the financial statements.

12. **False.** "Retained" earnings, not "related" earnings.

13. **False.** The balance sheet presents the financial position of a company at a given point in time -e.g., "as of December 31, 19xx".

14. **False.** The Income Statement presents the results of operations of a business over a specified period of time - e.g., "for the year ended December 31, 19xx".

15. **False.** Revenues (and expenses) occur in the normal course of business, while gains (and losses) arise from peripheral or incidental transactions.

16. **False.** Information about the source and use of actual cash generated during a company's operations is provided by the statement of cash flows.

17. **True.**

18. **True.**

Chapter 1: An Introduction to Accounting

Multiple Choice Answers

1. (c) The correct sequence is recording, processing, summarizing, and reporting.
2. (f) All of the above.
3. (d) C is frequent and usual, b is infrequent and usual, c is frequent and usual.
4. (d) A is infrequent and usual, b is infrequent and unusual, c is frequent and unusual.
5. (b) A is frequent and usual, and infrequent and unusual, c is infrequent and usual, and frequent and usual, d is infrequent and usual, and frequent and usual.
6. (f) All are true.
7. (e) All are true.

Answers to Questions 8 - 23 come from the definitions described in the chapter:

8. (c)
9. (n)
10. (f)
11. (m)
12. (a)
13. (o)
14. (h)
15. (d)
16. (g)
17. (e)
18. (b)
19. (l)
20. (j)
21. (p)
22. (l)
23. (k)

Short Essay Answers

1.

	frequent	infrequent
usual	B & H	D, E, & J
unusual	C, F, & I	A & G

Chapter 1: An Introduction to Accounting

2. Statements and Interpretations of FASB are the guidelines and procedures for reporting economic events developed by accountants and businesses, commonly known as GAAP. Statements on Auditing Standards issued by the AICPA are the standards that must be followed by independent CPAs who audit the financial statements of a company, commonly known as GAAS.

3.

CAPTAIN CABLE COMPANY
Balance Sheet
As of December 31, 19XX

Assets		Liabilities	
Cash	$205,000	Accounts Payable	$10,000
Accounts Receivable	$30,000	Total Liabilities	$10,000
Building	$95,000		
		Owner's equity	
		Common Stock	$20,000
		Retained Earnings	$300,000
		Total Equity	$320,000
Total Assets	$330,000	Total Liabilities and Owners' Equity	$330,000

4.

CAPTAIN CABLE COMPANY
Income Statement
For the year ended December 31, 19XX

Revenue		$100,000
Less: Salaries & Wages	$40,000	
Advertising	$10,000	
Utilities	$20,000	
Total Expenses		($70,000)
Net Income		$30,000

5.

CAPTAIN CABLE COMPANY
Statement of Retained Earnings
For the year ended December 31, 19XX

Retained Earnings, January 1, 19XX	$290,000
Plus: Net Income	$30,000
	$320,000
Less: Dividends	($20,000)
Retained Earnings, December 31, 19XX	$300,000

Chapter 1: An Introduction to Accounting

6.

Captain Cable Company
Statement of Cash Flows
For the year ended December 31, 19XX

Cash Flows from Operations:
Net Income		$86,000
Deduct: non-cash expenses & revenues included in net income		
Increase in accounts receivable	($52,000)	
Increase in accounts payable	$14,000	
Net cash provided by operating activities		($38,000)

Cash Flows from Investing:
Purchase of building	-38,000	
Sale of L/T Investment	70,000	
Net cash provided by investing activities		$32,000

Cash Flows from Financing:
Payment of dividends	($24,000)	
Issuance of stock	20,000	
Net cash provided by financing activities		($4,000)

Net Increase (decrease) in cash	$76,000
Cash at the beginning of the year	$330,000
Cash at the end of the year	$406,000

7.

Balance Sheet	Income Statement
Assets = Liabilities + Owners' Equity	Revenues - Expenses = Net Income

Statement of Cash Flows	Statement of Retained Earnings
<u>Operations:</u>	Retained Earnings, 1/1/XX
Net Income	Plus Net Income
Minus increase in receivables	Minus Dividends
Plus increase in payables	Equals Retained Earnings, 12/31/XX
<u>Investments:</u>	
Minus asset purchases	
Plus investment sales	
<u>Financing:</u>	
Minus dividends paid	
Plus stock issuance	

Chapter

Three Fundamental Rules of Accounting

2

Chapter 2: Three Fundamental Rules of Accounting

Overview

The accounting process requires both an understanding of the fundamental concepts that underlie every type of transaction and the ability to apply those concepts using a systematic method. Before we begin the application process in Chapter 3, we will outline and explain three important fundamental concepts.

1. It is necessary to understand the four basic principles of accounting to be able to A) identify an event that necessitates recording a transaction and B) determine the appropriate accounting for that transaction.

2. There is a fundamental accounting equation that must **always** be followed:

    Assets = Liabilities + Shareholders Equity

3. Net income flows to the balance sheet through retained earnings.

This chapter wil complete the foundation of our introductory accounting course. In the next chapter, we will introduce a methodical approach to recording transactions (the Journal Entry approach). But without the basics that we are covering here, that method will make little sense.

Chapter 2: Three Fundamental Rules of Accounting

Concepts

The Four Basic Principles...In Plain English

Full Disclosure Principle

In Chapter I, we explained that certain events occurring during the course of business give rise to an accounting transaction. The **full disclosure principle** serves as a guideline for determining exactly which events should be reported in a company's financial statements. For example, a company should report all of the following events:

- the sale of a piece of machinery
- the purchase of materials
- the retirement of debt
- information regarding a pending lawsuit

The **full disclosure principle** suggests that accountants follow the general practice of disclosing **material events**, which are events that could potentially influence the judgment and decisions of the informed user. The degree of potential influence directly affects the degree of disclosure. For example, consider information regarding a pending lawsuit against a company. If the outcome is not yet known the information would be disclosed in a footnote to the financial statements. However, if a loss is probable and the dollar amount of damages can be reasonably estimated, the loss must be shown within the main body of the company's financial statements. While knowledge about pending lawsuits is important to financial statement users, the dollar amount of a loss that a corporation has already sustained has greater likelihood of influencing the decision of a user. We can summarize the application of the full disclosure principle as follows:

- As a financial statement user, would disclosure of the event provide a better understanding of the financial position or results of operations of the company?
- If so, is the dollar amount reasonably estimable and does it have a material impact on the accuracy of the financial statements?

Chapter 2: Three Fundamental Rules of Accounting

Application of this test will ensure the successful completion of the first step in the accounting process: the identification of events that require recording a transaction. Here are some transactions commonly used in test questions that must be recorded in the financial statements:

- Transactions involving the sale of items that a corporation is in business to sell.

- Transactions involving the purchase of items used to help a corporation to sell its product or service.

- Transactions involving the purchase or sale of items that increase the long-term value of a corporation.

- Transactions involving the receipt of cash or other type of asset from an outsider (e.g. a bank or investor).

Historical Cost Principle

Generally accepted accounting principles require that most assets and liabilities be accounted for and reported on the basis of **acquisition cost.** This requirement is referred to as the **historical cost principle**. The historical cost principle provides a basis with which to present a company's balance sheet. Understanding this principle is the key to determining how to record transactions that affect balance sheet accounts. Although this principle may appear to be simple, determining acquisition cost is not always as easy as it seems. For example, determining the acquisition cost of a piece of equipment involves more than just finding out the manufacturer's price of the equipment. Other costs are included, such as freight, insurance, and installation costs. Inventory also includes costs other than the costs of the materials. The elements of acquisition cost of inventory and fixed assets will be covered in greater detail in later chapters.

Using historical cost (aquisition cost) to value assets and liabilities provides a stable and consistent benchmark that financial statement users can use to analyze a company's financial statements. However, the historical cost principle is not always the most informative method of valuing balance sheet items. When the value of assets increase or decrease due to changes in inflation or the market, these fluctuations are not reflected in the balance sheet — since the balance sheet reflects only the historical cost. As a result, there are some balance sheet items that are recorded at current market value because the current value provides more useful information to financial statement users about a company's financial position than a historical cost figure. The most important of these exceptions is the

Chapter 2: Three Fundamental Rules of Accounting

valuation of a company's long-term and short-term investments in debt and equity securities. Other balance sheet items valued on principles other than historical cost include:

- **inventory:** valued at the lower of either cost or market value
- **accounts receivable:** valued at net realizable value

These different valuation techniques will be covered in later chapters. For now, just remember the following key questions when determining the acquisition cost of a balance sheet item.

For **assets**: What is the cost to make this item ready and available for use in the company?

For **liabilities**: What is the "agreed upon" price at which the company is incurring the liability?

Revenue Recognition Principle

While the historical cost principle provides a basis for determining how to record transactions affecting the balance sheet, the revenue recognition principle provides a basis for determining how to record transactions affecting income statement accounts. The **revenue recognition principle** establishes the guideline that revenue should be recognized and recorded when it is 1) **realized** or **realizable** and 2) **earned** — which is generally at the time of sale. These two key elements are defined as follows:

1. a. Revenue is **realized** when goods or services are exchanged for cash or claims to cash.

   b. Revenue is **realizable** when goods or services are saleable in an active market at readily determinable prices (and without significant additional cost) in exchange for cash or claims to cash.

2. Revenues are considered **earned** when the company has "substantially completed" everything that it must do to be entitled to the revenue.

The first of these two tests is the easiest to apply. When XYZ company completes production of its product, and the product becomes a finished good, revenue is realizable. When a customer calls the local telephone company and requests that service be connected to his or her home, revenue is realized. In other words, as long a company has a product or service ready to sell, revenue is realizable. If someone agrees to buy that product or service, then revenue is realized.

Chapter 2: Three Fundamental Rules of Accounting

Determining when revenue is earned is somewhat more difficult. The company must "substantially complete" everything it must do to be entitled to the revenue. "Substantially complete" is a vague phrase and many companies today still dispute what they must do to substantially complete a sale. Even though XYZ company completed the production of its product, it has not earned any revenue, because no one has agreed to buy it. If someone agreed to buy the product under the condition that the product be delivered to Alaska, the company still will not earn any revenue until the product is delivered to Alaska. Similarly, simply because a customer wants a telephone line connected to his or her home, the telephone company cannot recognize any revenue until the telephone line is connected. In both of these situations, the two companies must provide additional service to the customer before they actually "earn" the revenue.

Recognizing revenue at the time of sale provides a uniform test that can be applied to all types of companies in a variety of industries. However, as with the historical cost principle, there are occasions when we use other criteria. Here are some of those exceptions.

During production: With certain long-term construction contracts, revenue recognition is allowed before production is complete based on the percent of the job complete. A quick example helps explain why this type of recognition is allowed. Suppose that a company has a three-year contract. If the revenue recognition principle were applied as usual, it would appear as though the company did not make a profit in the first two years and then made a huge profit in the third. Recognition during production allows a company to smooth out its earnings over the period the services are being performed even though the sale may not be complete until the end of the project.

End of production: In other situations, revenue may be recognized after production is complete but before the sale takes place. This can only occur when the selling price and the amount are certain. This sometimes occurs with mining for certain minerals, such as copper. Once mined, a readily available market exists for copper at a standard price.

Cash basis: In still other situations, revenue is recognized only when the actual cash is received (as opposed to the example of the credit card sale of the bicycle). This method is generally used only when collectibility of the cash is uncertain at the time of sale.

Proper recognition of revenue will be covered in greater detail in Chapter 9. For now, here are some tips for determining whether revenue that is realized or realizable has actually been earned.

- Is the company required to deliver the product at their expense? If so, is the delivery complete?
- Is the sale contingent on performance of some additional future services? If so, have those services been performed?

Chapter 2: Three Fundamental Rules of Accounting

Matching Principle

The matching principle provides a basis for determining how to record transactions affecting expense accounts in the income statement. The **matching principle** dictates that expenses are matched with revenues in the period that the revenues are earned. In other words, "expenses follow revenues." The primary justification for this principle is that expenses incurred while generating a product or service for sale should be recognized in the period in which the product or service is actually sold. However, this principle can only apply to certain types of costs. These types of costs are called **product costs**, which are defined as costs associated with the production of the product. Product costs include materials, labor, and overhead. Since product costs are associated in some way with the production of the product, it is easy to "match" them with the revenue earned from the sale of that product.

Period costs are costs incurred during a period that have no direct relationship with the revenue earned; these include officers' salaries and other general administrative expenses. Since these costs are not associated with the production of the product or service, they cannot be effectively matched in the period the revenues is earned. Instead, they are recognized immediately in the period incurred.

There is still a third type of cost: product costs that benefit more than one product and/or more than one revenue generating period. Consider a manufacturing company that has a machine that has a useful life of six years and produces 1,000 products per year. The machine will generate revenue for more than one year. In addition, each product sold benefits equally from the machine. Therefore, the cost of the machine will be "matched" with revenues by being systematically allocated over the useful life of the machine or over all of the products produced through a method of **depreciation**. The various depreciation methods will be covered in a later chapter. For now, follow these three steps to determine when to use the matching principle and how to record transactions involving expense accounts effectively:

- If the cost is associated with the production of the product (a product cost), "match" it and recognized it in the period in which the product is sold.

- If there is no determinable relationship between costs incurred during a period and the revenue earned from products sold (a period cost), recognize the expense immediately in the period incurred.

- If a relationship exists between the cost of the product and the revenue earned but the costs benefit more than one period or more than one product, allocate the costs systematically over the periods benefited or among the products produced.

Chapter 2: Three Fundamental Rules of Accounting

Assets = Liabilities + Equity (Always!)

Now that we have covered the fundamental accounting principles, we can turn to the fundamental accounting equation: Assets = Liabilities + Equity. The key to understanding this equation is to remember that debits must always equal credits. In accounting, the term **debit** means left, and the term **credit** means right. These terms are generated from the customary practice of recording debits on the left side of an account and credits on the right. The terms debit and credit do not mean increase or decrease in general because, depending on the type of account, the act of debiting an account could increase or decrease it. An **account** is a record of the increases, decreases, and balances of an individual asset, liability, capital, revenue, or expense (as opposed to overall assets, liabilities, etc.). The **double-entry accounting system** requires that both sides of each transaction be recorded in the appropriate account, meaning if one account is debited, another account must be credited in order to create a two-sided effect. If one account is debited while another account is credited every time a transaction is recorded, then the total debits will always equal total credits. Furthermore:

- All **asset** and **expense accounts** are increased on the debit side (the left side), decreased on the credit side (the right side), and normally **maintain debit balances.**

- All **liabilities, equity, income accounts** are increased on the credit side (the right side), decreased on the debit side (the left side), and normally **maintain credit balances.**

A good way to recall the places in which accounts increase and decrease is to remember that accounts increase on the same side that maintains its normal balance, as the table below summarizes:

Account Type	Normal Balance	Increase	Decrease
Asset	Debit	Debit	Credit
Expense	Debit	Debit	Credit
Liability	Credit	Credit	Debit
Equity	Credit	Credit	Debit
Income	Credit	Credit	Debit

Chapter 2: Three Fundamental Rules of Accounting

Asset accounts normally maintain debit balances — and liability and equity accounts normally maintain credit balances. If we couple these principles with the concept that total debits must always equal total credits, then we arrive at the rule that **assets must always equal liabilities plus equity**. This basic accounting equation is summarized by the following illustration:

Basic Equation	Assets	=	Liabilities	+	Stockholders Equity
Normal Balance	Debit		Credit		Credit

Expanded Basic Equation	Assets	=	Liabilities	+	Common Stock	+	Retained Earnings	
	Debit (Dr.) Increase	Credit (Cr.) Decrease	Debit (Dr.) Decrease	Credit (Cr.) Increase	Debit (Dr.) Decrease	Credit (Cr.) Increase	Debit (Dr.) Decrease	Credit (Cr.) Increase

	− (Expenses/Dividends)	+	Revenue
	Debit (Dr.) Increase / Credit (Cr.) Decrease		Debit (Dr.) Decrease / Credit (Cr.) Increase

Net Income Flows to the Balance Sheet through Retained Earnings

Look at the chart above carefully. Revenues and expenses have been included in the stockholders equity section of the basic accounting equation under retained earnings, with revenue appearing on the credit side and expenses appearing on the debit side. We have placed these accounts there because revenue increases retained earnings, and expenses decrease retained earnings. Recall from Chapter 1 that net income (or net loss) is reflected in the equity section of the balance sheet in the retained earnings account because it represents an increase or decrease in capital. This is because shareholders are entitled to income earned from the use of their resources after all other expenses have been paid. The additional resources (the net income) can either be paid out to shareholders in the form of dividends or retained in the business and used for future operations. Let's tackle this relationship between net income and the retained earnings account in three stages.

Step 1: Revenue

The account called "retained earnings" is increased when a company earns revenue because there is an additional inflow of resources. In addition, as the illustration above demonstrates, revenue and equity accounts normally maintain credit balances and therefore, increase on the credit side. Thus, in the financial statements, two things happen when a company earns revenue.

1. On the income statement, revenue increases, and the revenue account is increased on the credit side.

2. On the balance sheet, capital increases, and retained earnings is increased on the credit side.

Therefore, revenue is added (as an increase) to the retained earnings section of stockholders equity in the expanded accounting equation.

STEP 2: EXPENSES

Retained Earnings is decreased when a company incurs expenses because there is an outflow of resources. Furthermore, remember that expense accounts normally maintain debit balances and therefore increase on the debit side. However, since equity accounts normally maintain credit balances, they decrease on the debit side. Just as when a company earns revenue, two things happen when a company incurs expenses.

1. On the income statement, expenses increase and the expense account is increased on the debit side.

2. On the balance sheet, capital decreases and retained earnings is decreased on the debit side

Therefore, although expense accounts are increased when they are debited, expenses are deducted (as a decrease) from the retained earnings section of stockholders equity in the expanded accounting equation.

STEP 3: DIVIDENDS

Net income is reflected in (or "flows to") the balance sheet through retained earnings. Dividends paid to shareholders are not included in net income, because they are not considered expenses incurred during the course of a company's operations. Instead, dividends are considered a return on capital to shareholders. As we have discussed before, shareholders are entitled to any net income earned by the company and that income can either be retained in the company or paid out to shareholders. When payments are made to shareholders, they are made in the form of **dividends**. Just as net income increases a company's retained earnings and economic resources, the declaration of dividends directly reduces retained earnings and the amount of economic resources.

Chapter 2: Three Fundamental Rules of Accounting

KEY CONCEPT

To summarize, net income flows to the balance sheet through retained earnings because revenues increase retained earnings and expenses decrease retained earnings. When revenues exceed expenses, a company earns net income and, in effect, there is a net increase in retained earnings. When expenses exceed revenues, a company suffers a net loss and, in effect, there is a net decrease in retained earnings. Dividends are not considered expenses but are considered a return of capital, because shareholders have received a portion of the "retained earnings" from the company to which they are entitled.

Putting the Principles to Work: A Comprehensive Example

Let's put these fundamental concepts together by analyzing the effect of transactions upon the basic accounting equation. for a hypothetical company called Sports Agents, Inc.. Suppose that Sports Agents entered into the following transactions:

1. Issued common stock for $50,000 cash.
2. Purchased $4,000 in supplies on account.
3. Billed athletes $20,000 in commissions for services rendered.
4. Purchased office furniture for $10,000.
5. Received $14,000 for the services billed in #3.
6. Paid $750 for monthly utility bills.
7. Paid $4,000 for the supplies purchased in #2.
8. After taking inventory, realized that there were $3,000 in supplies remaining in storage.
9. Declared dividends of $5,000.

1. **Issued common stock for $50,000 cash.** In this transaction, Sports Agents received cash in exchange for common stock. The cash creates an economic resource and the investors now have a claim on those resources. Thus, assets increase by $50,000, and common stock increases by the same amount.

Assets	=	Liabilities	+	Equity	
Cash (Dr.) + $50,000				Common Stock (Cr.)	+ $50,000

Chapter 2: Three Fundamental Rules of Accounting

2. **Purchased $4,000 in supplies on account.** Here, Sports Agents received supplies but did not pay cash for them upon purchase. Instead, the company now owes its supplier for the supplies purchased. The supplies create an economic resource that can be used in the company's business, but the supplier has a claim on those resources until Sports Agents pay the bills. Thus, assets increase by $4,000, and liabilities increase by $4,000.

BROWNIE POINTS

TIP: Purchasing "on account" means that the company did not pay cash for the purchase and has a liability to pay later. Thus, purchases on account will always increase liabilities by increasing an account we will call "accounts payable."

Assets	=	Liabilities	+	Equity
Supplies (Dr.) + $4,000		Accounts Payable (Cr.) + $4,000		

3. **Billed athletes $20,000 in commissions for services rendered.** The company billed athletes for services rendered but did not receive cash. Since Sports Agents has already performed its services, the revenue has been earned. The athletes now owe Sports Agents $20,000 for their services. The amount owed is classified as a receivable in the asset section of the balance sheet because, once the money is received, it will create additional economic resources. The increase in revenue results in a corresponding increase in equity of $20,000.

BROWNIE POINTS

TIP: Billing for services or selling "on account" means that the company did not receive cash upon completion of the revenue earning process. Thus, sales on account and billings will always increase accounts receivable instead of cash.

Assets	=	Liabilities	+	Equity
Accounts Receivable (Dr.) + $20,000				Revenue (Cr.) + $20,000

4. **Purchased office furniture for $10,000.** Sports Agents used one economic resource (cash) to create another (fixed asset). Thus, assets decrease by $10,000 and simultaneously increase by $10,000. Note that the net effect of this transaction of the equation is zero.

Assets	=	Liabilities	+	Equity
Cash (Cr.) - $10,000				
Furniture (Dr.) + $10,000				

Chapter 2: Three Fundamental Rules of Accounting

5. **Received $14,000 for the services billed in #3.** This case is similar to #4 in that the transaction is simply an exchange of one economic resource for another. Here, cash is increased by $14,000 because previously billed services are actually paid. Correspondingly, accounts receivable is decreased by the same amount.

Assets	=	Liabilities	+	Equity
Cash (Cr.) + $14,000				
Accounts − $14,000				
Receivable (Cr.)				

6. **Paid $750 for monthly utility bills.** In this transaction, cash is being used to pay expenses incurred by Sports Agents during the normal operations of its business. Expenses are increased, meaning that equity is decreased (remember: when expenses are incurred, there is a reduction of capital). Therefore, assets decrease by $750, and equity decreases by $750 due to the outflow of resources.

Assets	=	Liabilities	+	Equity	
Cash (Cr.) − $750				Utilities Expense (Dr.)	− $750

7. **Paid $4,000 for the supplies purchased in #2.** Here Sports Agents is simply using its economic resources to pay off the previous debt it incurred to purchase supplies. As a result the supplier no longer has a claim on those resources. Thus, assets and liabilities both decrease by $4,000.

Assets	=	Liabilities	+	Equity
Cash (Cr.) − $4,000		Accounts Payable (Dr.) − $4,000		

8. **After taking inventory, realized that there were $3,000 in supplies remaining in storage.** In transaction #2, Sports Agents purchased $4,000 in supplies, thus creating $4,000 worth of economic resources. If only $3,000 in supplies remain in storage, then $1,000 must have been used in operations. The $1,000 supplies used represent expenses incurred during the period. Therefore, assets must be reduced by $1,000, and equity must be reduced by $1,000 to reflect this outflow of resources.

Assets	=	Liabilities	+	Equity	
Supplies (Cr.) − $1,000				Supplies Expenses (Dr.)	− $1,000

CHAPTER 2: THREE FUNDAMENTAL RULES OF ACCOUNTING

9. **Declared dividends of $5,000.** Recall that dividends are taken directly from retained earnings. In addition, since they have been declared but not paid, a liability has been created. As a result, equity decreases by $5,000, and liabilities increase by $5,000.

Assets	=	Liabilities	+	Equity	
		Dividend (Cr.) Payable (Cr.)	+ $5,000	Dividend Declared (Dr.)	- $5,000

The following is a summary of all transactions. Note that the basic accounting equation — total assets equals total liabilities plus total equity — remains balanced throughout.

Transaction	Assets		=	Liabilities		+	Equity	
1	Cash (Dr.)	+ $50,000					Common Stock (Cr.)	+ $50,000
2	Supplies (Dr.)	+ $4,000		Accounts Payable (Cr.)	+ $4,000			
3	Accounts Receivable (Dr.)	+ $20,000					Revenue (Cr.)	+ $20,000
4	Cash (Cr.)	- $10,000						
	Furniture (Dr.)	+ $10,000						
5	Cash (Dr.)	+ $14,000						
	Account Receivable (Dr.)	- $14,000						
6	Cash (Cr.)	- $750					Utilities Expense (Dr.)	- $750
7	Cash (Cr.)	+ $4,000		Accounts Payable (Dr.)	- $4,000			
8	Supplies (Cr.)	+ $1,000					Supplies Expense (Dr.)	- $1,000
9				Dividend Payable (Cr.)	+ $5,000		Dividend Declared (Dr.)	- $5,000
Totals	Assets	68,250	=	Liabilities	5,000	+	Equity	63,250

Chapter 2: Three Fundamental Rules of Accounting

Key Terms

account: a record of the increases, decreases, and balances of an individual asset, liability, capital, revenue, or expense.

debits and credits: these words mean "left" and "right," respectively. The terms debit and credit do not mean increase or decrease because, depending on the type of account, the act of debiting an account could increase or decrease it.

dividends: payments made to shareholders representing a return on capital. The declaration of dividends directly reduces retained earnings and does not flow through the income statement.

full disclosure principle: a guideline for determining what and how much information should be reflected in the four basic financial statements. The rule states that we should disclose information that could potentially affect the judgment and decisions of the informed user.

historical cost principle: a guideline for determining how to record transactions that affect balance sheet accounts. The rule states that we should value assets and liabilities based on acquisition cost, except in special situations.

matching principle: the guideline for determining how to record transactions that affect income statement accounts. The principle states that we should match expenses incurred with the revenue earned when a relationship between expenses and revenue can be determined; otherwise, expenses should be recognized immediately.

revenue recognition principle: the guideline for determining how to record transactions that affect income statement accounts. The principle states that we should recognize revenue when realized (or realizable) and earned.

Chapter 2: Three Fundamental Rules of Accounting

Thrills, Chills and Drills

True or False

1. Assets always equal liabilities plus shareholders' equity.

2. The balance sheet and income statement are tied together through the retained earnings account.

3. The full disclosure principle serves as a guideline for determining exactly which events should be reported in a company's financial statements.

4. The general practice of disclosing events that could potentially influence the judgment and decisions of the informed user is known as the full disclosure principle.

5. When applying the full disclosure principle, the degree of influence has little to do with the degree of disclosure.

6. The conditions that determine whether or not a transaction should be recorded are:

    a. The disclosure of the event should provide a better understanding of the financial position or results of the operations of a company.

    b. The dollar amount should be reasonably estimable or have a material impact on the accuracy of the financial statements.

7. According to the historical cost principle, all assets and liabilities are recorded on the basis of acquisition cost.

8. The historical cost principle provides a stable and consistent benchmark useful in the analysis of a company's financial statements.

9. In order to determine the acquisition cost of assets, one must consider all costs that make these items ready and available for use by the company.

10. The acquisition cost of liabilities is the "agreed upon" price at which the company incurs a liability.

11. Revenue is realizable when goods or services are exchanged for cash or claims to cash.

12. Revenues are considered earned when the company has "substantially completed" everything it must do to be entitled to the revenue.

Chapter 2: Three Fundamental Rules of Accounting

13. When a company completes production of its product and the product becomes a finished good, revenue is realizable.

14. Recognition of revenue at the time of sale provides a uniform test that can be applied to all types of companies in a variety of industries.

15. The matching principle dictates that expenses are matched with revenues in the period following the one in which revenues are earned.

16. The matching principle applies to both product and period costs.

17. Debit means right and credit means left.

18. Debits increase assets.

19. If the company's books showed net losses, the company has a debit balance in retained earnings.

20. Selling on account and purchasing on account create a debit to assets in both cases, and a credit to revenue and to liabilities, respectively.

Multiple Choice

1. All of the following events should be reported by a company except
    a) the sale of a piece of machinery
    b) the purchase of materials
    c) the retirement of debt
    d) information regarding a pending lawsuit
    e) all of the above
    f) none of the above

2. Which statement is not true?
    a) Assets equal liabilities plus owners equity.
    b) Owners equity equals assets minus liabilities.
    c) Liabilities equal assets minus owners' equity.
    d) None of the above.
    e) All of the above.

Chapter 2: Three Fundamental Rules of Accounting

3. Which of the following transactions do not require journal entries and the recording of the event in the financial statements?
    a) transactions involving the receipt of cash or some other type of asset from an outsider
    b) transactions involving the sale of items that the company is in business to sell
    c) transactions involving the purchase of items that increase the long-term value of the company
    d) transactions involving the hiring of employees
    e) none of the above

4. The acquisition cost of a piece of equipment includes which of the following?
    I. the manufacturer's price for the equipment
    II. installation costs
    III. freight costs
    IV. insurance
    a) I and II
    b) I, II and II
    c) I and III
    d) I, II, III and IV
    e) I, II, and IV
    f) I and IV

5. Which of the following statements about the revenue recognition principle is incorrect?
    a) The revenue recognition principle provides a basis for determining how to record transactions affecting income statement accounts.
    b) The revenue recognition principle establishes the guideline about when revenue should be recognized and recorded.
    c) The revenue recognition principle provides a basis for determining how to record transactions affecting balance sheet accounts.
    d) According to the revenue recognition principle, revenue should be recognized and recorded when it is realized and earned.

CHAPTER 2: THREE FUNDAMENTAL RULES OF ACCOUNTING

6. Which of the following statements is not true?
   a) In certain long-term construction contracts, revenue recognition is allowed before production is completed based on the percent of the job complete.
   b) When mining for minerals, revenue may be recognized after production is complete but before the sale takes place.
   c) When the collectibility of cash is uncertain at the time of sale, revenue is recognized when the actual cash is received.
   d) When products are bought under the condition that they be delivered to Pennsylvania, revenue is recognized when the goods leave the warehouse.

7. Which of the following is not a product cost?
   a) materials
   b) overhead
   c) labor
   d) officer salaries
   e) all are product costs
   f) none are product costs

8. Which of the following is a period cost?
   a) officer salary
   b) selling costs
   c) marketing costs
   d) administrative costs
   e) all are period costs
   f) none are period costs

9. There are two types of costs: period costs and production costs. While period costs have no direct relationship with the revenues earned, product costs
   I. are associated with the production of the product
   II. are matched and recognized in the period in which the product is sold
   III. can be allocated systematically over the periods benefited or products produced
   IV. include officers' salaries and other general administrative expenses
   a) I, II and III
   b) I and II
   c) I and III
   d) I, II, III and IV

Chapter 2: Three Fundamental Rules of Accounting

10. Assets and expenses are
    a). normally debit balances
    b) increased by debits
    c) decreased by credits
    d) all of the above
    e) none of the above

11. Liabilities, equity, and income accounts are
    a) increased on the credit side
    b) decreased on the debit side
    c) normally debit balances
    d) all of the above
    e) a and b only

12. Dividends are
    a) normally credit balances
    b) increased by crediting
    c) decreased by debiting
    d) handled the same as expenses

For Questions 13-20, decide what the effect of the transaction should have on the accounting equation.

13. The owner invested $20,000 in the company.
    a) debit equity, credit assets
    b) debit assets, credit equity
    c) increase assets, increase equity
    d) a and c
    e) b and c

14. The company purchased a building and land for $125,000. The company paid $10,000 cash and signed a note for the balance.
    a) debit assets, credit liabilities
    b) credit assets, debit liabilities
    c) debit assets $125,000, credit liabilities $125,000
    d) debit assets $125,000, credit assets $10,000, credit liabilities $115,000

Chapter 2: Three Fundamental Rules of Accounting

15. The company purchased $50,000 worth of inventory on account.
    a) debit assets, credit liabilities
    b) credit assets, debit liabilities
    c) increase assets, decrease liabilities
    d) decrease assets, increase liabilities

16. The company sold $25,000 worth of merchandise on account.
    a) debit assets, credit liabilities
    b) debit assets, credit equity
    c) increase assets, increase liabilities
    d) decrease assets, increase equity
    e) none of the above

17. The company paid $1,200 for insurance.
    a) debit expense, credit cash
    b) debit cash, credit expense
    c) debit equity, credit assets
    d) debit assets, credit equity
    e) a and c
    f) b and d

18. The company paid employees weekly salary of $5,000.
    a) debit cash, credit expense
    b) debit expense, credit cash
    c) debit equity, credit assets
    d) debit assets, credit equity
    e) a and d
    f) b and c

19. The company paid $20,000 for services not yet rendered.
    a) debit assets, credit equity
    b) debit assets, credit liabilities
    c) increase cash, increase revenues
    d) increase cash, increase receivables

20. The company owes employees three days' pay totaling $3000 by the end of the year.
    a) debit equity, credit liabilities
    b) debit expense, credit cash
    c) debit payable, credit expense
    d) none of the above

Chapter 2: Three Fundamental Rules of Accounting

Short Essays

1. Differentiate between the following four basic principles:

    a. full disclosure

    b. historical cost

    c. revenue recognition

    d. matching

2. What is the difference between product and period costs?

3. Explain why accounting is referred to as the double-entry system.

4. What is the basic accounting equation? What is the expanded basic equation? Show how the terms debit and credit can both mean increase and decrease.

5. Use the format provided below to identify the type of asset, normal account balance, and whether debits or credits increase or decrease the account for the following:

    a. utilities expense

    b. cash

    c. accounts payable

    d. owner's equity

    e. buildings

    f. note payable

    g. accounts receivable

    h. goodwill

    i. inventory

    j. common stock

    k. mortgage payable

Chapter 2: Three Fundamental Rules of Accounting

l. income tax return receivable

m. salary expense

n. supplies

o. accumulated depreciation - buildings

p. income tax expense

q. retained earnings

r. notes receivable

s. advertising expense

6. For the following transactions, indicate the effect on the expanded basic equation.

   a. The owner invested $25,000 in the company.

   b. The company purchased a building for $125,000 by signing a 10-year mortgage.

   c. The company purchased equipment for $50,000 on credit.

   d. The company purchased supplies for $5,000.

   e. The owner purchased inventory for $20,000 on credit.

   f. The company sold $50,000 worth of merchandise to customers on account.

   g. The company hired three employees.

   h. The company received $12,000 from customers on account.

   i. The company purchased insurance for $5,000.

   j. The company received $20,000 from customers on account.

   k. The company paid employees $1,000 for weekly salary.

7. Given the transactions in Problem 6, prepare an income statement and a balance sheet.

Chapter 2: Three Fundamental Rules of Accounting

Answers

True or False Answers

1. True.
2. True.
3. True.
4. True.
5. **False.** The degree of potential influence directly affects the degree of disclosure.
6. **False.** In order for a transaction to be recorded, the disclosure should provide a better understanding of the company's position, as well as, satisfy two conditions: the dollar amount should be reasonably estimable and it should have a material impact on the accuracy of the financial statements.
7. **False.** All assets and liabilities are originally recorded on the basis of acquisition cost; however, some are re-valued to provide more useful information to users.
8. True.
9. True.
10. True.
11. **False.** Realized.
12. True.
13. True.
14. True.
15. **False.** The principle dictates that expenses are matched in the period earned (expenses follow revenues).
16. **False.** Product costs are matched with revenues in the period the product is sold. Period costs have no direct relationship with the revenue earned and are expensed when incurred.
17. **False.** Debit means left and credit means right.
18. True.
19. True.
20. True.

Multiple Choice Answers

1. **(f)** All should be included.
2. **(d)** All are true.
3. **(d)** The mere act of hiring employees is not recorded in the financial statements, other than by memo entry. Transactions that require journal entries and recording in the financial statements involving employees deal with employees earning their pay or the company owing employees due to contractual agreements.

Chapter 2: Three Fundamental Rules of Accounting

4. **(d)** All are included.
5. **(c)** The historical cost principle provides a basis for determining how to record transactions affecting balance sheet accounts.
6. **(d)** Revenue is not recognized until the product is delivered to Pennsylvania --Free On Board-destination point.
7. **(d)** Period costs are not product costs.
8. **(e)** All are period costs.
9. **(a)** Number 4 describes period costs.
10. **(d)** Assets and expenses are described by all of these statements.
11. **(e)** Accounts on the right hand side of the equation normally have credit balances. Credits increase these accounts and debits decrease these accounts.
12. **(d)** Dividends reduce retained earnings, and as such are similar to expenses.
13. **(e)** Investing $20,000 in the company translates to debiting cash for $20,000 and crediting owner's equity for $20,000, which increases both accounts.
14. **(d)** Cash decreases by $10,000 paid for purchase of land and building, building and land increase by $125,000 value of property acquired, and note payable increases by $115,000 ($125,000 - $10,000).
15. **(a)** Assets/inventory increased/debited by $50,000, and liability/account payable increased/credited by same amount.
16. **(b)** Assets/accounts receivable increases by $25,000, and revenue/equity increases by the same amount.
17. **(e)** Cash/asset decreases/credited by $1200, and expense is increased/debited. Remember that expenses decrease equity, and revenues increase equity.
18. **(f)** Cash/asset is decreased/credited, and expense is increased/debited. Again, expenses reduce equity.
19. **(b)** Receipt of money for services not yet performed creates a liability to the company. If the services are not performed, the company owes the customer the money back.
20. **(a)** The company owes employees the money, creating a liability. This is an example of an adjusting entry for the end of an accounting period. The expenses are matched with the revenues generated.

Short Essay Answers

1) a. The practice of disclosing events that could influence the judgment and decisions of informed users. Test: Does disclosure provide a better understanding of the financial position or results of operations of the company? If so, is the dollar amount reasonably estimable and does it have a material impact on the accuracy of the financial statements?

   b. Provides a basis for determining how to record transactions affecting the balance sheet. Provides a stable and consistent benchmark that financial users can use to analyze a company's financial statements. Most assets and liabilities are accounted for and reported on the basis of acquisition cost.

   c. Provides a basis for determining how to record transactions affecting the income statement. Establishes a guideline that revenue should be recognized and recorded when it is 1) realized or realizable and 2) earned.

   d. Provides a basis for determining how to record transactions affecting expense accounts in the income statement. Dictates that expenses are matched with revenues in the period revenues are earned--i.e., expenses follow revenues.

Chapter 2: Three Fundamental Rules of Accounting

2. Product costs are inputs associated with the production of the product or output and include materials, labor, and overhead. Period costs are incurred during a period and have no direct relationship with the revenue earned and include officers salaries and other general administrative expenses.

3. Accounting is referred to as the double-entry system because it requires that both sides of each transaction be recorded in the appropriate account — i.e., if one account is debited, another account must be credited in order to create a two-sided effect. With each transaction, total debits must equal total credits. Therefore, the accounting equation always remains in balance. The manner in which the system operates provides users with a built-in system of checks and balances. If total debits do not equal total credits, you have done something wrong.

4. The basic accounting equation is: Assets = Liabilities + Owner's equity
   The expanded basic equation is: Assets = Liabilities + Common stock + Retained earnings + (Revenue - Expenses)

   Debit means left side, and credit means right side.

Expanded Equation:	Assets	=	Liabilities	+	Common stock	+	Retained Earnings
normal balances:	Debit +		Credit +		Credit +		Credit +
	Credit -		Debit -		Debit -		Debit -
				+	Revenue	-	Expenses
					Credit +		Debit +
					Debit -		Credit -

5.

	Account Name	Account Type	Normal Balance	Increase	Decrease
A	Utilities expense	Expense	debit	debit	credit
B	Cash	asset	debit	debit	credit
C	Accounts payable	liability	credit	credit	debit
D	Owner's equity	equity	credit	credit	debit
E	Buildings	asset	debit	debit	credit
F	Note payable	liability	credit	credit	debit
G	Accounts receivable	asset	debit	debit	credit
H	Goodwill	asset	debit	debit	credit
I	Inventory	asset	debit	debit	credit
J	Common stock	equity	credit	credit	debit
K	Mortgage payable	liability	credit	credit	debit
L	Income tax return receivable	asset	debit	debit	credit
M	Salary expense	expense	debit	debit	credit
N	Supplies	asset	debit	debit	credit
O	Accumulated depreciation	contra asset	credit	credit	debit
P	Income tax expense	expense	debit	debit	credit
Q	Retained earnings	equity	credit	credit	debit
R	Notes receivable	asset	debit	debit	credit
S	Advertising expense	expense	debit	debit	credit

Chapter 2: Three Fundamental Rules of Accounting

6.

		Assets	=	Liabilities	+	Equity	+	(Revenues − Expenses)
	a	25,000				25,000		
	b	125,000		125,000				
	c	50,000		50,000				
	d	5,000						
		-5,000						
	e	20,000		20,000				
	f	50,000						50,000
	g							
	h	12,000						
		-12,000						
	i	5,000						
		-5,000						
	j	20,000						
		-20,000						
	k	-1,000						-1,000
	total	269,000	=	195,000	+	25,000	+	50,000 −1,000

7.

XYZ Company
Income Sheet
For the period ended December 31, 19XX

Revenues	
Sales	$50,000
Less: Expenses	
Salaries	($1,000)
Net Income	**$49,000**

XYZ Company
Balance Sheet
December 31, 19XX

Assets			Liabilities	
Cash	46,000 **		Accounts Payable	20,000
Accounts Receivable	18,000 ***		Note Payable	50,000
Supplies	5,000		Mortgage	125,000
Prepaid Insurance	5,000			
Inventory	20,000		**Owners' Equity**	
Equipment	50,000		Capital	74,000 (Original Investment of $25,000 plus Net Income of $49,000)
Building	125,000			
Total assets	**$269,000**		**Total Liabilities and owners' equity**	**$269,000**

* Do Income Statement first otherwise Balance Sheet does not balance.
** Cash = +25,000 − 5,000 + 12,000 − 5,000 + 20,000 − 10,000 = **46,000**
*** Accounts Receivable = +50,000 − 12,000 − 20,000 = **18,000**

Chapter

The Six Steps to Stardom

3

Chapter 3: The Six Steps to Stardom

Overview

Recall that accounting is the process of **recording, processing, summarizing, and reporting** a series of **economic events** that affect the operations of a company for the purpose of evaluating the total effect of those economic events on a company's net worth over a specified period of time or at a given point in time. The first step in that process is the identification of economic events. In Chapter 1, you learned how to identify and classify economic events in order to determine the appropriate treatment of a transaction in the accounting process. Chapter 2 introduced you to the **full disclosure principle**, which establishes the guideline for determining exactly which events should be reported in a company's financial statements. By the end of this chapter, you will be able to complete the accounting process of recording, processing, summarizing, and reporting economic data. You will learn to:

- Use the Journal Entry Approach to record transactions
- Identify and understand adjusting and closing entries
- Prepare financial statements using a post-closing trial balance

This chapter is called the Six Steps to Stardom because you will learn six methodical procedures that will help you begin and complete the accounting process. The Journal Entry Abpproach is a simple, methodical approach that can be used to record the most complex types of transactions. This approach will be used to navigate our way through the complexities of the balance sheet, income statement, and statement of cash flow covered in later chapters.

Chapter 3: The Six Steps to Stardom

Concepts

Step 1: Identification of Events

This first step to approaching the accounting process is important because economic events are usually not handed to an accountant (or an accounting student) on a silver platter. They are often hidden in a tangled mess of paragraphs and sentences thay may divert and frustrate you. Therefore, you must be able to read a problem and identify the economics of the transaction. Let's review some of the concepts we learned in Chapters 1 and 2. Under the **full disclosure principle** the two tests for identifying economic events are:

- As a financial statement user, would disclosure of the event provide a better understanding of the financial position or results of operations of the company?

- If so, is the dollar amount reasonably estimable and does it have a material impact on the accuracy of the financial statements?

Once identified, economic events must be classified. Recall that there are four types of economic events:

	Frequent	**Infrequent**
Usual	Eg. Sales of merchandise Purchase of inventory	Eg. Effects of a strike Write-downs (changes in value)of receivables or inventories
Unusual	Eg. Foreign currency translations Purchase/sale of equipment	Eg. Natural Disasters Expropriations (takeovers)

Usual and frequent transactions are those transactions occurring in the normal course of business. In contrast, **unusual and infrequent transactions** are both "abnormal" in nature and rare in occurrence. The other two types of economic events — which do not occur on a regular basis but are not "abnormal", either — are considered to be "in-between" the two extremes. **The full disclosure principle is used as a guideline for what economic events should be recorded**. Proper classification of each economic event into one of the categories outlined above determines how the transactions should be recorded. Let's look at the identification and classification of transactions with an example.

Chapter 3: The Six Steps to Stardom

Jones Manufacturing, Inc. began operating on July 1, 1989, when Mr. Jones invested his entire savings of $45,000. By 1992, the company had grown to employ over 1,000 employees and boasted a market capitalization of over $5 million. In 1993, the company had revenues of $12 million, all of which was received in cash, representing a 25% increase over the prior year. During that year, Mr. Jones sold the company's office building at book value of $300,000 and moved to a new location where the company would be better positioned to enter international markets. In 1998, Jones Manufacturing, Inc. went public and issued $10 million of common stock to the open market.

To identify the economics events in this example, think about the exchanges that were made, i.e., what was given up and what was received in exchange. Using this process, there are four economic events that occurred in this situation, classified as follows:

Account Type	Classification	Accounts Affected
1. Mr. Jones used cash for a capital investment.	Unusual	Cash
	Infrequent	Owner's Equity
2. Jones Manufacturing, Inc. sold $12 million of goods for cash.	Usual	Cash
	Frequent	Revenue
3. Jones Manufacturing, Inc. sold its office building for cash.	Usual	Cash
	Infrequent	Fixed Assets
4. Jones Manufacturing, Inc. issued common stock for cash.	Unusual	Cash
	Infrequent	Common Stock

Note that the receipt of cash from the usual and frequent transaction affects revenue, and is reflected in the income statement. The receipt of cash from the unusual and infrequent transactions affect equity, which is reflected on the balance sheet. We should realize that proper classification of economic events plays an important factor in how every transaction is presented upon the balance sheet.

Step 2: Recording the Transaction Using a Systematic Method

After identifying and classifying each economic event that must be recorded, the next step is to actually record the transaction. Throughout this study guide, we will use the **Journal Entry Approach** to record transactions. This approach requires that for every transaction there must be a debit and a credit. In addition, after each transaction has been recorded, all debits must equal all credits. Recognizing that transactions are merely exchanges

Chapter 3: The Six Steps to Stardom

between parties, we must identify the accounts affected by the exchange and how they are affected (by an increase or a decrease). Note that in the four situations above, each economic event has two accounts listed. **If every transaction is an exchange that dictates a debit and a credit requirement, then at least two accounts are affected by every economic event.**

When recording entries using the Journal Entry Approach, we will use the following format. This example records the first event listed above:

	Debit	Credit
Cash (Dr.)	45,000	
Owners' Equity (Cr.)		45,000

Since debit means "left" and credit means "right," we will list all accounts requiring a debit first and on the left. Conversely, all accounts requiring a credit will be listed second and indented to the right. The advantage of this approach is two-fold:

1. After every transaction is recorded you can visually balance all debits and credits.

2. If you only know one half of the transaction, using this approach can help you figure out the other half.

Let's look at event #2. Suppose you could determine only that Jones Manufacturing, Inc. earned revenues of $12 million. Since revenues increase on the credit side, you record the following:

	Debit	Credit
Dr. ?	12,000,000	
Revenue (Cr.)		12,000,000

By recording the journal entry, you can determine that another account must be debited for $12 million. Jones Manufacturing, Inc. sold goods to earn revenue and received something in exchange for the goods sold. In this case, we must assume that cash was received since no other information was received. Therefore, the debit must be to increase cash.

	Debit	Credit
Cash (Dr.)	12,000,000	
Revenue (Cr.)		12,000,000

Chapter 3: The Six Steps to Stardom

The Journal Entry Approach is a constant application of the concept that debits must always equal credits, and the corollary that assets must always equal liabilities plus equity. This approach will become especially useful in later chapters when three or four accounts are affected by the same transaction, because it allows you to identify and record the "knowns" in order to figure out the "unknowns."

Even if you don't master it completely, using this approach will demonstrate that you understand the methodology involved in recording transactions. Let's practice the journal entry approach by recording a series of transactions for Just Toys Manufacturing Company.

Application: Comprehensive Example

Just Toys Manufacturing Company manufactures and distributes stuffed animals to toy stores around the country; it has been in business for over 15 years. Just Toys operates on a calendar year basis, meaning that its fiscal year ends December 31. Just Toys' balance sheet at the beginning of the year is as follows:

Just Toys Manufacturing Company
Balance Sheet
December 31, 1997

Assets		Liabilities & Shareholders Equity	
Current Assets		**Current Liabilities**	
Cash	14,000	Accounts Payable	17,000
Accounts Receivable	26,000	Wages Payable	6,000
Inventory	11,000	Total Current Liabilities	23,000
Prepaid Insurance	4,000		
Total Current Assets	55,000	**Non-Current Liabilities**	
		Bonds Payable	100,000
Non-Current Assets			
Land	100,000	Total Liabilities	123,000
Machinery & Equipment	300,000	**Stockholders Equity**	
Less: Accumulated Depreciation	(75,000)	Common Stock	100,000
Patent	22,000	Additional Paid-in Capital	81,000
Total Non-Current Assets	347,000	Retained Earnings	98,000
		Total Liabilities & Equity	279,000
Total Assets	402,000	Total Liab & Stockholders Equity	402,000

The following transactions occurred at Just Toys during the month of December:

1. Purchased inventory on account for $200,000.

2. Purchased equipment for $50,000.

Chapter 3: The Six Steps to Stardom

3. Sold goods totaling $300,000, of which $176,000 was received in cash.

4. Paid water, electric, and gas bills totaling $7,000.

5. Paid $90,000 in salaries and wages.

6. Received $145,000 in payments from customers.

7. Paid $163,000 for inventory purchased in #1.

8. Paid $6,000 in interest on outstanding bonds payable.

The journal entries for each of these transactions are illustrated below. Remember to ask yourself what is exchanged, what accounts are affected (at least two in each transaction), and how they are affected.

1. **Purchased inventory on account for $200,000.** In this transaction, the receipt of inventory is exchanged for a promise to pay later. The two accounts affected are Inventory and Accounts Payable, both of which increase.

	Debit	Credit
Inventory	200,000	
Accounts Payable		200,000

2. **Purchased equipment for $50,000.** In this transaction, cash is exchanged for equipment — one economic resource for another. The two accounts affected are Cash (decrease) and Equipment (increase). Note that this purchase does not affect Inventory, because the equipment will be used in the business and not resold to customers.

Helpful Hint: If the transaction does not state otherwise, assume that the purchase was made with cash.

	Debit	Credit
Machinery & Equipment	50,000	
Cash		50,000

3. **Sold goods for $300,000, of which $176,000 was received in cash.** In this transaction, inventory is exchanged for cash and accounts receivable. If only part of the revenue was received in cash, then customers must owe the remainder. Knowing this, you can fill in the journal entry with the "known" values to determine the amount owed by customers to Just Toys. Thus, three accounts are affected: revenue (increase), cash (increase), and accounts receivable (increase). This type of entry is called a **compound entry** because it involves more than one debit or more than one credit. When recording a compound entry, always group the debits and credits together, as shown below.

Chapter 3: The Six Steps to Stardom

Helpful Hint: If only part of revenue earned is received in cash, the remainder is probably accounts receivable.

	Debit	Credit
Cash	176,000	
Accounts Receivable	124,000	
Sales Revenue		300,000

4. **Paid water, electric, and gas bills totaling $7,000.** In this transaction, cash is exchanged as payment for utility usage in December. Since utility bills do not provide any future benefits to Just Toys, they are considered expenses and not assets. Recall that these types of expenses are period costs, because they are not directly associated with production and should be expensed in the period incurred. The two accounts affected are Utilities Expense (increase) and Cash (decrease).

	Debit	Credit
Utilities Expense	7,000	
Cash		7,000

5. **Paid $60,000 in officers' salaries and $30,000 wages to factory workers for inventory produced during December.** In this transaction, cash is exchanged as payment for services provided during this month. The officers salaries are considered period costs, but the wages to factory workers are considered product costs because they are directly associated with December production. Thus, the two accounts affected are cash (decrease) and salaries and wages expense (increase).

	Debit	Credit
Salaries & Wages Expense	90,000	
Cash		90,000

6. **Received $145,000 in payments from customers.** In this transaction, cash is received as settlement of the customer's obligation to pay for goods purchased from Just Toys. The two accounts affected are Cash (increase) and Accounts Receivable (decrease).

	Debit	Credit
Cash	145,000	
Accounts Receivable		145,000

Chapter 3: The Six Steps to Stardom

7. **Paid $163,000 for inventory purchased in #1.** Here, Just Toys is exchanging cash as settlement of its obligation to pay its suppliers for inventory purchased. The two accounts affected are Accounts Payable and Cash, both of which decrease.

	Debit	Credit
Accounts Payable	163,000	
Cash		163,000

8. **Paid $6,000 for December interest on outstanding bonds payable.** In this transaction, Just Toys is exchanging cash as part payment of its obligation for debt issued. Interest paid on bonds is a period cost and expensed as incurred, because the interest being paid on a period that has already passed. The two accounts affected are Cash (decrease) and Interest Expense (increase).

	Debit	Credit
Interest Expense	6,000	
Cash		6,000

Step 3: Summarize Transactions to Arrive at the Trial Balance

The transactions listed above are initially recorded in a **journal**. Afterward, the transactions are then **posted** to the individual accounts at the end of the accounting period to determine the account balances in order to prepare financial statements. Before actual preparation of the balance sheet, a **trial balance** is prepared that summarizes the transactions recorded and provides the accountant a way to test the equality of debits and credits in the accounts. Before we prepare a trial balance, let's define a few terms.

Accounting period: The time period over which the accounting process is completed and financial statements are prepared. An accounting period can be one month, three months (quarterly), or one year (annually). Most companies use an annual accounting period that coincides with the calendar year. However, some companies and organizations, use a **fiscal year** that sets a year end of something other than December 31.

Journal: Often called "the book of original entry," the journal is where transactions first enter the accounting records. General journals are the simplest type because they can be used to record all types of transactions. Specialized journals, such as a cash receipts journal or sales journal, are used to record repetitive transactions that affect the same accounts.

Chapter 3: The Six Steps to Stardom

Entries: Entries in the general journal should include the following information about each transaction.

1. the date
2. the account names (remember there should be at least two)
3. the dollar amounts debited and credited
4. an explanation of the transaction
5. the account identification numbers (the entry number)

Brownie Points: Don't lose points on an examination because of labeling. Even if you can't figure out the numbers or the accounts, make sure that everything else is properly labeled. In addition, remember that it is customary to skip a line after each journal entry.

Ledger: A book that contains all of the company's accounts. Each account is listed on a separate page, typically in the order they appear in the financial statements.

Posting: The act of transferring the information from the journal entry to the ledger by debiting or crediting the respective accounts. Posting can be done daily or weekly, depending on the frequency of the transactions. The balance at the end of the accounting period is determined by adding all the debits and credits in each ledger account after all transactions have been posted. These balances are then used to prepare a trial balance.

Key Concept: **Trial balance:** A list of all of the accounts in a ledger with their balances. The trial balance gives the accountant a chance to double check whether the debits and credits are equal. However, it does not provide a mechanism for detecting all errors in recording transactions. The following errors cannot be detected simply by preparing a trial balance.

1. **Determining whether transactions were recorded in the correct account.** For example, if a sale on account was incorrectly recorded as a debit to cash instead of a debit to accounts receivable, the trial balance will not detect this error because debits will still equal credits, even though the debit is in the wrong account.

2. **Omission of entire transactions.** This error cannot be detected through the trial balance because both the debit and the credit are omitted and the remaining entries recorded will still balance.

3. **Errors of the same amount on both the debit and the credit side.** For example, if actual salaries paid were $50,000, but salaries expense was debited for $30,000 and cash was also credited for $30,000, then this error could not be detected.

Chapter 3: The Six Steps to Stardom

For these three reasons, it is important to ensure that each transaction is analyzed correctly and that the correct amounts are recorded. Here are some troubleshooting tips if total debits and credits in the trial balance do not balance:

1. Look for debits entered into the account as a credit, or credits entered into the account as debits. This error will cause the discrepancy to be divisible by 2.

2. Check to see if numbers were transposed when transferring them from the ledger to the trial balance. This error will cause the discrepancy to be divisible by 9.

3. Check to see if the individual balance was computed correctly.

4. Check to see if the sums of the trial balance were added correctly.

Application: Comprehensive Example (continued)

Let's prepare the trial balance for Just Toys Manufacturing, Inc. by using the concepts defined above. First, record the journal entries from Step 2 in a general journal:

Just Toys Manufacturing Company
General Journal

Entry No.	Date	Account Name & Explanations	P.R.	Debit	Credit
1	12/5	Inventory		200,000	
		Accounts Payable			200,000
		To record inventory purchases on account.			
2	12/11	Machinery & Equipment		50,000	
		Cash			50,000
		To record equipment purchases.			
3	12/12	Cash		176,000	
		Accounts Receiveable		124,000	
		Sales Revenue			300,000
		To record this month's sales.			
4	12/15	Utilities Expense		7,000	
		Cash			7,000
		To record payment of utilities.			
5	12/15	Salaries & Wages Expense		90,000	
		Cash			90,000
		To record payment of salaries.			
6	12/17	Cash		145,000	
		Accounts Receivable			145,000
		To record cash receipts from customers.			
7	12/29	Accounts Payable		163,000	
		Cash			163,000
		To record payment for inventory purchased.			
8	12/30	Interest Expense		6,000	
		Cash			6,000
		To record payment of interest on bond.			
		Total		961,000	961,000

This P.R. (Posting Reference) column is used when the transaction is posted to the general ledger. The accountant either places the account number or a checkmark here to indicate that a transaction was posted.

CHAPTER 3: THE SIX STEPS TO STARDOM

Note that each transaction has been recorded in a way that includes all five of the labeling requirements. Note also that the total of all debits equals the total of all credits. Therefore, if transferred correctly, the general ledger account balances will be correct.

Listing items in a general journal in this format is more of a formality than a learning tool. By just using the Journal Entry Approach and the T-account format shown on the next page, you can successfully prepare a trial balance. However, it is good to know how to present a general journal, because it will help you earn easy points on an exam.

To post the transactions to the general ledger, we will use "T-accounts" for each of the company's accounts. In setting up the T-accounts, list them in order of appearance on the balance sheet. After listing balance sheet accounts, list income statement accounts with revenues first and expenses following. After all accounts have been listed, enter the beginning balances into the balance sheet accounts. Note that there will be no beginning balances in the income statement accounts, because the income statement reflects only information for the current period. Since we have not recorded anything in the general ledger yet for the current period, the beginning balances in these accounts will be zero. After entering the beginning balances, transfer entries from the general journal to their respective account. Remember to list the entry number from the general journal next to the amounts in the ledger as a way of keeping track of the source of the numbers.

Chapter 3: The Six Steps to Stardom

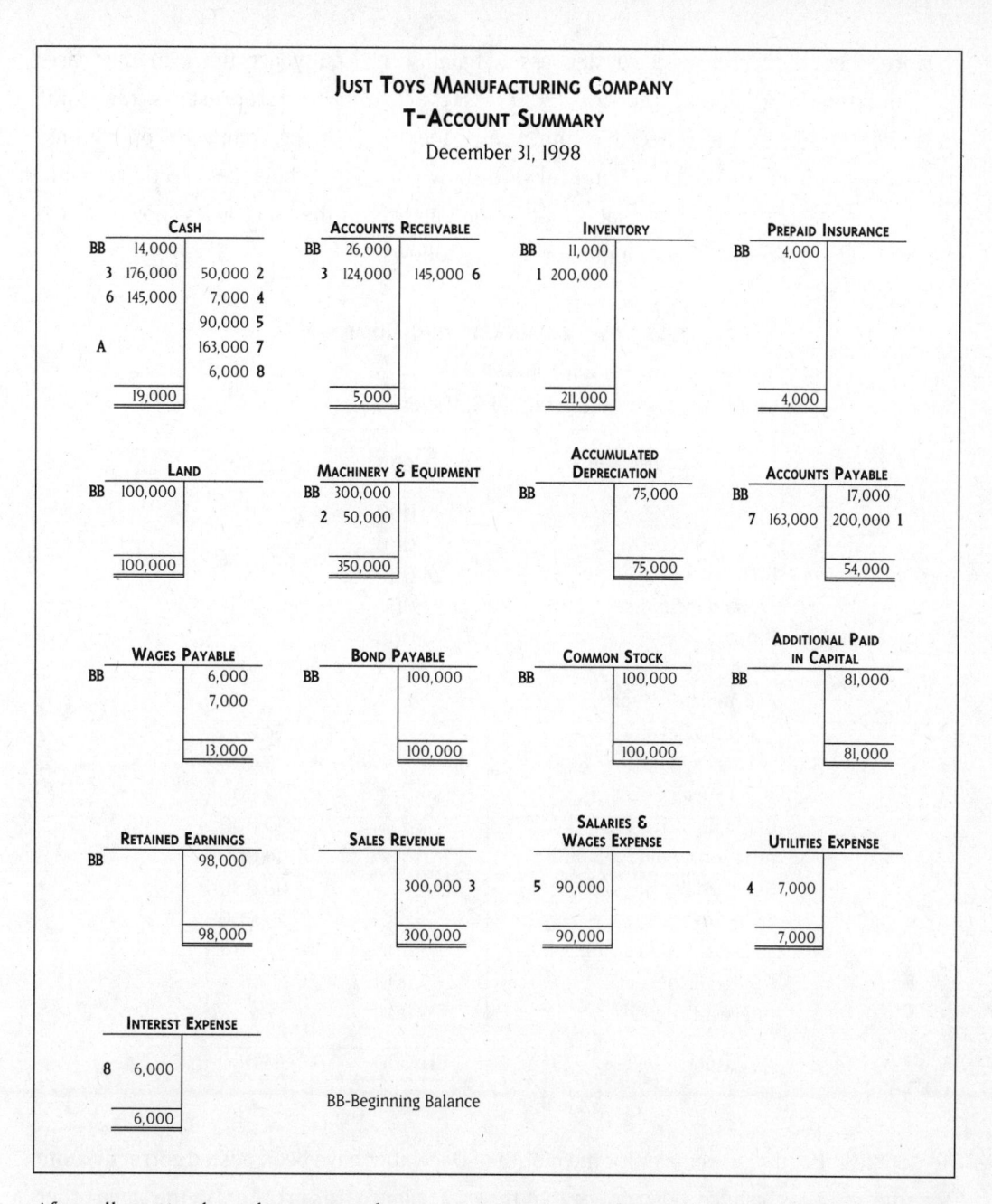

JUST TOYS MANUFACTURING COMPANY
T-ACCOUNT SUMMARY
December 31, 1998

CASH		ACCOUNTS RECEIVABLE		INVENTORY		PREPAID INSURANCE	
BB 14,000		BB 26,000		BB 11,000		BB 4,000	
3 176,000	50,000 2	3 124,000	145,000 6	1 200,000			
6 145,000	7,000 4						
	90,000 5						
A	163,000 7						
	6,000 8						
19,000		5,000		211,000		4,000	

LAND		MACHINERY & EQUIPMENT		ACCUMULATED DEPRECIATION		ACCOUNTS PAYABLE	
BB 100,000		BB 300,000			75,000 BB		17,000 BB
		2 50,000				7 163,000	200,000 1
100,000		350,000			75,000		54,000

WAGES PAYABLE		BOND PAYABLE		COMMON STOCK		ADDITIONAL PAID IN CAPITAL	
	6,000 BB		100,000 BB		100,000 BB		81,000 BB
	7,000						
	13,000		100,000		100,000		81,000

RETAINED EARNINGS		SALES REVENUE		SALARIES & WAGES EXPENSE		UTILITIES EXPENSE	
	98,000 BB		300,000 3	5 90,000		4 7,000	
	98,000		300,000	90,000		7,000	

INTEREST EXPENSE	
8 6,000	
6,000	

BB-Beginning Balance

After all entries have been posted, we can now prepare the trial balance. We prepare the trial balance by computing the balance in each of the accounts and listing them in two columns, one for debits and one for credits, based on the type of normal balance that the account maintains. Recall that assets and expenses normally maintain debit balances, while liabilities, equity, and revenues normally maintain credit balances.

KEY CONCEPT: Notice that the account "Accumulated Depreciation" has a credit balance at the end of the period. This account normally maintains a credit balance, but it is not a liability, capital, or revenue account. Accumulated Depreciation is a **contra account**, which is an account on the balance sheet that reduces a specific asset, liability, or equity account. In this case, Accumulated Depreciation reduces fixed asset accounts and represents the total depreciation recorded to reflect the total use of the assets in the company's operations. Therefore, accumulated depreciation is always shown as a credit balance directly after the fixed asset account to which it relates. Using the balances in the T-accounts shown above, the trial balance for Just Toys Manufacturing is as follows:

JUST TOYS MANUFACTURING COMPANY
Trial Balance
December 31, 1998

Account Name	Debit	Credit
Cash	19,000	
Accounts Receivable	5,000	
Inventory	211,000	
Prepaid Insurance	4,000	
Land	100,000	
Machinery & Equipment	372,000	
Accumulated Depreciation		75,000
Accounts Payable		54,000
Wages Payable		6,000
Bond Payable		100,000
Common Stock		100,000
Additional Paid in Capital		81,000
Retained Earnings		98,000
Sales Revenue		300,000
Salaries & Wages Expense	90,000	
Utilities Expense	7,000	
Interest Expense	6,000	
Total	814,000	814,000

To double check that the entries for the month of December have been posted correctly, note that the accounts balance. Also notice that the trial balance lists accounts in the same order as presented in the general ledger, with the balance sheet accounts appearing first and the income statement accounts following.

Chapter 3: The Six Steps to Stardom

Step 4: Record Period-End Adjustments, Adjusted Trial Balance

The revenue recognition principle and the matching principle are the two important rules to follow when recording adjusting entries. Under the revenue recognition principle, revenues are recognized when earned and realizable. Under the matching principle, expenses are matched with revenues and recognized in the period in which they are incurred to produce revenue. It is important to understand that the principles do not recognize revenue when cash is received and expenses when cash is paid. Thus, the purpose of adjusting entries is to reflect income and expenses in the appropriate accounting period by recording revenues earned but not yet received for the period, as well as expenses incurred but not yet paid. There are five basic types of adjusting entries.

A. Prepaid expenses: Prepaid expenses are expenses paid in cash in the current period that will benefit future periods. They are similar to fixed asset purchases, except that they are not long-term in nature. Examples of expenses that are often prepaid by companies are insurance, supplies, advertising, and rent. Prepaid expenses expire either with the passage of time (e.g. rent) or consumption (e.g. supplies). For example, suppose you decided to move off-campus next year and, for your birthday, your grandparents decided to give you $2700, just enough money for the entire rent for the year. Because you are such a busy college student and do not want the hassle of paying rent every month, you decide to pay your landlord the full $2700 at the beginning of the year for the entire 9 months of the school year. Because you have not lived in the apartment for the entire year, your landlord is by no means entitled to the full payment. You have a prepaid expense, because you have paid your monthly expenses up front. So instead of recording an expense, you would decrease one asset (cash), increase another asset (prepaid rent), and recognize the expense only when the landlord earns the revenue. The entry to record the initial payment is as follows.

	Debit	Credit
Prepaid Rent	2,700	
Cash		2,700

When one month passes, your landlord will be entitled to one-ninth of the prepayment, or $300. In addition, since the landlord has earned his revenue, one month's rent will no longer be prepaid, because it has expired. You would then record the expense by increasing expenses for $300 and decreasing prepaid rent for the same amount.

Chapter 3: The Six Steps to Stardom

	Debit	Credit
Rent Expense	300	
Prepaid Rent		300

KEY CONCEPT: The entry to record the expiration and/or usage of prepaid expenses is always a debit to an expense account and a credit to an asset account.

B. **Unearned revenues:** Unearned revenues are revenues received in cash before they are earned. Recall that revenues are recognized when they are both realized and earned. Many types of companies receive cash from their customers before the services have been performed or the goods have been delivered to earn the cash received. For example, when you subscribe to a magazine for a year, you normally pay the company in advance for your subscription. That company has not earned the revenue that you paid, because you haven't received all of you magazines. Therefore, instead of recording revenue in the income statement, they record a liability in the balance sheet. A liability is recorded because the company has an obligation to deliver the magazines to you for the entire year, and you still have a claim on the cash you paid if the company doesn't deliver them. Using the prepaid rent example above, let's consider another situation in which unearned revenue may be recorded. When you paid your rent in advance to your landlord for the 9-month lease, you considered the payment as prepaid rent. From your landlord's perspective, the $2,700 payment is unearned revenue because he still has an obligation to perform any services agreed upon in the lease agreement every month. In essence, unearned revenues are the opposite of prepaid expenses. So instead of recording revenue, your landlord recognizes an increase to his assets (cash) and his liabilities (unearned revenue), as follows.

	Debit	Credit
Cash	2,700	
Unearned Revenue		2,700

After one month expires, your landlord is entitled to one-ninth of the prepayment, as he has earned his revenue and is no longer obligated to you for that period. He then recognizes one month's revenue as follows.

	Debit	Credit
Unearned Revenue	300	
Revenue		300

CHAPTER 3: THE SIX STEPS TO STARDOM

KEY CONCEPT: The entry to record the recognition of unearned revenue is always a credit to unearned revenue and a debit to a liability account.

C. **Accrued expenses:** Accrued expenses are expenses incurred but not paid by the end of the accounting period. Some common examples of accrued expenses include salaries, interest, taxes, rent and utilities. Many types of accrued expenses are not paid by the end of the accounting period because the bill has not been received. As a result, many accrued expenses are often estimates, because the actual bills for these expenses are not received until after the accounting period. For example, utilities such as electricity, gas, and telephone are all incurred on a daily basis. At the end of the month, companies have a liability to the respective utility company for the usage of the service. However, the bills for these services are often not received until the beginning of the next month. In these situations, companies usually estimate how much the expenses will be based on actual amounts paid in prior periods. They then make appropriate adjustments when the bills are actually received. Returning to the rent example, suppose you didn't prepay your rent every month but waited for the bill from your landlord to come. Suppose that the bill arrives at the beginning of the next month. At the end of the month, you owe your landlord one month's rent, even though you have not been billed yet. Since you have incurred a liability that you are obligated to pay, you would increase your expenses (rent expense) and your liabilities (accrued expenses) as follows.

	Debit	Credit
Rent Expense	300	
Accrued Expenses		300

KEY CONCEPT: The entry to record the accrued expenses incurred but not paid is always a debit to an expense account and a credit to a liability account.

D. **Accrued revenues:** Accrued revenues are revenues earned but not yet received in cash by the end of the accounting period. The most common type of accrued revenue is revenue categorized as accounts receivable. Recall that in Step 3 of the accounting process, we recorded the following transaction for Just Toys Manufacturing:

Sold goods for $300,000, of which $176,000 was received in cash.

	Debit	Credit
Cash	176,000	
Accounts Receivable	124,000	
Sales Revenue		300,000

Chapter 3: The Six Steps to Stardom

In this transaction, only $176,000 was received in cash, but we still recorded $300,000 in revenue. We discussed that if only part of revenue earned is received in cash, the remainder is probably accounts receivable.

We record this amount in accounts receivable because Just Toys sold $300,000 of goods and is entitled to the revenue, even though it has not received full payment for delivering the goods. As a result, instead of recording cash for the remaining $124,000, Just Toys increases a different asset account and records the remainder as an account receivable.

The entry to record the accrued revenues earned but not yet received is always a debit to an asset account (specifically, a receivable account) and a credit to a revenue account.

E. **Estimated items:** Estimated items are expenses recorded based on estimates of future unknown events. The most common types of estimated items are depreciation expense and bad debt expense. We will cover depreciation expense here and bad debt expense in the next chapter. **Depreciation expense** represents an estimate of how much of a fixed asset was used during the accounting period to generate revenue. It is recorded based on the company's estimate of the useful life of its fixed assets. Entries for depreciation expense are similar to entries for reducing prepaid expenses, in that an expense account is debited and a credit reduces an asset account. However, instead of reducing an asset directly, a credit is made to the asset's **contra account,** "Accumulated Depreciation". For example, suppose you decide to start a business and purchase a computer for $3,000 which you intend to use for the first three years of operations. You record this purchase as an asset, because it is an economic resource that provides benefits to more than one accounting period. Instead of expensing all the costs of the computer in the current period, you will allocate the costs equally over the three years that you will benefit from the computer. After the first year, some of its usefulness is gone and you must, therefore, depreciate the asset. As stated above, you would increase your expenses (Depreciation Expense) and decrease your assets using the contra account (Accumulated Depreciation) as follows:

	Debit	Credit
Depreciation Expense	1,000	
Accumulated Depreciation		1,000

After recording this asset, the book value of the asset is now reduced to $2,000 (original cost of $3,000 less accumulated depreciation of $1,000).

The entry to record expenses for estimated items is normally a debit to an expense account and a credit to a contra asset account.

Chapter 3: The Six Steps to Stardom

Application: Comprehensive Example (continued)

Let's record the following adjusting entries for Just Toys Manufacturing:

9. Cost of Goods Sold for the period totaled $147,000.

10. Prepaid Insurance at the end of the year was $3,000.

11. Depreciation Expense for the period is $30,000.

12. Unpaid Salaries for the period are $7,000.

9. Cost of Goods Sold for the period totaled $147,000. Cost of Goods Sold is an expense account and represents the actual costs to purchase the goods that were sold. In this example, Just Toys purchased goods that cost $147,000 and sold them for $300,000. As we will discuss in Chapter 5, Cost of Goods Sold is often determined at the end of the period by calculating the ending inventory balance and reconciling this amount with the beginning balance. For this entry we will increase expenses to match them with the revenues earned, and decrease Inventory.

	Debit	Credit
Cost of Goods Sold	147,000	
Inventory		147,000

10. Prepaid Insurance at the end of the month was $3,000. Recall from our trial balance in Step 3 that Prepaid Insurance at the beginning of the year was $4,000. If the balance is now $3,000, then $1,000 of insurance must have expired during the year. Therefore, the following adjusting entry must be recorded.

	Debit	Credit
Insurance Expense	1,000	
Prepaid Insurance		1,000

Remember: The entry to record the expiration and/or usage of prepaid expenses is always a debit to an expense account and a credit to an asset account.

11. Depreciation Expense for the period is $30,000. For this transaction, the following entry must be recorded.

	Debit	Credit
Depreciation Expense	30,000	
Accumulated Depreciation		30,000

Chapter 3: The Six Steps to Stardom

Remember: The entry to record expenses for estimated items is always a debit to an expense account and a credit to a contra asset account.

12. **Unpaid Salaries for the period are $7,000.** In this transaction, salaries were incurred during the period in addition to those already paid in Entry #5, resulting in an accrued expense. Therefore, the following transaction muse be recorded.

	Debit	Credit
Salaries & Wages Expense	7,000	
Accrued Expenses		7,000

After recording adjusting entries, an adjusted trial balance is normally prepared to doublecheck the equality of all debits and credits made. Using the trial balance prepared in Step 3, the following adjusted trial balance for Just Toys Manufacturing is assembled.

Account Name	Trial Balance Debit	Trial Balance Credit	Adjusting Entries Debit		Adjusting Entries Credit		Adjusted Trial Balance Debit	Adjusted Trial Balance Credit
Cash	19,000						19,000	
Accounts Receivable	5,000						5,000	
Inventory	211,000				147,000	9	64,000	
Prepaid Insurance	4,000				1,000	10	3,000	
Land	100,000						100,000	
Machinery & Equipment	372,000						372,000	
Accumulated Depreciation		75,000			30,000	11		105,000
Accounts Payable		54,000						54,000
Wages Payable		6,000			7,000	12		13,000
Bond Payable		100,000						100,000
Common Stock		100,000						100,000
Additional Paid in Capital		81,000						81,000
Retained Earnings		98,000						98,000
Sales Revenue		300,000						300,000
Cost of Goods Sold			147,000	9			147,000	
Salaries & Wages Expense	90,000		7,000	12			97,000	
Utilities Expense	7,000						7,000	
Interest Expense	6,000						6,000	
Insurance Expense			1,000	10			1,000	
Depreciation Expense			30,000	11			30,000	
Total	814,000	814,000	185,000		185,000		851,000	851,000

Adjusting entries are normally posted to the T-accounts described in Step 3 before the adjusted trial balance is recorded. However, once you have prepared the trial balance using the T-accounts, the adjusted entries may be posted directly to the worksheet shown above to prepare the adjusted trial balance.

Chapter 3: The Six Steps to Stardom

Three income statement accounts — Cost of Goods Sold, Insurance Expense, and Depreciation Expense — were added to the adjusted trial balance. Income statement accounts are the most common types of accounts that will be added to your trial balance. In your exams, all accounts may not always be listed, and you may need to create a few. Don't assume that the list of accounts given to you is comprehensive (unless, of course, you are told otherwise). Making such an assumption and ignoring the possibility of adding an account can cause you to record transactions in the wrong accounts. Also, don't assume that just because an account is not listed, a transaction does not need to be recorded.

Step 5: Record Closing Entries and Prepare Post-Closing Trial Balance

After all adjusting entries have been made, there is one last step we must take before we can prepare financial statements. Recall that net income flows to the balance sheet through retained earnings. Using the expanded accounting equation, we learned that revenues increase retained earnings and that expenses and dividends decrease retained earnings. Throughout the accounting process, we have been recording transactions affecting income statement accounts in their respective accounts. However, we have not yet reflected the effect of these transactions on the retained earnings account. This is done by preparing closing entries.

Closing entries are entries prepared after all transactions have been recorded. They serve the purpose of providing a summary of income and expenses, and recording net income in the balance sheet. Recall that the balance sheet reports information about a company *at a specific point in time*, the balance sheet accounts are cumulative and reflect all information about a company since its inception. For this reason, balance sheet accounts are called **permanent (or real) accounts** and are never closed out at the end of a period. In contrast, the income statement reflects information about a company's operations *over a certain period of time*. After the period is over, the balance in the account must be reduced to zero in order to start a new accounting period. For this reason, income statement accounts are called **temporary accounts.** When you close an account, you are essentially reducing the balance to zero by making the appropriate debit or credit for the balance in the account. There are two primary steps in this closing process.

1. Transfer the balances in the income statement accounts to an intermediate account, commonly referred to as the "Income Summary" account. For revenues, we can do this by debiting the Revenue account and crediting the Income Summary account. For

expenses, we can do this by crediting the expense account and debiting the Income Summary account. In normal practice, step one in the closing process is typically one journal entry.

Revenue Accounts	Expense Accounts
Revenue	Income Summary
Income Summary	Expenses

2. Transfer the balance in the Income Summary to the Retained Earnings account. The net of all the debits and credits in the Income Summary account is the net income or loss. If total credits exceed total debits, you have a net income, and the income summary account will have a credit balance. To close the Income Summary account if there is net income, debit Income Summary and credit Retained Earnings. Conversely, if total debits exceed total credits, you have a net loss and the Income Summary will have a debit balance. To close the Income Summary account if there is a net loss, credit Income Summary and debit Retained Earnings.

Net Income	Net Loss
Income Summary	Retained Earnings
Retained Earnings	Income Summary

After you have completed step 2 of the closing process, you will have increased Retained Earnings by the excess of revenues over expenses or decreased Retained Earnings by the excess of expenses over revenues and thereby reflected net income (net loss) in the balance sheet

We recommend using the two steps listed above because, as you will see, they will assist you in the preparation of financial statements. However, if you are running short on time during an exam, and your teacher does not require you to show entries for the income summary account (or you just have become an accounting wiz and want a shortcut), you may record net income or net loss directly in retained earnings. Do this by closing the respecting revenue and expense accounts in one journal entry, and then debiting or crediting the balance to retained earnings. As long as you remember that total debits must equal total credits, you can arrive at the net income or net loss that must be reflected in the retained earnings account.

Chapter 3: The Six Steps to Stardom

Following steps 1 and 2 of the closing process, the following closing entries are made:

Just Toys Manufacturing Company
Closing Entries

Step 1	Debit	Credit
Revenue	300,000	
Cost of Goods Sold		147,000
Salaries & Wages Expense		97,000
Utilities Expense		7,000
Interest Expense		6,000
Insurance Expense		1,000
Depreciation Expense		30,000
Income Summary (Net Income)		12,000
Step 2		
Income Summary (Net Income)	12,000	
Retained Earnings		12,000
Total Debits & Credits	312,000	312,000

Using the short-cut method, the following closing entry is made:

Just Toys Manufacturing Company
Shortcut Closing Entry

	Debit	Credit
Revenue	300,000	
Cost of Goods Sold		147,000
Salaries & Wages Expense		97,000
Utilities Expense		7,000
Interest Expense		6,000
Insurance Expense		1,000
Depreciation Expense		30,000
Retained Earnings		**12,000**
Total Debits & Credits	300,000	300,000

Computed by subtracting total revenues from total expenses.

Chapter 3: The Six Steps to Stardom

The following T-account summary represents all the transactions posted, including adjusting and closing entries, for Just Toys Manufacturing. Note that the balances in all temporary accounts (revenue and expense accounts) have been reduced to zero.

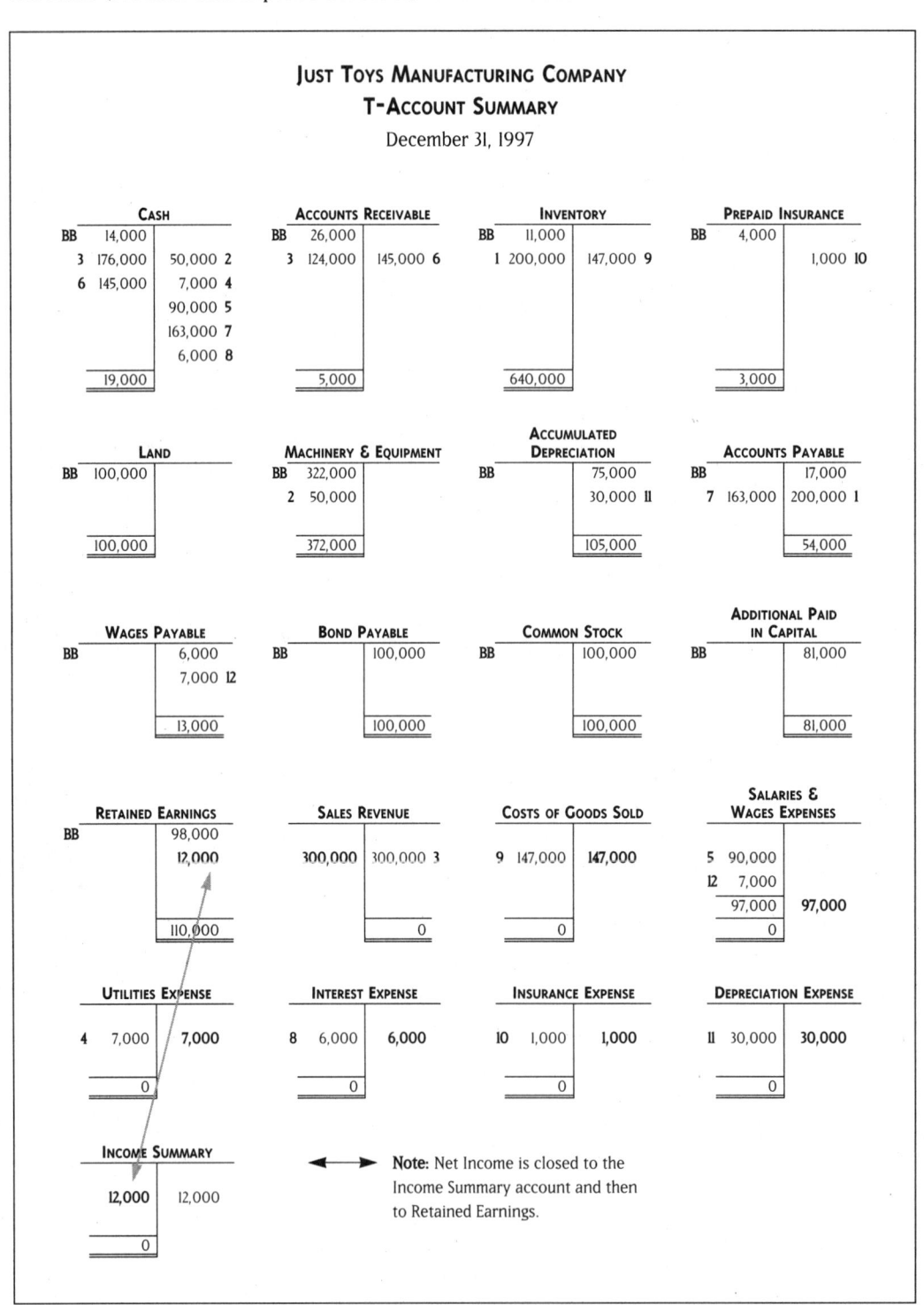

Just Toys Manufacturing Company
T-Account Summary
December 31, 1997

CASH
BB	14,000		
3	176,000	50,000	2
6	145,000	7,000	4
		90,000	5
		163,000	7
		6,000	8
	19,000		

ACCOUNTS RECEIVABLE
BB	26,000		
3	124,000	145,000	6
	5,000		

INVENTORY
BB	11,000		
1	200,000	147,000	9
	640,000		

PREPAID INSURANCE
BB	4,000		
		1,000	10
	3,000		

LAND
BB 100,000	
100,000	

MACHINERY & EQUIPMENT
BB	322,000		
2	50,000		
	372,000		

ACCUMULATED DEPRECIATION
	BB	75,000
		30,000 11
		105,000

ACCOUNTS PAYABLE
		BB	17,000
7	163,000	200,000	1
		54,000	

WAGES PAYABLE
	BB	6,000
		7,000 12
		13,000

BOND PAYABLE
	BB	100,000
		100,000

COMMON STOCK
	BB	100,000
		100,000

ADDITIONAL PAID IN CAPITAL
	BB	81,000
		81,000

RETAINED EARNINGS
	BB	98,000
		12,000
		110,000

SALES REVENUE
300,000	300,000	3
0		

COSTS OF GOODS SOLD
9	147,000	147,000	
	0		

SALARIES & WAGES EXPENSES
5	90,000		
12	7,000		
	97,000	97,000	
	0		

UTILITIES EXPENSE
4	7,000	7,000	
	0		

INTEREST EXPENSE
8	6,000	6,000	
	0		

INSURANCE EXPENSE
10	1,000	1,000	
	0		

DEPRECIATION EXPENSE
11	30,000	30,000	
	0		

INCOME SUMMARY
12,000	12,000
0	

Note: Net Income is closed to the Income Summary account and then to Retained Earnings.

Chapter 3: The Six Steps to Stardom

After closing entries are recorded and posted, the post-closing trial balance is prepared. If done properly, only balance sheet accounts – the permanent accounts – should have balances. The post-closing trial balance for Just Toys Manufacturing Inc. is shown on the below.

Account Name	Adjusted Trial Balance Debit	Adjusted Trial Balance Credit	Closing Entries Debit	Closing Entries Credit	Post-Closing Trial Balance Debit	Post-Closing Trial Balance Credit
Cash	19,000				19,000	
Accounts Receivable	5,000				5,000	
Inventory	64,000				64,000	
Prepaid Insurance	3,000				3,000	
Land	100,000				100,000	
Machinery & Equipment	372,000				372,000	
Accumulated Depreciation		105,000				105,000
Accounts Payable		54,000				54,000
Wages Payable		13,000				13,000
Bond Payable		100,000				100,000
Common Stock		100,000				100,000
Additional Paid in Capital		81,000				81,000
Retained Earnings		98,000		12,000		110,000
Sales Revenue		300,000	300,000			
Cost of Goods Sold	147,000			147,000		
Salaries & Wages Expense	97,000			97,000		
Utilities Expense	7,000			7,000		
Interest Expense	6,000			6,000		
Insurance Expense	1,000			1,000		
Depreciation Expense	30,000			30,000		
Income Summary			12,000	12,000		
	851,000	851,000	312,000	312,000	563,000	563,000

Step 6: Prepare Financial Statements

The final step in the accounting process is the preparation of financial statements. Financial statements can be prepared using the post-closing trial balance and the closing entries. If all entries have been made correctly, this step should be simple to complete and the balance sheet should balance. Since the post-closing trial balance contains only balance sheet accounts, we have all the information we need to prepare the balance sheet. Moreover, since all income statement accounts were closed to Retained Earnings, the short-cut closing entry has all the information we need to prepare the income statement.

KEY CONCEPT

However, properly classifying assets and liabilities on the balance sheet can be complicated. Assets and liabilities are classified into two categories, current or long-term, based on their relative liquidity. In addition, within each category, the assets and liabilities are listed based on the relative liquidity. Recall that liquidity refers to how "near to cash" a company's assets and liabilities are. In general, assets that are expected to be converted into cash within one year and liabilities expected to be paid within one year are classified as current and the remainder are classified as long term. The following chart will assist you properly classify balance sheet items.

Classification Type	General Rule	Common Examples (appearing in order of relative liquidity within the category)
current asset	Plan to convert into cash within one year or one operating cycle, if longer.	cash available for sale securities accounts receivable notes receivable (due within one year) inventory supplies prepaid expenses
non-current assets (also called long-term assets)	Plan to hold for more than one year or one operating cycle, if longer.	notes receivable (due after one year) long-term investments land buildings furniture & fixtures machinery & equipment intangible assets (goodwill, patents, etc.)
current liabilities	Due to be paid within one year or one operating cycle, if longer.	notes payable (due within one year) accounts payable income taxes payable interest payable salaries payable unearned revenue
non-current liabilities (also called long-term liabilities)	Not payable within the year or one operating cycle, if longer.	notes payable (due after one year) bonds payable

Equity accounts are commonly listed in the following order:

1. Common Stock (or Owners' Capital)

2. Additional Paid-in Capital

3. Retained Earnings

Using the chart above as a guide, the balance sheet, income statement, and statement of retained earnings for Just Toys Manufacturing is arranged as follows:

Chapter 3: The Six Steps to Stardom

Just Toys Manufacturing Company
Balance Sheet
As of December 31, 1998

Assets		Liabilities & Shareholders Equity	
Current Assets		**Current Liabilities**	
Cash	19,000	Accounts Payable	54,000
Accounts Receivable	5,000	Wages Payable	13,000
Inventory	64,000	Total Current Liabilities	67,000
Prepaid Insurance	3,000		
Total Current Assets	91,000	**Non-Current Liabilities**	
		Bonds Payable	100,000
Non-Current Assets			
Land	100,000	Total Liabilities	167,000
Machinery & Equipment	372,000	**Stockholders Equity**	
Less: Accumulated Depreciation	(105,000)	Common Stock	100,000
Total Non-Current Assets	367,000	Additional Paid-In Capital	81,000
		Retained Earnings	110,000
		Total Liabilities & Equity	291,000
Total Assets	458,000	Total Liab & Stockholders Equity	458,000

Just Toys Manufacturing Company
Income Statement
For the year ended December 31, 1998

Revenue		
Sales Revenue		300,000
Expenses		
Costs of Goods Sold	147,000	
Salaries & Wages Expenses	97,000	
Utilities Expense	7,000	
Interest Expense	6,000	
Insurance Expense	1,000	
Depreciation Expense	30,000	
Total Expenses		288,000
Net Income		12,000
Retained Earnings 1/1/98		98,000
Retained Earnings 12/31/98		110,000

CHAPTER 3: THE SIX STEPS TO STARDOM

JUST TOYS MANUFACTURING COMPANY
Statement of Retained Earnings
For the year ended December 31, 1998

Retained Earnings	1/1/98	98,000
Add: Net Income for the year		12,000
		110,000
Less: Dividends Declared		0
Retained Earnings	12/31/98	110,000

This income statement presents an alternative presentation of the statement of retained earnings. Smaller companies that do not have a lot of activity in their retained earnings accounts often present the statement of retained earnings through their income statement. Both methods of presentation are acceptable under Generally Accepted Accounting Principles.

Brownie Points: Do not forget to label each financial statement with the name of the company, the name of the financial statement, and the period covered. Note that the balance sheet is labeled "as of" December 31, 1998, while the income statement is labeled "for the year ended" December 31, 1998. The balance sheet is cumulative and covers the period from inception and is appropriately always labeled "as of." The income statement covers only a certain period (in this case, one year) and should appropriately be labeled as such.

Chapter 3: The Six Steps to Stardom

Key Terms

accrued expenses: expenses incurred but not paid by the end of the accounting period. The entry to record the accrued expenses incurred but not paid is always a debit to an expense account and a credit to a liability account.

accrued revenues: revenues earned but not yet received in cash by the end of the accounting period. The entry to record the accrued revenues earned but not yet received is always a debit to an asset account (specifically, a receivable account) and a credit to a revenue account.

adjusting entries: entries recorded after all transactions have been posted. Adjusting entries reflect income and expenses in the appropriate accounting period by recording revenues earned but not yet received for the period and expenses incurred but not yet paid.

closing entries: entries prepared for all temporary accounts to provide a summary of income and expenses and to record net income in the balance sheet. When you close an account, you are essentially reducing the balance to zero by making the appropriate opposing debit or credit for the balance in the account.

compound entry: a journal entry that involves more than one debit or more than one credit.

contra account: an account on the balance sheet that reduces a specific asset, liability, or equity account

entries: entries in the general journal should include the following information about each transaction:
1. The date
2. The account names (remember there should be at least two)
3. The dollar amounts debited and credited
4. An explanation of the transaction
5. The account identification numbers (the entry number)

estimated items: expenses recorded based on estimates of future unknown events. Estimated items are normally recorded as a debit to an expense account and a credit to a contra asset account.

Chapter 3: The Six Steps to Stardom

journal: often called "the book of original entry" because it is where transactions first enter the accounting records. General journals are the simplest type, because they can be used to record all types of transactions. Specialized journals, such as a cash receipts journal or sales journal, are used to record repetitive transactions that affect the same accounts.

prepaid expenses: prepaid expenses are expenses paid in cash in the current period that will benefit future periods. The entry to record the expiration and/or usage of prepaid expenses is always a debit to an expense account and a credit to an asset account.

trial balance: a list of all of the accounts in a ledger with their balances. The trial balance gives the accountant a chance to double check the equality of debits and credits, but it does not provide a mechanism for detecting all errors in recording transactions.

unearned revenues: revenues received in cash before they are earned. The entry to record the recognition of unearned revenue is always a credit to unearned revenue and a debit to a liability account.

Chapter 3: The Six Steps to Stardom

Thrills, Chills and Drills

True or False

1. If Johnny B. Good uses cash to invest in his new company, B. Good Productions, he will record the transaction as usual and frequent.

2. When Johnny B. Good records the above transaction on the books of the company, he will debit cash and credit owner's equity.

3. Up, Up and Away Company located in Florida, where Class 1 but not Class 2 and Class 3 hurricanes are common, loses a building in a Class 3 hurricane. This is recorded as an unusual and infrequent occurrence.

4. The building of Flying High Company, located in Philadelphia, Pennsylvania, where hurricanes rarely visit, is destroyed in a Class 1 hurricane. This is recorded as an unusual and infrequent occurrence.

5. The Journal Entry Approach applies the concept that debits must always equal liabilities plus owners' equity.

6. The trial balance is always completed after the balance sheet to check if the debits equal the credits in all the journal entries.

7. All transactions are recorded in their individual accounts first, and are then posted to the journal.

8. Sally Straightline likes everything neat and in rows. She was hired to help Shirley I. Kant, to enter transactions into the journal. Sally put all the debits in first and then all the credits. Shirley I. Kant couldn't believe her eyes. Sally said, "As long as the debits equal the credits, the order in which the transactions are entered doesn't matter." Sally was correct.

9. The revenue recognition principle and the matching principle ask us to recognize revenue when cash is received and to recognize expenses when cash is paid.

10. The entry to record the expiration and/or usage of prepaid expenses is always a debit to an expense account and a credit to an asset account.

11. Unearned revenue is recorded on the income statement.

12. Lan D. Lord's tenants pay him 6 months rent in advance when they sign their leases. He should record each transaction as a debit to cash and a credit to revenue.

Chapter 3: The Six Steps to Stardom

13. In the situation in question 12, the tenants would record the rent on their books as a credit to Rent Expense and a debit to Accrued Rent.

14. The entry to record an expense for an estimated item is always a debit to an expense account and a credit to a contra asset account.

15. Revenues increase Retained Earnings, and expenses decrease Retained Earnings.

16. Closing entries close the balance sheet accounts at the end of the period.

17. The balance in the income summary account is transferred to the Retained Earnings account at the beginning of the period.

18. Les N. Perfect Company had more expenses than revenues for the period. To close the Income Summary account, the bookkeeper, Mr. Slick, should debit the Income Summary account and credit Retained Earnings.

19. The post-closing trial balance contains all the accounts for the company.

20. The balance sheet should be labeled "for the year ended."

Multiple Choice

Use the following information to answer questions 1 and 2.

Superman Imports was started by four friends: Lois, Clark, Jimmy, and Perry. Lois invested cash of $45,000. Clark donated a building and land worth $45,000. Jimmy donated his truck worth $45,000. Perry donated a computer worth $45,000. The company had revenue of $1,000,000 during its first year and expenses of $985,000.

1. **The entry to record the investment into the company should be:**

   a)
Owner's Equity	$45,000	
Cash		$45,000

   b)
Owner's Equity	$180,000	
Cash		45,000
Building & Land		45,000
Truck		45,000
Computer		45,000

c)
Cash	180,000	
Owner's Equity		180,000

d)
Cash	45,000	
Building & Land	45,000	
Truck	45,000	
Computer	45,000	
Owner's Equity		180,000

2. The entry to record the income (loss) for the year should be:

a)
Retained Earnings	$15,000	
Cash		$15,000

b)
Income Summary	$15,000	
Retained Earnings		$15,000

c)
Cash	$15,000	
Retained Earnings		$15,000

d)
Retained Earnings	$15,000	
Income Summary		$15,000

3. Waves, Inc. had a warehouse located on the Mississippi River for easy access to the river traffic for both sales to the boat owner's and for deliveries from their suppliers. Recently, the river overflowed its banks and destroyed the inventory stored on the bottom floor. This event should be recorded as

   a) usual and frequent
   b) unusual and infrequent
   c) usual and infrequent
   d) unusual and frequent

4. Imagine that the warehouse described above is located at 30th and Market Streets in Philadelphia. This event should be recorded as

   a) usual and frequent
   b) unusual and infrequent
   c) usual and infrequent
   d) unusual and frequent

Chapter 3: The Six Steps to Stardom

5. The journal entry approach is
    I. a constant application of the concept that debits must always equal credits
    II. assets must always equal liabilities
        a) I only
        b) II only
        c) both I and II
        d) Neither

6. Too Good to be True, Inc. has sold goods for $6,000,000. Cash received was $2,500,000. What is the entry to record this event?

    a)
Cash	$6,000,000	
Sales		$6,000,000

    b)
Cash	$2,500,000	
Sales		$2,500,000

    c)
Sales	$6,000,000	
Cash		$6,000,000

    d)
Cash	$2,500,000	
Accounts Receivable	$3,500,000	
Sales		$6,000,000

7. The journal entry should contain
    I. the date the event is recorded
    II. the account names
    III. an explanation of the transaction
    IV. the account identification numbers
    V. the dollar amount debited and credited
    VI. the date the event happened
        a) all of the above
        b) none of the above
        c) I, II, III, IV, and V only
        d) II, III, IV, V and VI only

Chapter 3: The Six Steps to Stardom

8. The trial balance includes
   a) assets and liabilities only
   b) revenues and expenses only
   c) assets, liabilities, and owners' equity only
   d) a and b
   e) b and c

9. An example of an adjusting entry is

   a)
Depreciation Expense
Accumulated Depreciation

   b)
Insurance Expense
Prepaid Insurance

   c)
Salaries and Wages Expense
Cash

   d) all of the above
   e) a and b only
   f) b and c only

10. The income statement
    a) reports information about a company at a specific point in time
    b) reports information about a company over a certain period of time
    c) is debited by revenue amounts
    d) is credited by the expense amounts

11. To close the income summary account when there is a net loss
    a) debit income summary; credit retained earnings
    b) credit income summary; debit retained earnings
    c) debit income summary; credit revenue
    d) debit cash; credit income summary

12. The post-closing trial balance consists of
    a) assets and liabilities only
    b) revenues and expenses only
    c) assets, liabilities, and owners' equity only
    d) b and c
    e) a and b

CHAPTER 3: THE SIX STEPS TO STARDOM

13. The first step in preparing the financial statements is to
    a) enter the transactions in the ledger
    b) enter the transactions in the journal
    c) enter the transactions in the balance sheet
    d) enter the transactions in the trial balance

14. Accrued revenue is
    a) an asset
    b) a liability
    c) an income statement account
    d) a contra account

15. Accumulated depreciation is
    a) an asset
    b) a liability
    c) an income statement account
    d) none of the above

16. The entry to record depreciation expense on the office furniture is
    a) debit depreciation expense; credit office furniture
    b) debit accumulated depreciation; credit office furniture
    c) debit depreciation expense; credit accumulated depreciation
    d) debit accumulated depreciation; credit depreciation expense

17. ShooFly Inc. needed to buy insurance on the building it used to house its business equipment. The policy cost $1,200 a year. In January, the bookkeeper needed to make an entry to record this purchase. She should
    a) debit cash; credit insurance
    b) debit prepaid insurance; credit cash
    c) debit prepaid insurance; credit insurance
    d) debit insurance expense; credit cash

18. The bookkeeper also needs to make a second entry for the month of January. She should
    a) debit cash; credit insurance
    b) debit prepaid insurance; credit cash
    c) debit insurance expense; credit cash
    d) debit insurance expense; credit prepaid insurance

Chapter 3: The Six Steps to Stardom

For questions 19 and 20, refer to the following information.

George's Vending Machine Company was started when he invested his savings. His business grew so quickly that he needed more financial backing. He decided to go public and issue $10,000,000 of common stock. Classify the two transactions (the founding and the public offering) and tell which accounts are affected.

19. Initial investment in business
   a) unusual-cash
      infrequent-owner's equity
   b) usual-cash
      frequent-owner's equity
   c) unusual-cash
      frequent-owner's equity
   d) usual-cash
      infrequent-owner's equity

20. The sale of common stock
   a) usual-cash
      infrequent-common stock
   b) unusual-cash
      frequent-common stock
   c) usual-cash
      frequent-common stock
   d)i unusual-cash
      infrequent-common stock

Chapter 3: The Six Steps to Stardom

Short Essays

1. List the following accounting events in the order that they should occur.

    a. record adjustments

    b. analyze and record transactions in journal

    c. prepare financial statements

    d. post transactions to ledger

    e. prepare adjusting trial balance

    f. collect and prepare source documents

    g. prepare trial balance

    h. record closing transactions

2. John E. Rebel did not get along with the management of the bill collecting firm for which he worked. He decided to start his own collection agency on July 4, 1999. The following events occurred during his first month of business.

    July   4   John started firm by investing $20,000.

              5   An office suite was rented for $12,000 per year up front.

              6   Furnishings for the office were purchased for cash at a cost of $7000.

              7   Three employees were hired. They were scheduled to start training the next week.

              8   A $15,000 loan was obtained from a relative at 10% annual interest.

             11   John had promotional literature printed and distributed to potential clients. The cost was $2,100, paid in full.

             23   Services were provided for clients totaling $4500. Of the fees, 20% was collected in cash, with the balance due August 15.

             31   Utilities used during the month totaling $480 and had not been paid.

             31   Employee wages for the month were $3,200, of which 30% was still owed at the end of the month.

Chapter 3: The Six Steps to Stardom

31 Three more clients contracted for services to begin during the following month. John estimated that these clients would generate $6,000 of billings per month. No cash had been received. Depreciation expense for the month was $300.

a. Decide which events qualify as economic events. For those that do, prepare the necessary journal entries. For those that do not, write N/E.

b. Prepare a trial balance for the end of the month. Remember to include the adjusting journal entries if any. Do not make closing entries.

3. Below is the trial balance for Tell Me More, Ltd. The company provides flowers, greeting cards, and specialty packages that ship all over the country. Using this trial balance, prepare the necessary closing entries and prepare the post-closing trial balance. (Remember to be precise in your labeling and form).

TELL ME MORE LTD.
Adjusted Trial Balance
December 31, 1998

Account	Debit	Credit
Cash	$ 1,300	
Inventory	5,600	
Supplies	2,000	
Prepaid Insurance	900	
Equipment	7,100	
Accumulated Depreciation		$ 3,400
Interest Payable		300
Notes Payable		4,000
Investment by Owner		8,350
Sales Revenue		4,400
Costs of Goods Sold	1,800	
Wages Expense	700	
Utilities Expense	300	
Depreciation Expense	100	
Insurance Expense	200	
Supplies Expense	150	
Interest Expense	300	
	$ 20,450	$ 20,450

4. Using the information provided in Question #3, prepare the income statement and statement of retained earnings for Tell Me More, Ltd.

Chapter 3: The Six Steps to Stardom

5. The Shelly Shores Co. closes its books on September 15, marking the end of its accounting period. Explain what is meant by "closing the books" and "accounting period."

6. Listed below are account balances for Run-A-Muck Co. for the fiscal year ended October 31, 1997:

Accounts Payable	$ 22,000
Accounts Receivable	11,000
Accumulated Depreciation	164,000
Buildings	412,000
Cash	16,000
Equipment	245,000
Dividends (declared not paid)	245,000
Notes Payable	45,000
Selling Expense	13,000
Supplies	13,000
Wages Payable	18,000
Retained Earnings	357,000
Net Income	25,000
Salary Expense	100,000
Unearned Revenue	30,000
Prepaid Insurance	1,000
Cost of Goods Sold	10,000
Prepaid Rent	12,000
Rent Expense	1,000
Accrued Vacation Pay	200

For each of the accounts listed above, state which financial statement (balance sheet, income statement, or statement of retained earnings) the account should be recorded in. Also state whether the account has a debit or credit balance.

Chapter 3: The Six Steps to Stardom

7. A series of financial statement items is listed below.

1. Accounts Receivable
2. Inventory
3. Supplies
4. Prepaid Insurance
5. Accounts Payable
6. Dividends
7. Wages Expense
8. Cash Paid for Equipment
9. Buildings
10. Wages Payable
11. Sales/Service Revenue
12. Retained Earnings
13. Rent Expense
14. Unearned Revenue
15. Depreciation Expense
16. Patents
17. Contributed Capital
18. Notes Payable
19. Interest Payable
20. Cost of Goods Sold
21. Accrued Vacation Pay
22. Net Income

For each account, indicate the financial statement on which the account would appear. Then, describe the information provided by the account to someone reading the financial statements.

Example:

1. Accounts Receivable   Balance Sheet   Money that will be received in the future from sales made in the past.

Chapter 3: The Six Steps to Stardom

Answers

True or False Answers

1. **False.** It is classified as unusual and infrequent.
2. **True.** The journal entry is correct because cash is an asset and debited to increase, and owners' equity carries a credit balance and is credited to increase.
3. **False.** It would be usual and infrequent. Hurricanes are common in Florida but a force 3 is an infrequent occurrence
4. **True.** Hurricanes are not a common occurrence in Pennsylvania. No matter what the force, they are infrequent.
5. **False.** Assets must always equal liabilities plus owners' equity.
6. **False.** The trial balance is completed first.
7. **False.** All transactions are recorded in the journal first and then to individual accounts.
8. **False.** For each transaction, we must have at least one debit and at least one credit (double-entry bookkeeping system).
9. **False.** These two principles do not require us to recognize revenue when cash is received and expenses when cash is paid.
10. **True.** Prepaid expenses are assets to the paying entity and are decreased when used or expired. Assets are decreased with a credit, and expenses are increased with a debit entry.
11. **False.** Unearned revenue is a liability until the service is performed that the client paid for in advance.
12. **False.** He should record it as a debit to Cash and a credit to Unearned Revenue.
13. **False.** The tenants would record it as a debit to Prepaid Rent and a credit to Cash.
14. **True.** An example is the recording of depreciation expense (debit Depreciation Expense and credit Accumulated Depreciation.)
15. **True.** Revenues over expenses is reflected in net income, and net income increases Retained Earnings. This is also true because revenues increase the net worth of the company. This is shown in Retained Earnings.
16. **False.** Closing entries close the income and expense accounts at the end of the period.
17. **False.** The transfer takes place at the end of period when the books are closed.
18. **False.** Mr. Slick should debit Retained Earnings and credit the Income Summary account.
19. **False.** The post-closing trial balance contains only the balance sheet accounts. The income accounts were closed.
20. **False.** The balance sheet should be labeled "as of " December 31, 1998. It is a snapshot of the company at this particular time, not over a period.

CHAPTER 3: THE SIX STEPS TO STARDOM

Multiple Choice Answers

1. **(d)** Not a, because you do not record only the cash. Not b, because assets are increased by a debit and Owners' Equity is increased by a credit. Not c, because all received was not cash. Therefore d is correct as each asset is entered.

2. **(b)** Not a, because revenue increased Retained Earnings, which has a credit balance. Not c, because revenue does not run through Cash at the end of the period, but rather through the Income Summary. Not d because of a. Therefore c is the correct choice.

3. **(d)** Not a, because this expense does not occur as a result of regular business transactions. Not b, because the Mississippi does overflow its banks occasionally. Not c, because it is not a usual occurrence. Therefore d is the correct choice.

4. **(b)** Because of the location, the answer is b.

5. **(a)** Remember the basic equation: Assets = Liabilities + Owners' Equity + (Revenues - Expenses). Therefore, the only possible choice is a.

6. **(d)** d is the correct choice. All sales must be accounted for, and if some are paid in cash, the others must have been on account.

7. **(d)** The date the event is recorded in not necessary, but the date used to record the transaction should be the date the transaction occurred.

8. **(e)** The trial balance contains both the balance sheet and the income statement accounts.

9. **(e)** Adjusting entries are those entries that are posted after all transactions are posted to reflect income and expenses in the appropriate accounting period by recording revenues earned but not yet received for the period (and expenses incurred but not yet paid).

10. **(b)** The income statement reports the information about a company over a certain period of time.

11. **(b)** Not a or c because Retained Earnings is decreased by a debit entry, and a net loss will decrease Retained Earnings. Not d, because cash is not debited to close the Income Summary. Therefore, b is the correct choice.

12. **(c)** Not a, because the post closing trial balance also included Owners' Equity. Not b, because all revenue and expense accounts were closed for the period. Therefore, the correct choice is c.

13. **(b)** The correct choice is b, because step 2 of the "6 steps to stardom" is to record the transactions in the journal.

14. **(a)** Not b, because accrued revenue is revenue earned but not yet received and similar to accounts receivable (and therefore an asset not a liability). Not c, because it is a balance sheet account, not an income statement account. Therefore, the correct answer is a.

15. **(d)** Not a, because depreciation does not increase the value of the asset, but rather decreases it. Not b, because depreciation is not a liability. It is a contra asset account. Not c, because depreciation is not an expense. Therefore the correct answer is d, none of the above.

16. **(c)** The correct choice is c, because the entry to record expenses for estimated items are always a debit to an expense account and a credit to a contra asset account.

17. **(b)** Not a, because cash is decreased by a credit. Not c, because the cash was not accounted for in this entry. Not d, because the company is paying in advance for insurance that has been used. Therefore, b is the correct choice because an asset is recorded and cash is spent.

Chapter 3: The Six Steps to Stardom

18. **(d)** The entry to record the expiration and/or usage of prepaid expenses is always a debit to an expense account and a credit to an asset account.

19. **(a)** The investment of the cash into the business by other investors is not part of the of the regular course of business and occurs infrequently, only once when the business is started. The investment of the money is recorded as a debit to Cash and credit to Owners' Equity.

20. **(d)** The sale of stock is not related to the regular course of business; it is an infrequent occurrence and is unusual in nature. Cash is affected by the selling price, and Common Stock is affected by the distribution of the stock to the purchaser.

Short Essay Answers

1. F   One must collect the source documents in order to analyze the transaction.
   B   One must next analyze and record the transaction.
   D   Posting the transactions to the ledger.
   G   Prepare the trial balance.
   A   Record any adjustments that need to be made.
   E   Prepare the adjusting trial balance.
   H   Record the closing transactions.
   C   Prepare the financial statements.

2. a.

Date	Account	Debit	Credit
4-July	Cash	20,000	
	Owners' Equity		20,000

To record the investment of cash by John E. Rebel.

Date	Account	Debit	Credit
5-July	Prepaid Rent	12,000	
	Cash		12,000

To record signing of lease paid in full for one year.

Date	Account	Debit	Credit
6-July	Furniture	7,000	
	Cash		7,000

To record the purchase of furniture for the office in cash.

Date	Account	Debit	Credit
7-July	N/E		

Date	Account	Debit	Credit
8-July	Cash	15,000	
	Loan Payable		15,000

To record loan from Bill E. Rebel at 10% interest.

Date	Account	Debit	Credit
11-July	Advertising Expense	2,100	
	Cash		2,100

To record the purchase and distribution of advertising material.

23-July	Cash		900	
	Client Services			900
	Accounts Receivable		3,400	
	Client Services			3,400
	To record services rendered to clients.			
31-July	Utilities Expense		480	
	Accounts Payable			480
	To record utility bill not yet paid.			
31-July	Salary Expense		960	
	Wages Payable			960
	Salary Expense		2,240	
	Cash			2,240
	To record salaries for the month.			
31-Jul	N/E			

2. b.

JOHN E. REBEL
For the month ended July 31, 1998

	Trial Balance		Adjusting Entries		Adjusted Trial Balance	
Cash	12,560				12,560	
Accounts Receivable	3,400				3,400	
Furniture & Fixture	7,000				7,000	
Prepaid Rent	12,000			1,000 (b)	11,000	
Accumulated Depreciation				300 (a)		300
Accounts Payable		480				480
Wages Payable		960				960
Loan Payable		15,000				15,000
Owners' Equity		20,000				20,000
Service Income		4,300				4,300
Advertising Expense	2,100				2,100	
Salaries Expense	3,200				3,200	
Utilities Expense	480				480	
Depreciation Expense			300 (a)		300	
Rent Expense			1,000 (b)		1,000	
Total	40,740	40,740	1,300	1,300	41,040	41,040

(a) To record Depreciation Expense for the month of July.

(b) To record Rent Expense for the month of July.

Chapter 3: The Six Steps to Stardom

3. **Part 1**

TELL ME MORE, LTD.
Adjusted Trial Balance
December 31, 1998

Account	Debit	Credit
Cash	$1,300	
Inventory	5,600	
Supplies	2,000	
Prepaid Insurance	900	
Equipment	7,100	
Accumulated Depreciation		$3,400
Interest Payable		300
Notes Payable		4,000
Investment by Owner		8,350
Sales Revenue		4,400
Cost of Goods Sold	1,800	
Wages Expense	700	
Utilities Expense	300	
Depreciation Expense	100	
Insurance Expense	200	
Supplies Expense	150	
Interest Expense	300	
	$20,450	$20,450

TELL ME MORE, LTD.
Closing Entries
December 31, 1998

Step 1

	Debit	Credit
Sales Revenue	4,400	
Cost of Goods Sold		1,800
Wages Expense		700
Utilities Expense		300
Depreciation Expense		100
Insurance Expense		200
Supplies Expense		150
Interest Expense		300
Income Summary		850
Total Debits & Credits	4,400	4,400

Step 2

Income Summary	850	
Retained Earnings		850
Total Debits & Credits	850	850

Part 2

TELL ME MORE, LTD.
Balance Sheet
December 31, 1998

Cash	$1,300	
Inventory	5,600	
Supplies	2,000	
Prepaid Insurance	700	
Equipment	7,100	
Accumulated Depreciation		$3,500
Interest Payable		0
Notes Payable		4,000
Investment by Owner		9,200
	$16,700	$16,700

4. Part 1

TELL ME MORE, LTD.
Income Statement
For the year ended December 31, 1998

<u>Revenue</u>

Sales revenue		$4,400

<u>Expenses</u>

Cost of Goods Sold	1,800	
Wages Expense	700	
Utilities Expense	300	
Depreciation Expense	100	
Insurance Expense	200	
Supplies Expense	150	
Interest Expense	300	
Total Expenses		3,550
Net Income		850
Retained Earnings 1/1/98		8,350
Retained Earnings 12/31/98		9,200

Part 2

TELL ME MORE, LTD.
Statement of Retained Earnings
For the year ended December 31, 1998

Retained Earnings	8,350
Add: Net income for the year	850
	9,200
Less: Dividends Declared	0
Retained Earnings 12/31/98	9,200

5. Part 1

<u>Closing the books:</u>

Closing the books relates to the process of transferring revenue and expense account balances to the owners' equity. This involves adjusting each revenue and expense account so that it has a zero balance at the end of the accounting period.

Part 2

<u>Accounting period:</u>

An accounting period is any length of time used to measure the effects of transactions. This period could be a month, a quarter or a year. An accounting period is often called a fiscal period because it may not end with a calendar year. For example, a corporation's year-end may be June 30, instead of December 31.

Chapter 3: The Six Steps to Stardom

6.

Account Description	Balance	Financial Statement	Debit/Credit
Accounts Payable	$22,000	Balance Sheet	Credit
Accounts Receivable	11,000	Balance Sheet	Debit
Accumulated Depreciation	164,000	Blaance Sheet	Credit
Buildings	412,000	Balance Sheet	Debit
Cash	16,000	Balance Sheet	Debit
Equipment	245,000	Balance Sheet	Debit
Dividends (declared not paid)	245,000	Statement of Retained Earnings	Credit
Notes Payable	45,000	Balance Sheet	Credit
Selling Expense	13,000	Income Statement	Debit
Supplies	13,000	Balance Sheet	Debit
Wages Payable	18,000	Balance Sheet	Credit
Retained Earnings	357,000	Balance Sheet & Statement of Retained Earnings	Credit
Net Income	25,000	Statement of Retained Earnings	Credit
Salary Expense	100,000	Income Statement	Debit
Unearned Revenue	30,000	Balance Sheet	Credit
Prepaid Insurance	1,000	Balance Sheet	Debit
Cost of Goods Sold	10,000	Income Statement	Debit
Prepaid Rent	12,000	Balance Sheet	Debit
Rent Expense	1,000	Income Statement	Debit
Accrued Vacation Pay	200	Balance Sheet	Credit

Chapter 3: The Six Steps to Stardom

7.

Account Description	Financial Statement	What the account represents
Accounts Receivable	Balance Sheet	Revenues earned but not yet received
Inventory	Balance Sheet	Goods available to convert to cash in the future
Supplies	Balance Sheet	Cost of supplies purchased in the past to be used in the future
Prepaid Insurance	Balace Sheet	Cash paid in the present or past period for insurance consumed in the future
Accounts Payable	Balance Sheet	Expenses incurred but not yet paid
Dividends (delcared not paid)	Statement of Retained Earnings	Cash paid or promised to shareholders as a result of operations
Wages Expense	Income Statement	Cost of services for the present period
Cash Paid for Equipment	Balance Sheet	Cash paid for resources acquired
Buildings	Balance Sheet	Historical Cost of assets acquired to be consumed in the future
Wages Payable	Balance Sheet	Cash to be paid in the future for services used in the past
Sales/Service Revenue	Income Statement	Cash received or owed by clients for goods/services rendered in current period
Retained Earnings	Balance Sheet & Statement of Retained Earnings	Profits from operations put aside for future future use
Rent Expense	Income Statement	Amount due in current period
Unearned Revenue	Balance Sheet	Revenues received in cash before they are earned
Depreciation Expense	Income Statement	Current cost of using up of an asset
Patents	Balance Sheet	Cost of asset paid in the past used in the future
Contributed Capital	Balance Sheet & Statement Retained Earnings	Cash received from owners to acquire resources
Notes Payable	Balance Sheet	Cash borrowed in the past to acquire resources but paid in the future
Interest Payable	Balance Sheet	Cash due in the future on funds borrowed
Cost of Goods Sold	Income Statement	Cost of resources consumed in current period
Accrued Vacation Pay	Balance Sheet	Expenses incurred but not paid before the end of the period
Net Income	Statement of Retained Earnings	Profit for the period

Chapter

Cash, Accounts Receivable, and Marketable Securities

4

Chapter 4: Cash, Accounts Receivable, and Marketable Securities

Overview

The first three chapters of this book provided a general overview of the accounting process. By now, you should have a firm grasp of the importance of financial statements, recorded transactions, and the completed accounting process. Starting with Chapter 4, we will look at individual accounts in the balance sheet to identify their complexities and provide easy ways to solve problems when they arise. In this chapter, we will cover **cash, accounts receivable, and marketable securities.** Cash, accounts receivable, and marketable securities are a company's three most liquid assets. When financial statement users analyze a company's liquidity, they want to know if the company will be able to pay their bills in the short term. The value of these three accounts in the balance sheet gives financial analysts a good starting point. For this reason, in this chapter we will focus on the presentation and valuation of these accounts. While marketable securities and accounts receivable are the more complex topics, the cash and cash equivalents sections are crucial if you ever have to prepare a bank reconciliation.

Chapter 4: Cash, Accounts Receivable, and Marketable Securities

Concepts

Cash and Cash Equivalents

Cash is a company's most liquid asset. Because of its liquidity, it is used to execute most business transactions. However, the liquidity of this asset also means that there is a high risk of loss associated with its use, because of the risk of theft or embezzlement.

COMPOSITION OF CASH

To be classified as "cash and cash equivalents" on the balance sheet, an asset must be currency or easily convertible into currency. Common cash items include coins, currency on hand and in the bank, undeposited checks, money orders, savings deposits, and certificates of deposit. Postage stamps, postdated checks, and IOUs are not cash. Compensating balances are also excluded from cash. A **compensating balance** is a minimum checking account balance that must be maintained as a requirement of a borrowing agreement with the bank. The use of compensating balances is restricted; having such balances reduces a company's liquidity. Since the cash item on the balance sheet indicates a company's liquidity, compensating balance arrangements must be shown separately on the balance sheet.

CASH MANAGEMENT

Because of its liquidity and high risk of loss, the management of cash requires effective **internal controls**. Internal controls are procedures adopted by companies to ensure the safeguarding of company assets, the operational effectiveness and efficiency of the financial reporting process, and the overall reliability of financial reporting. The most common control procedure over cash is the bank account. Another consideration in managing cash is maintaining the appropriate level of cash in the bank to conduct business while simultaneously receiving the highest possible return on investments. Companies usually use a budget process or another comparative analysis to determine how much cash is required to conduct day-to-day operations. Any excess or "idle" cash is often invested in short-term investments, such as US Treasury notes, certificates of deposits, commercial paper, and other highly liquid securities. If these investments have an original maturity date of 90 days or less, they are classified as **cash equivalents**. We use this term because the investments convert into cash so quickly that they are considered the equivalent of cash on the balance sheet.

Chapter 4: Cash, Accounts Receivable, and Marketable Securities

Remember, when reading problems on cash equivalents, focus on the maturity date, with the respect of the purchase date. Consider the following scenarios, that may seem like they represent cash equivalents, but do not.

1. Suppose you purchased a US Treasury bill five years ago that it is maturing tomorrow. This investment would not be considered a cash equivalent since the **original** maturity date is not within 90 days or less of its purchase.

2. Suppose that on March 1 you purchased a certificate of deposit (CD) that will mature in 120 days. It is now April 1, and you have to prepare financial statements. This CD is not considered a cash equivalent — although it will mature in 90 days — because the **original** maturity date is not within 90 days or less.

3. Suppose you purchased a US Treasury bill with a maturity date 10 years from the date of purchase. You are now in year four and decide that you want to sell the investment. In the year you sell the T-Bill, the investment would not be considered a cash equivalent, because the **original** maturity date is not within 90 days or less.

Petty Cash

Not all of a company's money is kept in a bank account. Most companies also keep a **petty cash** account in order to keep some currency and coins on hand to pay for incidental expenses or to fill cash registers. This account is normally funded using an **imprest system**, which establishes a fixed amount in the account. As the funds are used, the account is periodically reimbursed to maintain the fixed amount.

The Bank Account

A bank account allows for an external record of total cash held by a company. To ensure that the cash reflected on the books is what is actually held by the bank, companies often prepare monthly bank reconciliations. There are two common reconciling items that appear on a bank reconciliation:

outstanding checks: These are cash disbursements in the form of checks that have been issued by a company and recorded on the books as paid but have not been cashed by the payee. For example, say University Services, Inc. receives an invoice from Supply Me Company in June in the amount of $4,000 for supplies purchased in May. When University Services writes and mails the check to Supply Me, they no longer have an obligation to this supplier and would record the entry shown on the adjacent page:

Chapter 4: Cash, Accounts Receivable, and Marketable Securities

	Debit	Credit
Accounts Payable	40,000	
Cash		40,000

Suppose Supply Me doesn't cash the check until July. If this happens, the payment will not be reflected in the June bank statement. When University Services prepares its June bank reconciliation, its cash balance in the bank will be higher than what is recorded in the books by $40,000. The check written to Supply Me has not been cashed and is, therefore, considered "outstanding."

deposits in transit: These are cash receipts recorded on the books and mailed or taken to the bank but not reflected on the bank statement. For example, suppose that University Services, Inc. receives $10,000 in collections on account on June 30, but is unable to deposit the cash receipts before the bank closed for the day. University Services would record the following entry on the books to reflect the cash receipt:

	Debit	Credit
Cash	100,000	
Accounts Receivable		100,000

But since the money was not deposited, it will not be reflected before the end of the month in the June bank statement. As a result, when University Services prepares its June bank reconciliation, its cash balance in the bank will be lower than what is recorded on the books by $100,000. The deposit has not reached the bank and is still "in transit."

Other types of reconciling of items appearing on the bank statement include:

bank charges: Many banks charge a service fee for maintaining the account. This fee is often based on the average account balance or the number of checks drawn. Because these charges are automatically deducted from the checking account, a company does not know how much these charges are until after it receives the bank statement.

NSF (Non-Sufficient Funds) checks: An NSF check is a bounced check that a company could not deposit because the maker of the check had insufficient funds in his account to cover the amount written on the check. A company's bank charges a fee for NSF checks and returns the check to the company. It is not until the company receives the NSF check that the incomplete transaction can be reflected on the books.

interest income: Some checking accounts are interest-bearing accounts, on which interest is earned and credited to the account once per month. A company does not know how much interest it has earned until it receives the bank statement.

Chapter 4: Cash, Accounts Receivable, and Marketable Securities

bank and book errors: Errors in posting or recording a transaction by the bank or by the company also require reconciliation:

- Payments posted in error by the company are added to the book balance.
- Deposits posted in error by the company are subtracted from the book balance.
- Payments deducted in error by the bank are added to the bank balance.
- Deposits made in error by the bank are subtracted from the bank balance.

Bank overdrafts occur when the total amount of checks outstanding exceeds the total available cash balance. Although total payments exceed cash availability, the company has an obligation to honor all checks written and mailed. As a result, a current liability is recorded for all bank overdrafts for the amount of the overdraft and cash balance is brought to zero as follows:

```
Cash
     Overdraft Liability
```

The ultimate objective of the bank reconciliation is to start with the bank balance and arrive at the book balance using the reconciling items defined above. Therefore, the book balance generally reflects the company's true cash position. The following is a sample bank reconciliation for University Services, Inc. for the month ended June 30, 1998. You may want to use this example as a guide when preparing other bank reconciliations.

UNIVERSITY SERVICES, INC.
Bank Reconciliation
June 30, 1998

Balance per Bank @ 6/30/98	56,784
Less: Outstanding Checks	
No. 987	(40,000)
Plus: Deposits in Transit	100,000
Adjusted bank balance @ 6/30/98	116,784
Balance per Books @ 6/30/98	113,684
Less:	
Bank Service Charges	(68)
NSF Check	(500)
Add:	
Interest Income	2,668
Payment posted in error	1,000
Adjusted book balance @ 6/30/98	116,784

Annotations:
- Balance per Bank: This amount should be taken directly from the bank statement.
- Outstanding Checks: Outstanding checks are always subtracted from the bank balance, because the bank has not yet subtracted this payment, which is already recorded on the book balance.
- Deposits in Transit: Deposits in transit are always added to the bank balance, because the bank has not yet reflected cash receipts already recorded in the books.
- Adjusted bank balance: This amount normally agrees with the book balance. However, if it does not agree, then there are probably transactions reflected on the bank statements but not recorded in the books, such as the four items shown below.
- Balance per Books: This amount should be taken directly from the company's general ledger.
- Bank Service Charges / NSF Check: Bank service charges and NSF checks are always deducted from the books when the banks statements are received, because they have already been automatically deducted from the bank balance.
- Interest Income: Interest income is always added to the book balance, because additional cash has already been credited (added) to the account by the bank.
- Payment posted in error: This payment posted in error is a book error made by the University Services that was not discovered until the bank statement was received. It must be added back to the book balance, since the payment was not really made.

Chapter 4: Cash, Accounts Receivable, and Marketable Securities

Marketable Securities

Cash management technique

Marketable securities are long-term or short-term investments in **securities**. Securities are documents indicating ownership or potential ownership other than cash equivalents, such as bonds and stocks. Investment in these types of securities is another cash management technique used by companies to create additional sources of income.

Categories of marketable securities

The three basic categories of marketable securities are defined as follows:

trading securities: Investments in equity or debt securities that are held primarily for sale in the near term. The most common types of companies that buy and sell trading securities are commercial banks, mutual funds, insurance companies, and other types of financial institutions. These securities are characterized by "active and frequent" buying and selling with the objective of making short-term profits and are always classified as current assets on the balance sheet. Since the primary objective is to sell them, trading securities are not the same as cash equivalents. Trading securities are not to be confused with cash equivalents. Recall that the primary objective of holding cash equivalents instead of cash is to earn a profit by purchasing securities that mature within 90 days and then holding them to maturity.

held-to-maturity: Investments in debt securities for which management has A) the intent and B) the ability, to hold to maturity. Note that equity securities such as common stock cannot be categorized as held-to-maturity. Depending on the maturity date, held-to-maturity securities are classified on the balance sheet as either current or non-current assets.

   Less than one year: Current asset commonly labeled as marketable securities
   Greater than one year: Non-current asset commonly labeled as investments in securities

available-for-sale: These are investments in equity or debt securities that are not categorized as trading or held-to-maturity. For this reason, this category is often called the "catch-all" category. The most common types of companies that purchase securities and hold them as available for sale are manufacturers, retailers, and other non-financial companies. Available-for-sale securities can be classified as either current or non-current. If they are debt securities, we use the same test that we apply to held-to-maturity securities. If they are equity securities, read the problem to try to determine management's intent. This classification is not always easily discernible, so read carefully. If the problem does not state the requirements of a trading or held-to-maturity security, then it is probably available-for-sale. Another common example of long-term available for sale securities are debt securities that meet one, but not both, of the two requirements for held-to-maturity securities.

At its core, the classification of marketable securities depends on the company's objective with respect to the individual security. A company's objective determines whether a transaction affects income statement accounts and/or balance sheet accounts. The following chart summarizes the classification of marketable securities based on the company's objectives.

Company Objective	Category	Types of Securities	Accounting Treatment	Balance Sheet Classification	Keywords to look for in problem sets
Sell in near term	Trading	Equity & Debt	Market to Market	Always current	"for trading purposes" "intent to sell in near term"
Hold to maturity	Held-to-Maturity	Debt only	Amortized Cost	Matures in: < 1yr - Current > 1yr - Non-current	"intent and ability hold to maturity"
No real objective	Available for Sale	Equity & Debt	Market to Market	Debt securities matures in: < 1yr - Current > 1yr - Non-current Equity securities Depends on management intent	"available-for-sale" "management does not intend to sell in near term"

Notice that this chart provides keywords to look for in problem sets. These keywords will be useful in Step 1 of the accounting process — identifying and classifying the transactions the require recording.

Market to Market Approach: Departure from Historical Cost

In Chapter 2, we explained that balance sheet items are reflected at historical cost, with the exception of three common accounts: Marketable Securities, Accounts Receivable, and Inventory. Two types of marketable securities — trading securities and available-for-sale securities — are recorded using a **market to market approach,** by which the value of the security is adjusted upward or downward to reflect its current market value at the end of the

Chapter 4: Cash, Accounts Receivable, and Marketable Securities

accounting period. The theoretical justification for the use of this approach (based largely on the full disclosure principle), is that the market value of marketable securities provides more useful information to financial statement users about a company's financial position than a historical cost number. By reading about the market value of securities in the financial statements, users are better able to analyze a company's success at its trading activities.

Amortized Cost: Departure from Historical Cost

A third type of marketable security, the held-to-maturity security, is recorded using an **amortized cost** method, in which the security is initially recorded at acquisition cost and allocated over its life to the ending maturity value. Since these types of securities will not be sold until they mature, it is not useful to record them at their market value every time financial statements are prepared. Investors and financial statement users are really only concerned with the maturity value, because this is the amount that will actually be received when the investment matures. The acquisition cost of a held-to-maturity security is often different from the maturity value, because the company that purchases the security earns interest for agreeing to exchange cash for the investment. The difference between the acquisition cost and the maturity value is considered interest revenue and must be recognized over the life of the investment. Amortization techniques will be covered in Chapter 8 on **bonds**, which are debt securities representing the evidence of a loan. The chapter focuses on amortization techniques from the debtor's, or borrower's perspective. However, from the investor's perspective, a bond investment is considered a held-to-maturity security. Therefore, the same concepts learned in Chapter 8 can be applied in amortizing the cost of held-to-maturity investments.

In the next two sections, we will cover the appropriate accounting for trading and available for sale securities.

Recording Transactions: Trading Securities

To illustrate the proper recording of transactions affecting trading securities, consider the following scenario.

Images National Bank acquired 10,000 shares of Pierce Technologies' common stock on December 26 of Year 1 for $35/share. On December 31, Year 1, the market value of the shares was $37/share. Images National Bank sold these shares on January 2, Year 2, for $40/share. Images National Bank operates on a calendar year-end (it's fiscal year coincides with the calendar year).

Chapter 4: Cash, Accounts Receivable, and Marketable Securities

Even though the problem does not mention the word "trading," this transaction is still considered a trading activity based on the dates that the securities were bought and sold. Since the securities were bought and sold within one week, it fits the description of "active and frequent" buying and selling; it is therefore, considered a trading security. There are three basic transactions involved in a trading securities scenario.

1. **Record the purchase of the security.** In this example, the total cost of the purchase of Pierce Technologies' stock is $350,000 ($35/share x 10,000 shares) and would be recorded by increasing one liquid asset and decreasing the other:

	Debit	Credit
Marketable Securities – Pierce Technologies	$350,000	
Cash		$350,000

   Note: It is a good idea to record the name of the security when recording the debit to the marketable securities accounts, because many problem sets involve the purchase and sale of several different securities. By recording the name in the account description, it will be easier to identify the transactions affecting each individual security.

2. **Mark the security to market at the end of the period.** This step essentially means adjusting the value of the security at the end of the period to reflect its current market value. In our case, the end of the period is the end of the year, because that is the time at which we must prepare financial statements. We adjust a security to market value by directly increasing (debiting) or decreasing (crediting) the marketable securities account by the change in market value of the security and recording a corresponding **unrealized holding gain or loss.** In Chapter 1, we defined gains as sources of income from peripheral or incidental transactions and losses as expenses incurred as a result of peripheral or incidental transactions. These peripheral or incidental transactions generally relate to non-operating activities – activities unrelated to a company's core revenue generating source. Thus, gains and losses are differentiated from revenues and expenses, because they generally relate to non-operating activities. For most companies, buying and selling securities is not a principal source of income. As a result, income earned from trading activities are classified as gains and losses. Let's refine our definitions of gains and losses as they apply to marketable securities.

   Unrealized Holding Gains: The excess of the market value of a security at its valuation date over the market value at the time of purchase. This excess is an additional source of income earned from the increase in market value of a security, but it has not been realized because the security has not been sold (the company is still "holding" it). Unrealized holding gains are realizable, however, because the securities are saleable in an active market at readily determinable prices (through the stock market).

Chapter 4: Cash, Accounts Receivable, and Marketable Securities

Unrealized Holding Losses: The excess of the market value of a security at the time of purchase over its market value at the valuation date. This excess is an expense incurred from holding a security that is trading in an active market, but it has not been paid because the company has not sold the security. In accordance with the matching principle, unrealized holding losses must be recognized in the period incurred.

KEY CONCEPT

Unrealized holding gains and losses on trading securities are *always* reflected in the income statement. The theoretical justification for this approach is that the company's primary objective for buying and selling trading securities is to generate short-term profits. Thus, to properly reflect any profits or losses realizable from holding the securities, gains and losses are included as a part of income in the income statement. In our example, the market value of the Pierce Technologies' stock increased $2 from $35/share on December 26 to $37/share on December 31. Since Images National Bank owns 10,000 of Pierce stock at December 31, the current market value of their holding is $370,000 ($37 x 10,000). Therefore, they have an unrealized holding gain of $20,000 ($2 x 10,000), which would be recorded as follows:

	Debit	Credit
Marketable Securities – Pierce Technologies	20,000	
Unrealized Holding Gain on Trading Securities (IS)		20,000

After this entry, the balance sheet will show the Pierce Technologies stock at its current market value of $370,000 (initial entry of $350,000 plus $20,000 market adjustment). The designation "IS" indicates that the account is an income statement account and appears on the income statement.

3. **Record realized gain or loss when the security is sold by using the market value at last valuation date.** When the security is actually sold, the gain or loss is realized because cash is received or paid. The realized gain or loss is recorded in the income statement as the difference between the market value on the date of sale and the market value on the last valuation date. Realized gains and losses as they relate to trading securities can be defined as follows:

Realized Gains: The excess of the market value of a security at the date of sale over the market value at the last valuation date.

Realized Losses: The excess of the market value of a security at the time of purchase over its market value at the last valuation date.

Note that realized gains and losses are determined by using the market value of the security at its valuation date instead of the market value at the original date of purchase. We use this later figure because the change in market value up to the valuation date was recognized in the prior period. Therefore, at the time of sale, only the additional change in market value should be recognized. Using our example, Images sold its holdings in Pierce stock on January 2, Year 2 for $40/share or $400,000. On that date, the market value of the stock had increased by an additional $3 from $37/share to $40/share, creating an additional $30,000 gain ($3 x 10,000). To record the cash received, remove the investment from the accounting records, and record the additional gain, the following entry would be made:

Cash	400,000	
Marketable securities – Pierce Technologies		370,000
Unrealized Holding Gain on Trading Securities (IS)		30,000

Note that the marketable securities account is credited for $370,000 (the initial entry of $350,000 plus $20,000 market adjustment). Note also that the total cash received in excess of the cost of the original purchase is $50,000 ($400,000-$350,000). The amount of $20,000 was recognized as an unrealized holding gain in Year 1; the remaining $30,000 was recognized as a realized gain at the time of sale, in Year 2.

RECORDING TRANSACTIONS: AVAILABLE-FOR-SALE SECURITIES

To illustrate the proper recording of transactions affecting available for sale securities, consider the following scenario.

Lifestyles Insurance acquired 10,000 shares of Sneakers, Inc. common stock on September 1, Year 1, for $26/share. At that time, management had no intention of selling the securities in the near term. On December 31, Year 1, the market value of the shares was $32/share. Lifestyles Insurance sold these shares on April 2, Year 2 for $34/share. Lifestyles operates on a calendar year end.

Based on the keywords provided in the problem, this security would be classified as available-for-sale. This security could not be considered held-to-maturity because it is an equity security. In addition, the time period between the date of purchase and date of sale spans eight months, another indication that there was no intent to use the security for "active and frequent" trading. As with trading securities, there are three basic transactions in a problem involving available-for-sale securities:

1. **Record the purchase of the security.** This step is the same as the first transaction used for trading securities. In this example, the total cost of the purchase of Pierce Technologies' stock is $260,000 ($26/share x 10,000 shares). It is recorded by increasing one liquid asset and decreasing the other as follows:

Chapter 4: Cash, Accounts Receivable, and Marketable Securities

	Debit	Credit
Marketable Securities – Sneakers, Inc.	$260,000	
Cash		$260,000

2. **Mark the security to market at the end of the period.** The entry to adjust an available-for-sale security to market value at the end of the period is similar to trading securities. **However, the unrealized holding gain or loss is recorded as a separate line item in the equity section of the balance sheet and not in the income statement.** With available-for-sale securities, the company's objective is not to generate additional income. Thus, any profits or losses from holding the security should not be reflected in the income statement as a part of net income. If we were to record unrealized holding gains and losses in the income statement, the income statement would appear more volatile than it actually is. However, it is also the management's intention not to hold the security to maturity. Therefore, the company should still be required the adjust the security to its market value. In addition, the change in market value of a marketable security does change a company's net worth, because increasing the value of an asset increases a company's value and decreasing the value of an asset decreases a company's value [assets - liabilities = equity (or net worth)]. With trading securities, net worth is effectively adjusted when the net income is closed to retained earnings. By recording the unrealized gain or loss on available-for-sale securities in the equity section of the balance sheet, net worth can be adjusted to reflect the increase or decrease in the value of the asset without the change being reflected in the income statement.

In our example, the market value of the Sneakers, Inc. stock increased $6 from $26/share on September 1 to $32/share on December 31. Since Lifestyles Insurance owns 10,000 shares of Sneakers stock on December 31, the current market value of their holding is $320,000 ($32 x 10,000). Therefore, the company has an unrealized holding gain of $60,000 ($6 x 10,000), which is recorded as follows:

	Debit	Credit
Marketable Securities – Sneakers, Inc.	60,000	
Unrealized Holding Gain on available-for-sale Securities (BS)		60,000

After this entry, the balance sheet will show the Sneakers, Inc. stock at its current market value of $320,000 (the initial entry of $260,000 plus $60,000 market adjustment). The designation "BS" indicates that the account is a balance sheet account and appears on the balance sheet. Unrealized holding gains and losses on available-for-sale securities appear after retained earnings in the equity section of the balance sheet.

3. **Record realized gain or loss when the security is sold based on market value at time of purchase.** When the security is actually sold, the gain or loss on holding the security is realized, because cash is received or paid. The realized gain or loss is recorded in the income statement as the difference between the market value on the date of sale and the market value on the original purchase date. Recall that for trading securities, a portion of the gain or loss (the unrealized portion) is included as a part of income when the security is adjusted to market value at the end of the accounting period. The remaining portion (the realized portion) is included as a part of income when the security is sold in the next accounting period. With available-for-sale securities, the entire gain or loss (unrealized and realized) is included as a part of income only in the period of sale. Thus, realized gains and losses as they relate available-for-sale securities can be defined as follows:

> **Realized Gains:** The excess of the market value of a security at the date of sale over the market value at the date of purchase.
>
> **Realized Losses:** The excess of the market value of a security at the time of purchase over its market value at the date of sale.

In our example, Lifestyles sold its holdings of Sneakers, Inc. on April 2, Year 2, for $34/share or $340,000. On that date, that market value had increased by $8 from $26/share to $34/share since the original purchase date, resulting in a total gain of $80,000. However, we have already adjusted the "marketable securities" account by $60,000 by recording an unrealized holding gain in the equity section of the balance sheet. Thus, to record the realized gain of $80,000 in the income statement, we must use the following procedure.

1. Debit cash for the amount received at time of sale.

2. Debit (or credit) the unrealized holding gain (or loss) to remove this account from the equity section of the balance sheet. Do this by reducing the unrealized holding gain to a zero balance, since we have now realized the gain.

3. Credit marketable securities for the value at the valuation date (the end of the accounting period) to remove the investment from the books by reducing it to a zero balance.

4. Credit (or debit) realized gain (or loss) to recognize the total income (or loss) from the security.

Chapter 4: Cash, Accounts Receivable, and Marketable Securities

Using these steps, the final entry to record the sale of Sneakers, Inc. securities should be recorded as:

	Debit	Credit
Cash	340,000	
Unrealized Holding Gain on Available-for-Sale Securities (BS)	60,000	
Marketable Securities		320,000
Realized Gain on Available-for-Sale Securities (IS)		80,000

The following chart summarizes the entries to be made when recording transactions for trading or available-for-sale securities:

STEP 1: Record the purchase of the security

TRADING SECURITIES		AVAILABLE-FOR-SALE SECURITIES	
Cash	market value at time of purchase	Cash	market value at time of purchase
Marketable securities	market value at time of purchase	Marketable Securities	market value at time of purchase

STEP 2: Mark the security to market at the end of the period

TRADING SECURITIES		AVAILABLE-FOR-SALE SECURITIES	
Gain Situation		**Gain Situation**	
Marketable Securities	increase in market vaule since date of purchase	Marketable Securities	increase in market vaule since date of purchase
Unrealized holding gain on trading securities (IS)	increase in market value since date of purchase	Unrealized Holding Gain on Available for Sale Securities (BS)	increase in market value since date of purchase
Loss Situation		**Loss Situation**	
Unrealized holding loss on trading securities (IS)	decrease in market vaule since date of purchase	Unrealized Holding Loss on Available for Sale Securities (BS)	decrease in market vaule since date of purchase
Marketable securities	decrease in market value since date of purchase	Marketable Securities	decrease in market value since date of purchase

STEP 3: Record the gain or loss when the security is sold

TRADING SECURITIES		AVAILABLE-FOR-SALE SECURITIES	
Total Realized Gain Situation		**Total Realized Gain Situation**	
Cash	total cash received	Cash	total cash received
Marketable securities	market value at valuation date	Unrealized Holding Gain on Available for Sale Securities (BS)	increase in market value since date of purchase
Realized gain on Trading securities (IS)	increase in market value since valuation date	Marketable Securities	market value at valuation date
		Realized Gain on Available for Sale Securities (BS)	increase in market value since date of purchase
Total Realized Loss Situation		**Total Realized Loss Situation**	
Cash	total cash received	Cash	total cash received
Marketable Securities	market value at valuation date	Unrealized Holding Loss on Available for Sale Securities (BS)	decrease in market vaule since date of purchase
Realized Loss on Trading Securities (IS)	decrease in market vaule since valuation date	Marketable Securities	market value at valuation date
		Realized Loss on Available for Sale Securities (BS)	decrease in market vaule since date of purchase

Chapter 4: Cash, Accounts Receivable, and Marketable Securities

Trade Accounts Receivable

Another departure from the Historical Cost Principle

In addition to marketable securities, accounts receivable is a current asset that is not presented in the balance sheet at historical cost. Instead, accounts receivable is presented at its net realizable value. **Net realizable value** is the value of the accounts receivable that a company can actually expect to receive in cash. It is computed using the following format:

Total sales on account
Less: Estimates for uncollectible accounts
Less: Sales discounts, returns, and allowances
Equals: Net realizable value of accounts receivable

After cash and marketable securities, accounts receivable is the third most liquid asset a company can have. Therefore, it is beneficial to financial statement users to present accounts receivable at its value in the event of liquidation.

Recall from Chapter 3 that when we sell goods on account, we credit Revenue and debit Accounts Receivable instead of cash. However, when a company extends credit to a customer, it recognizes that all customers will not pay their bills. Thus, we can assume that not all sales on account will be converted into cash in the short term to be available for use in current operations. This conclusion holds especially true in the retail industry, in which companies have millions of customers who own store credit cards. It would be unfair to financial statement users to present accounts receivable at its total amount when the company knows that not all of the money will be collected. In addition, any losses associated with the sale of goods should be recognized in the period that the revenue is recognized (consistent with the matching principle). This is why we must determine how much will not be collected and recognize a loss (called a bad debt expense) for that amount. There are two methods for accounting for uncollectible accounts:

1. The Direct Write-Off Method

2. Allowance Method

CHAPTER 4: CASH, ACCOUNTS RECEIVABLE, AND MARKETABLE SECURITIES

DIRECT WRITE-OFF METHOD

Under the **direct write-off** method, bad debt expense is not recorded until a specific customer actually defaults on their payments. Companies usually implement a series of collection procedures to collect long outstanding sales on account and most often have a separate collection department. Normally, if a customer has not paid his or her bill after a certain number of days, the account is sent to the collection department, which makes an attempt to collect the outstanding receivable. If the collection department is unable to collect the receivable and all other collection efforts have been exhausted, the account may then be written off. For example, in Year 5 of Hi-Tech Calculators' operations, the collection department sends a memo to the company's controller, indicating that the following specific customer accounts have been labeled as uncollectible:

Customer Name	Year Sale Made	Amount Outstanding
Frank Johnson & Co.	Year 3	$12,000
Warehouse Unlimited	Year 3	9,000
Supply Me Corp	Year 4	30,000
		$51,000

The entry to write-off the uncollectible accounts under the direct write-off method is as follows:

	Debit	Credit
Bad Debt Expense	51,000	
Accounts Receivable		51,000

When the sale to these customers was initially made, the entry to record the sale was a debit to accounts receivable and a credit to revenue. Therefore, when the account becomes uncollectible we must credit the customer's account in the Accounts Receivable ledger and reduce the balance to zero. Finally, Bad Debt Expense is debited to increase expenses for the amount of the loss.

ALLOWANCE METHOD

The direct write-off method has three major flaws:

1. The loss is not recognized in the period that the actual sale occurred. In the example above, the accounts were written off in Year 5, when they were determined to be uncollectible, although the sales were made in prior years.

CHAPTER 4: CASH, ACCOUNTS RECEIVABLE, AND MARKETABLE SECURITIES

2. There is no strict process of determining when accounts actually become uncollectible. The company exercises a significant amount of subjective judgment in determining that the customer cannot or will not pay and that the company expended sufficient energy to collect the outstanding bill. In the absence of a set of hard-and-fast rules, companies have an opportunity to manipulate earnings by delaying the write-off of accounts that are uncollectible.

3. The balance in Accounts Receivable on the balance sheet is not presented at net realizable value, because it does not reflect the amount the company expects to collect in cash. This is because the company has only recognized bad debt expense for what actually became uncollectible. No estimate has been made for additional sales made during the year that may not be collected in the future.

The **allowance method** corrects these flaws. Under this method, the company makes an estimate every year of the amount of sales made during the year that it expects to be uncollectible. The company then recognizes an expense for that amount in the year of sale. The estimates are made based on an established methodology using a balance sheet approach or an income statement approach. By making estimates in the year of sale and before the accounts actually become uncollectible, accounts receivable can be stated at net realizable value. In addition to recognizing an expense, an allowance account is set up in the balance sheet to reduce accounts receivable by the estimated uncollectible accounts. The standard entry to record the allowance for uncollectible accounts is as follows:

	Debit	Credit
Bad Debt Expense	XXXX	
Allowance for Uncollectible Accounts		XXXX

"Allowance for Uncollectible Accounts" is a contra account, similar to accumulated depreciation, and is used to record a company's estimate of how much of its total sales on account it will not be able to collect. Allowance for Uncollectible Accounts is presented directly after Accounts Receivable in the current assets section of the balance sheet. It is a direct reduction of Accounts Receivable. Like Accumulated Depreciation, it normally maintains a credit balance. Note that this account is credited instead of Accounts Receivable (which is credited under the direct write-off method). This is because the allowance is an estimate based on total sales and does not relate to specific customer accounts.

Chapter 4: Cash, Accounts Receivable, and Marketable Securities

There are two approaches to the allowance method:

1. **Income Statement Approach:** Under this approach, bad debt expense is calculated based on a **percentage of sales** for the year. The balance in Allowance for Uncollectible Accounts has no effect on the expense recognized in the income statement for the year.

2. **Balance Sheet Approach:** Under this approach, bad debt expense is determined based on the number of days outstanding, and the allowance account is adjusted to the necessary required balance. To calculate the expense, an **aging of receivables** is prepared that categorizes accounts receivable based on the number of days outstanding. The following is a sample of intervals that many companies use to prepare an aging analysis.

   a. outstanding 30 days or less

   b. outstanding 31 to 60 days

   c. outstanding 61 to 90 days

   d. outstanding 91 to 180 days

   e. outstanding more than 180 days

If the receivable is outstanding more than a company-specified number of days (for example, more than 180 days), the company will adjust the allowance for uncollectible accounts and record bad debt expense for the adjusted amount.

Income Statement Approach: An Example

Lotsa Furniture provides customer financing for sales of its bedroom and living room furniture. At the time the sale is made, customers typically enter into an arrangement to pay monthly cash payments for the full cost of the furniture and any interest over a period of 24 to 36 months. Past experience has indicated to Lotsa Furniture that approximately 2% of total sales in the year of sale, 7% in the next year, and 5% in the third year become uncollectible. Accounts receivable for Lotsa Furniture at the beginning of Year 3 is as follows.

Accounts Receivable	150,000
Less: Allowance for Uncollectible Accounts	(25,000)
Net Accounts Receivable	125,000

Sales for Year 3 through Year 5 are given below.

Year 3	700,000
Year 4	900,000
Year 5	1,200,000

Chapter 4: Cash, Accounts Receivable, and Marketable Securities

In addition we know that of the $700,000 sales made during Year 3, $275,000 was collected. Based on these sales, an analysis of uncollectible accounts can be summarized below.

Year	Sales	$ Deemed Uncollectible in Year 3	4	5	6	7	Total Uncollectible
3	700,000	14,000	49,000	35,000			98,000
4	900,000		18,000	63,000	45,000		126,000
5	1,200,000			24,000	84,000	60,000	168,000
		14,000	67,000	122,000	129,000	60,000	

The chart above indicates that the total estimated uncollectible accounts for sales made in Year 3 is $98,000. This is the amount that will be recognized as bad debt expense. It does not matter when the account actually becomes uncollectible. The purpose of the allowance method is to match expenses with revenues in the year the revenues are earned. Therefore, we must recognize the full $98,000 in Year 3. Likewise, $126,000 of bad debt expense will be recognized in Year 4, and $168,000 will be recognized in Year 5. The entry to record bad debt expense in Year 3 is as follows:

	Debit	Credit
Bad Debt Expense	98,000	
Allowance for Uncollectible Accounts		98,000

After this entry is made, the new balance in Accounts Receivable is $575,000, and the Allowance for Uncollectible Accounts at the end of Year 3 is $123,000 calculated as follows:

Accounts Receivable, beginning of year	150,000
Plus: Total sales for the year	700,000
Less: Collections during the year	(275,000)
Accounts Receivable, end of year	575,000
Allowance for Uncollectibles, beginning of the year	25,000
Plus: Bad Debt Expense for the year	98,000
Allowance for Uncollectibles, end of year	123,000

The net realizable value of accounts receivable at the end of year 3 is $452,000 (575,000 - 123,000).

Chapter 4: Cash, Accounts Receivable, and Marketable Securities

Note that under the direct write-off method, only $14,000, $67,000, and $122,000 in uncollectible accounts will be recognized in Year 3, Year 4, and Year 5, respectively, while $129,000 and $60,000 will be recognized in Years 6 and 7. The direct write-off method will therefore result in an understatement of expenses for those years and an overstatement of expenses related to Years 6 and 7.

Balance Sheet Approach: An Example

Assume that instead of using the percentage of sales method for estimating bad debt expense, Lotsa Furniture prepares an aging analysis of their accounts receivable at the end of Year 3. The $575,000 in accounts receivable at the end of the year are divided as follows, based on the number of days outstanding as shown below.

	Amount	Estimated Uncollectible Percentage	Estimated Uncollectible Amounts
Outstanding 30 days or less	425,000	8.4%	35,750
Outstanding 31 to 60 days	65,000	40.0%	26,000
Outstanding 61 to 90 days	40,000	50.0%	20,000
Outstanding 91 to 180 days	25,000	85.0%	21,250
Outstanding more than 180 days	20,000	100.0%	20,000
	575,000		123,000

Based on this analysis, the total estimated uncollectible accounts at the end of Year 3 is $123,000. However, the balance in the allowance account at the beginning of the year is $25,000. Therefore, we only need an additional $98,000 (not $123,000) to present accounts receivable at its net realizable value of $452,000 (575,000 - 123,000). Therefore, the entry to record bad debt expense for the year is the same entry made using the percentage of sales method.

	Debit	Credit
Bad Debt Expense	98,000	
Allowance for Uncollectible Accounts		98,000

Direct Write-off or Allowance? Income Statement Approach or Balance Sheet Approach?

Both the direct write-off method and the allowance method are acceptable accounting practices under Generally Accepted Accounting Principles (GAAP). But the direct write-off method may only be used if bad debt expense is an immaterial item on a company's income statement. An item is immaterial if it is a small amount relative to the other expense items on the income statement. Under the allowance method, a company may choose between using the percentage of sales approach or an aging analysis approach. Most companies select the percentage of sales approach, because it is easier to apply and provides a reasonable estimate of uncollectible accounts. However, although time consuming, the aging analysis provides the most accurate estimate because each individual account is examined and categorized. Also, a different uncollectible percentage is applied to each category. Even if a company uses the percentage of sales approach, it must age the accounts periodically to make sure that the percentage it is using is accurate. In our example, the percentages used (2% of total sales in the year of sale, 7% in the next year, and 5% in the third year) proved to be accurate, because we recorded the same amount of bad debt expense under both methods. If they had not been accurate, Lotsa Furniture would have had to adjust its percentages for future years.

Recovering Accounts Written Off

Recall that the entry to write off accounts and record bad debt expense under the direct write-off method is as follows:

	Debit	Credit
Bad Debt Expense	XXXX	
Accounts Receivable		XXXX

Under the allowance method, the bad debt expense has already been recognized in the year an account actually becomes uncollectible. In the year of sale, an entry is made to debit Bad Debt Expense and credit the Allowance for Uncollectible Accounts. Therefore, it is not necessary to record an additional expense in the year that the account actually becomes uncollectible. However, because we now know for certain that we will not collect the cash, we must still remove the Accounts Receivable (with a credit) from the books. To do this, we make the following entry:

	Debit	Credit
Allowance for Uncollectible Accounts	XXXX	
Accounts Receivable		XXXX

Instead of recording bad debt expense, we debited the allowance account. Since we determined that we will not collect the cash, we no longer need the allowance amount on the books for this amount. Therefore, we must remove the Allowance for Uncollectibles (with a debit) as well as the receivable from the books.

Chapter 4: Cash, Accounts Receivable, and Marketable Securities

Sometimes, even after a company has already written off a customer's account as uncollectible, the customer pays. In this situation, the following entries must be made to "recover" the account and record the cash received:

1. Reverse the entry made to write the account off and put the receivable back on the books.

	Debit	Credit
Accounts Receivable	XXXX	
Allowance for Uncollectible Accounts		XXXX

2. Record the cash received and remove the accounts receivable from the books.

	Debit	Credit
Cash	XXXX	
Accounts Receivable		XXXX

The recovered allowance amount remains on the books until it is written off against another uncollectible account or adjusted based on an aging analysis of uncollectible accounts.

Chapter 4: Cash, Accounts Receivable, and Marketable Securities

Key Terms

aging of receivables: a balance sheet approach to recognizing bad debt expense. Under this approach, bad debt expense is determined based on the number of days a receivable is outstanding. The allowance account is adjusted to the necessary required balance. Even if a company uses the percentage of sales approach, it must periodically age its accounts receivable to determine that the percentages it is using are correct.

allowance method: a method of recording bad debt expense in which management makes an estimate every year for the for the amount of sales made during the year that it expects to be uncollectible. The company then recognizes an expense for that amount in the year of sale. The two basic approaches under this method are the income statement approach and the balance sheet approach.

available-for-sale: investments in equity or debt securities that are not categorized as trading or held-to-maturity. This category is often called the "catch-all" category. These types of securities are recorded using the market-to-market approach and can be classified as either current or non-current, depending on the maturity date or the investor's intent. Unrealized holding gains and losses are reflected as a separate line item in the equity section of the balance sheet. Realized gains and losses are reflected in the income statement.

cash equivalents: any short-term investment having an original maturity date of 90 days or less. Examples include US Treasury notes, certificates of deposits, commercial paper, and other highly liquid securities.

deposits in transit: cash receipts recorded on the books and mailed or taken to the bank – but not reflected in the bank statement. In a bank reconciliation, deposits in transit are added to the bank balance.

direct write-off method: a method of recording bad debt expense through which the expense is not recorded until a specific customer actually defaults on his or her payments.

held-to-maturity: investments in debt securities for which management has the intent and the ability to hold to maturity. This type of investment is recorded using the amortized cost approach. These types of securities can be classified as either current or non-current, depending on the maturity date.

Chapter 4: Cash, Accounts Receivable, and Marketable Securities

marketable securities: long-term or short-term investments in securities other than cash equivalents, such as bonds and stocks. Investment in these types of securities is another cash management technique used by companies to create additional sources of income.

outstanding checks: cash disbursements in the form of checks that have been issued by a company and recorded on the books as paid but not cashed by the payee. In a bank reconciliation, outstanding checks are deducted from the bank balance.

percentage of sales: an income statement approach to recognizing bad debt expense. Under this approach, bad debt expense is calculated based on a percentage of sales for the year. The balance in the allowance for uncollectible accounts has no effect on the expense recognized in the income statement for the year.

realized losses: for trading securities, the excess of the market value of a security at the most recent valuation date over its market value at the date of purchase (value at purchase - value at last valuation). For available-for-sale securities, the excess of the market value of a security at the date of purchase over its market value at the date of sale (value at purchase - value at sale).

realized gains: for trading securities, the excess of the market value of a security at the date of sale over the market value at the last valuation date (value at sale - value at last valuation). For available-for-sale securities, the excess of the market value of a security at the date of sale over the market value at the date of purchase (value at sale - value at purchase).

trading securities: investments in equity or debt securities that are held primarily for sale in the near term and are recorded using the market-to-market approach. Trading securities are always classified as current assets. Both unrealized and realized gains and losses are reflected in the income statement.

unrealized holding gains: the excess of the market value of a security at its valuation date over the market value at the time of purchase (value at valuation date - value at purchase). This excess is an additional source of income earned from the increase in market value of a security but not realized because it has not been sold (the company is still "holding" it).

unrealized holding losses: the excess of the market value of a security at the time of purchase over its market value at the valuation date (value at purchase - value at valuation date). This excess is an expense incurred from holding a security that is trading in an active market but not yet paid, because the company has not sold the security.

Chapter 4: Cash, Accounts Receivable, and Marketable Securities

Thrills, Chills and Drills

True or False

1. To be considered a cash equivalent, an investment should have an original maturity date of no longer than one year.

2. Historical cost is used to value trading securities and available-for-sale securities.

3. Held-to-maturity securities are recorded using the amortized cost method.

4. Trading securities are always classified as non-current assets on the balance sheet.

5. Held-to-maturity securities are always classified as non-current assets.

6. Available-for-sale investments can be classified as either current or non-current assets.

7. In 1997, Crying Shame Company purchased a bond with a maturity date of January 1, 2007. In 1999, the company decided to cash in the bond to raise money for a loan payment. The bond would still be considered a held-to-maturity security, because its original maturity date is longer than 90 days.

8. The adjustment of a marketable security at the end of the period is conducted by debiting the security and crediting revenue if the value increases, or by debiting revenue and crediting the security if the value decreases.

9. Unrealized holding gains and losses are always reflected in the balance sheet.

10. A realized gain is recognized when a security is sold. It is determined by taking the difference between the market value on the date of purchase and the value on the date of the sale.

11. Nobody Knows, Inc. purchased 10,000 shares of Everybody Does, Inc. common stock for $100/share on March 1, 1998. The bookkeeper should classify the securities as held-to-maturity.

12. The entry to adjust an available-for-sale security to market value at the end of the period when the value increases is to debit the security and credit the unrealized holding gain on the balance sheet.

13. There are two methods for determining the amount to be placed in the allowance for uncollectible accounts: the income statement approach and the direct write-off approach.

Chapter 4: Cash, Accounts Receivable, and Marketable Securities

14. An aging of receivables is used with the balance sheet approach of valuing the accounts receivable balance sheet account.

15. When a previously written-off accounts receivable account is paid, the entry to record the transaction is a debit cash and a credit to accounts receivable.

16. Let's Make Money, Inc. purchased a CD on January 1, 1998 that will mature on May 1, 1998. On April 1, 1998, the company's bookkeeper, prepares the financial statements for the period ending March 31, 1998. He correctly classifies the CD as a cash equivalent.

17. Because of its liquidity, cash requires minimum internal controls.

18. Compensating balances are excluded from the cash account and must be shown separately on the balance sheet.

19. Rolling A. Long Investment Company purchased a security on January 1, 1990 with a maturity date of January 1, 2000. The value at maturity will be $1,000,000. Rolling A. Long paid $800,000. The security is correctly shown on the balance sheet dated December 31, 1998 as $1,000,000.

20. In question 19, the difference between the acquisition cost of the security and the maturity value is a realized gain.

Multiple Choice

1. Which item is not considered a cash equivalent?
    a) certificate of deposit
    b) money order
    c) $2,000 minimum deposit in a checking account
    d) undeposited check

2. Which of the following is a cash equivalent on the 12/31/96 balance sheet?
    a) U.S. Treasury Bill purchased in 1993, maturing in 1997
    b) Certificate of Deposit purchased 12/1/96, maturing 2/1/97
    c) U.S. Treasury bill purchased in 1995, maturing in 2005, but that will be sold 1/10/97
    d) Municipal bond with a maturity date of 6/31/97

Chapter 4: Cash, Accounts Receivable, and Marketable Securities

3. Short-term equity securities should be accounted for by using
    a) historical cost
    b) amortized cost
    c) market to market approach
    d) none of the above
    e) any of the above, depending on the facts of the transaction

4. An unrealized gain is
    a) the excess of the market value of a security at the time of purchase over its maturity value at the valuation date
    b) the excess of the market value of a security at its valuation date over the market value at the time of the purchase
    c) always reflected in the income statement
    d) always reflected in the balance sheet

5. Run-A-Muck, Inc. purchased 10,000 shares of Run Long, Inc. stock on July 1, 1995 for $10/share. Run Long, Inc. raised its annual income to $30,000,000, and the price of its stock rose to $40/share. This increase is recorded by Run-A-Muck, Inc. by which of the following entries?

    a)
Marketable Securities – Run Long, Inc	$400,000	
Unrealized Holding Gain – Trading Securities		$400,000

    b)
Marketable Securities – Run Long, Inc	$30,000,000	
Unrealized Holding Gain – Trading Securities		$30,000,000

    c)
Unrealized Holding Gain – Trading Securities	$300,000	
Marketable Securities – Run Long, Inc		$300,000

    d)
Marketable Securities – Run Long, Inc	$300,000	
Unrealized Holding Gain – Trading Securities		$300,000

6. On January 5, 1999, Ernie Lot bought a certificate of deposit from Merging Big Time. It had a maturity date of March 7, 1999. The CD is considered:
    a) held-to-maturity
    b) a trading security
    c) available-for-sale
    d) a cash equivalent

Chapter 4: Cash, Accounts Receivable, and Marketable Securities

7. Crazy Mary, Inc.'s investment consultant gave the bookkeeper a tip to buy the stock of Crazy Louie, Inc. Joe Slick, the consultant, recommended a short term investment of 3 months. Crazy Mary bought 10,000 shares at $100/share on March 15, 1997. Mel Snell, the bookkeeper for Crazy, would classify these securities as
   a) held-to-maturity
   b) trading securities
   c) available-for-sale
   d) cash equivalents

8. Penny Pincer, a mutual fund set up with the middle class in mind, also bought stocks in Crazy Louie under the same recommendation from Joe Slick. But Penny Pincer sold the shares on March 22, 1997. Happy Mack, the bookkeeper for Penny Pincer classified the stocks as
   a. a held-to-maturity security
   b. a trading security
   c. an available-for-sale security
   d. a cash equivalent

9. The balance sheet of Penny Pincer on December 31, 1997 showed these securities as
   a) current assets
   b) non-current assets
   c) stockholders' equity
   d) a or b

10. During its fiscal year 1997, Running on Empty, Inc. began looking over its investments. The company had taken its excess cash and invested it in several vehicles. One of the vehicles was a municipal bond that was purchased in 1990 with an original maturity date of 2000. How should this investment be classified?
    a) as a held-to-maturity security
    b) as a trading security
    c) as an available-for-sale security
    d) as a cash equivalent

Chapter 4: Cash, Accounts Receivable, and Marketable Securities

11. In 1995, Looking for a Break, Co. had invested in the common stock of Rocky Franconi, the junior welterweight champion. The company was looking for a long-term investment to be used for the acquisition of a new plant in Hong Kong. Franconi won a spot on the 1996 Olympic team as a welterweight and the company's stock increased by $10 per share. When he returned to America in 1997, he lost his first fight and the stock decreased in value by $5 per share. He went on to win his next several fights, and in 1998 his stock again increased by $50 per share. In its 1997 balance sheet, how should the company account for the stock investment in Franconi?
    a) debit unrealized holding gain/loss
    b) credit unrealized holding gain/loss
    c) debit investment-Franconi.
    d) credit investment-Franconi.
    e) a and d
    f) b and c

12. Funland Bank has invested in GNMA Stock and its value has increased by $30 per share. How is this increase in value is recorded?
    a) credit unrealized holding gain/loss (income statement)
    b) credit GNMA Stock
    c) debit GNMA Stock
    d) credit unrealized holding gain/loss (balance sheet)
    e) a and c
    f) c and d

13. The Dave Matthews Band (DMB) is planning a world tour starting in January 2000. They decide that they need money to pull this tour off. They have some excess cash from album sales and personal appearances. They do not have money from the gates at concerts because they were in the studio recording their new single "Don't Drink the Water" from the new album, "Beyond These Crowded Streets." They put their excess cash to work by buying 1000 shares of the band Blues Traveler. They bought the shares in January 1998 for $100/share. In June 1998, the stock reached an all-time high of $400/share; they sold the stock. How should the sale be recorded?
    a) credit unrealized holding gain/loss
    b) credit investment-Blues Traveler
    c) debit cash
    d) b and c
    e) a and c
    f) all of the above

Chapter 4: Cash, Accounts Receivable, and Marketable Securities

14. The Dave Mathews Band bought the common stock of "Blues Traveler" as a
    a) held-to-maturity security
    b) trading security
    c) available-for-sale security
    d) cash equivalent

15. In December 1997, the Edmonton Oilers hockey team realized that they would be involved in the 1998 playoff games. At their club meeting in 1995, they had decided to put money into a bond with an original maturity date of May 30, 2007. The owners of Moosehead Beer decided to help them out by buying the bond for much needed cash. In their balance sheet dated December 31, 1996, the bond would be recorded as
    a) a held-to-maturity security
    b) a trading security
    c) an available-for-sale security
    d) a cash equivalent.

16. The Side-Kick soccer club had several means of raising funds to send itself to Florida for the East Coast Soccer Championship. These included standing on the corner for a bucket drive, selling cheesecakes, selling candy, and running a beef and beer stand. The boys and girls used all of the above fundraisers to help. They completed all the necessary steps and collected well over the required $215,000 needed for the trip. Since they had over three months before the money was due, one of the soccer moms decided to invest their take. On December 23, 1997, he took the $300,000 and invested it in a certificate of deposit at a bank run by an alumnus of the team. The certificate paid 6.5% compounded daily. The maturity date was March 1, 1998. The team would record this CD as
    a) a held-to-maturity security
    b) a trading security
    c) an available-for-sale security
    d) a cash equivalent

Chapter 4: Cash, Accounts Receivable, and Marketable Securities

17. Starting out in the business of managing professional boxers, Mickey Stromboli decided to open a bank account at Corestates. He met the required minimum deposit of $3,000 and also deposited an extra $10,000 of his own hard-earned money so he could pay the expenses related to his boxers and his boxing club, Mickey's Gym. He signed a star boxer named Rocky in the hope of increasing his investment. When he went public with his company to attract outside investors, he had to file his financial statements. To record his initial investment of $13,000, he would credit owner's equity and debit which of the following?
    a) $13,000 cash
    b) $10,000 cash; $3,000 liability
    c) $10,000 cash; $3,000 compensating balance
    d) $10,000 bank balance; $3,000 petty cash

18. What type of company is likely to invest in trading securities?
    a) a manufacturing company
    b) a retailing company
    c) a mutual fund
    d) all of the above
    e) none of the above

19. Looking at the statement of retained earnings for First National Bank of Eutopia, you notice a line item called unrealized holding gain. This entry should make you aware of the fact that the bank has an investment in which kind of securities?
    a) trading securities
    b) available-for-sale
    c) held-to-maturity
    d) a and b

20. Under the allowance method, a company would make which entry into its ledger when it determines that Johnny Come Lately will not pay its account?
    a) credit accounts receivable / debit cash
    b) debit accounts receivable / credit allowance for doubtful accounts
    c) credit accounts receivable / debit allowance for doubtful accounts
    d) none of the above

Chapter 4: Cash, Accounts Receivable, and Marketable Securities

Short Essays

1. Explain the difference between trading securities, available-for-sale, and held-to-maturity securities. Include in your explanation, the proper recording of these securities in the balance sheet.

2. Explain the difference between realized gain/loss and unrealized gain/loss. Include in the explanation, the proper recording of these gains/losses on the balance sheet and/or income statement.

3. Describe the concept of cash equivalents and give several examples.

4. What are the two approaches for determining the balance in the "Allowance for Doubtful Accounts" account? Explain in detail by telling which accounts are affected and which financial statements are affected.

5. At the end of fiscal year 1999, Hopeless, Inc. owned the following investments.

    a. $100,000 of bonds of Costly Chairs, Inc. with a maturity date of 2/1/09

    b. $160,000 of common stock of You Like 'Em Hot Company

    c. $ 95,000 of certificates of deposit in Mellon Bank with maturity periods of 6 months

    d. $ 45,000 of Pennsylvania municipal bonds not readily marketable with a maturity date of 3/1/97

    e. $ 50,000 of bonds in New Jersey with a maturity date of 12/1/99

    Determine the amount that Hopeless would report as current assets, assuming its management plans to sell the bonds and common stock during the next fiscal year.

Chapter 4: Cash, Accounts Receivable, and Marketable Securities

6. During fiscal year 1999, Show Me the Money Insurance Co. engaged in the following transactions.

   a. Investment in Gotcha, Inc. with 300 shares of common stock at $45/share.

   b. Increase in market value of stock purchased in prior year (Show Me, Inc.) of $100/share for the 100 shares. These securities were entered into the books as available-for-sale securities.

   c. Decrease in the market value of municipal bonds purchased in 1999 of $100,000 (maturity date 1/1/2004).

   d. Sold the securities in statement "b" for $700,000. Original purchase price was $300,000.

   For each of the above transactions, record the appropriate journal entries and tell which financial statement will be affected.

7. During fiscal year 2000, Hopeless, Inc. had the following transactions.

   a. Total sales of $400,000.

   b. Set aside an Allowance for Doubtful Accounts; with beginning balance of $120,000.

   c. Accounts Receivable for Joe Shmoe, Inc. of $20,000, previously written off, was paid on February 3, 1998

   d. Hopeless accounts for their Allowance for Doubtful Accounts using the allowance method. It determined that 2% of sales are uncollectible.

   e. Shelly, Inc. had a bad summer and it was determined that their account for $20,000 was uncollectible.

   f. Accounts Receivable had a beginning balance of $250,000.

   Calculate the balance of the Allowance for Doubtful Accounts and Accounts Receivable accounts using the income statement method. Use T-accounts where necessary and show journal entries for amounts to be recorded (do not make an entry for sales).

Chapter 4: Cash, Accounts Receivable, and Marketable Securities

Answers

True or False

1. **False.** The investment can not have an original maturity date longer than 90 days.
2. **False.** They are recorded using the market to market approach to reflect current value or market value at the end of the period.
3. **True.** Held-to-maturity securities are usually bought at above or below their market price, depending on their interest rate, and must therefore be recorded at their amortized cost, not their market value.
4. **False.** They are recorded as current assets, because they are frequently bought and sold to make short term profits.
5. **False.** If they are held for less than one year, they are classified as current assets.
6. **True.** It depends on how long they have been held.
7. **False.** The company may have the intent to hold the bond to maturity, but it doesn't have the ability.
8. **False.** When the value is up: debit security; credit unrealizable gain. When the value is down: debit unrealized loss; credit security.
9. **False.** They may be reflected in the income statement.
10. **False.** It is the difference between the market value on the date of the sale and the market value on the last valuation date.
11. **False.** These are equity securities, they have no maturity dates. They would be available-for-sale.
12. **True.** The gain/loss is recorded as a separate line item on the balance sheet after retained earnings.
13. **False.** Direct write-off uses the bad debt expense and the accounts receivable accounts because it is an actual amount determined for a specific client. When allowance for uncollectible account is used, it is an estimate.
14. **True.** The balance sheet approach determines bad debt expense based on the number of days outstanding for accounts receivable.
15. **False.** It is a two step entry:

    Step 1 - To record the amount back into the accounts receivable:

        1 - Accounts Receivable

            Allowance for Uncollectible Accounts

    Step 2 - To record the collection of cash:

        2- Cash

            Accounts Receivable

16. **False.** The original maturity date is greater than 90 days.
17. **False.** Liquidity and high risk of loss mean cash management needs effective internal controls.
18. **True.**
19. **False.** The amount should be shown based on the amortized cost, which would be neither $800,000 nor $1,000,000, but some value between. (How to determine this value is shown in a later chapter.)
20. **True.**

Chapter 4: Cash, Accounts Receivable, and Marketable Securities

Multiple Choice Answers

1. **(c)** Compensating balances are not cash equivalents; they are restricted to use and reduce a company's liquidity.
2. **(b)** A cash equivalent is currency or easily convertible to currency. A CD with an original maturity date of less than 90 days is a cash equivalent.
3. **(c)** The recording of marketable securities at their current market value gives the users of financial statements more useful information than the historical cost.
4. **(b)** Not a, because this is a loss. Not c, because unrealized gain for available-for-sale securities is a separate line item in the equity section of the balance sheet. Not d, because the unrealized gain for trading securities is reflected in the income statement. Therefore, the correct answer is b.
5. **(d)** Not a, because the unrealized gain is the change in the value of the security. Not b, because the net income is not the unrealized gain of the investing company. Not c, because unrealized holding gain is an increase to income, which is a credit on the income statement. Therefore, the correct answer is d.
6. **(d)** The original maturity date is less than 90 days.
7. **(c)** Not a, because they do not have a maturity date. Not b, because the company's intention was to hold the securities for 90 days or less. Not d, because it is not a cash equivalent. Therefore, the correct choice is c.
8. **(b)** Not a, because they do not have a maturity date. Not c, because of the dates of purchase and sale. Not d, because they are not currency or easily converted to currency. Therefore, the answer is b, because the securities fit the description "active and frequent."
9. **(a)** Not b, because the securities are to be sold in the current term. Not c, because they are not Penny Pincer's own stock. Not d, because they are only current assets to be sold in the near term — answer a.
10. **(a)** Not b, because it is not considered "active or frequent." Not c, because it will be held until maturity. Not d, because it is not a cash equivalent. The correct answer is a: held-to-maturity.
11. **(e)** The 1997 outcome is a loss. A loss is a credit to the investment to lower its value and a debit to record the unrealized loss.
12. **(f)** The unrealized gain is recorded as a separate line item in stockholders' equity, and the increase as a debit to the investment.
13. **(f)** The realized gain is recorded on the income statement as a credit, the cash as a debit, and the sale of the investment as a credit to take it off the books of the seller.
14. **(c)** Not a, because it is an equity investment (no maturity date). Not b, because the company's intention was to hold for 2 years. Not d, because it is not considered a cash equivalent since it is not currency nor easily converted. Therefore, c is the correct choice.
15. **(a)** The original maturity date was longer than 90 days.
16. **(d)** Not a, because it is not a debt instrument. Not b, because it was not intended to be sold in the near term. Not c, because it is a cash equivalent that matures in less than 90 days. Therefore, the correct choice is d.
17. **(c)** Compensating balances must be a separate line item on the balance sheet.
18. **(c)** A mutual fund is in the business of buying and selling securities.
19. **(b)** The available-for-sale unrealized gain is a separate line item in the statement of retained earnings.
20. **(c)** The account should be written off the accounts receivable ledger as a credit, and then taken out of the allowance for doubtful accounts with a debit to that account.

Chapter 4: Cash, Accounts Receivable, and Marketable Securities

Short Essay Answers

1. **a.** Trading securities are investments in equity or debit securities that are frequently bought and sold. They are recorded on the balance sheet as current assets. Purchased by financial institutions and mutual funds.

   b. Available-for-sale securities are investments of debit or equity that are expected to be sold at some point in the future. These are recorded as either current or non-current.

   c. Held-to-maturity securities are debt investments with a maturity date that the company has the intent and ability to hold to maturity. These are recorded as non-current assets based on their original maturity date.

2. Realized gains and losses are recorded when an investment is sold. These are recorded on the income statement. Unrealized gains and losses are recorded on the valuation date of the investment at the end of the period. These are recorded in the balance sheet under retained earnings or on the income statement, depending on the type of security valued.

3. A cash equivalent is an investment vehicle that has a fast turnover: less than 90 days.

   Examples of this type of investments include:

   a. Certificates of deposit held in banks with maturity dates of less than 90 days

   b. Undeposited checks

   c. U.S. Treasury notes with an original maturity date of less than 90 days from date of purchase

4. The two approaches to determine the balance in the allowance for doubtful accounts are:

   a. Income statement approach

   The income statement approach uses a percentage of sales for the period to calculate the bad debt expense for the period. The balance in the allowance for uncollectible accounts has no effect on the income statement for the period.

   b. Balance sheet approach

   Under this approach, bad debt expense is calculated based on the number of days outstanding and the allowance account is adjusted to the required balance. This approach uses an aging of receivable.

5.
a. original maturity date is greater than one year: non-current asset	
b. investment in common stock that is available-for-sale with no maturity date: current asset	160,000
c. CD with a maturity date of less than one year: current asset	95,000
d. municipal bond with an original maturity of greater than one year: non-current asset	
e. NJ bonds with an original maturity date of less than one year: current asset	50,000
Total current assets	**305,000**

Chapter 4: Cash, Accounts Receivable, and Marketable Securities

6. a.

Investment in Gotcha	$13,500	
Cash		$13,500

To record the purchase of 300 shares of Gotcha common stock at $45/share.
Balance sheet.

b.

Investment in Shoe Me, Inc.	$10,000	
Unrealized Holding Gain		$10,000

To record the increase in market value of available-for-sale securities in Shoe Me, Inc.
Balance Sheet and Statement of Retained Earnings.

c.

Unrealized Holding Loss – Municipal Bonds	$10,000	
Investment in Municipal Bonds		$10,000

To record the decrease in market value of held-to-maturity securities in Municipal Bonds.
Balance Sheet decrease, Income Statement decrease

d.

Unrealized Holding Gain	$10,000	
Cash	$700,000	
Investment in Shoe Me, Inc.		$300,000
Gain on Sale of Investment		$410,000

To record the sale of Investment in Shoe Me, Inc.
Balance Sheet no effect due to the increase in asset (cash) and decrease in asset (investment) as well as the decrease in Retained Earnings (Unrealized Gain). Also, an increase in income statement (Gain Sale of Investment).

7. c.

Accounts Receivable – Joe Schmoe	$20,000	
Allowance for Doubtful Accounts		$20,000
Cash	$20,000	
Accounts Receivable – Joe Schmoe		$20,000

To record a previously written-off Accounts Receivable that was collected.

d.

Bad Debt Expense	$8,000	
Allowance for Doubtful Accounts		$8,000

To record Bad Debt Expense based on 2% of sales for the period.

e.

Allowance for Doubtful Accounts	$20,000	
Accounts receivable – Shelly, Inc.		$20,000

To record the write-off of Shelly Inc. Accounts Receivable when determined uncollectible.

	ALLOWANCE FOR DOUBTFUL ACCOUNTS			ACCOUNTS RECEIVABLE	
Beg Bal		120,000	Beg Bal	250,000	
c.		20,000	c.	20,000	20,000
d.		8,000	d.		
e.	20,000		e.		20,000
Ending Bal		128,000	Ending Bal	230,000	

Chapter

Inventory

5

Chapter 5: Inventory

Overview

In Chapter 4, we covered the three most liquid assets: cash, accounts receivable, and marketable securities. In this chapter, we will focus on the complexities of the **inventory** account. The inventory account is normally presented in the current assets section of the balance sheet following accounts receivable. Inventory is usually defined as the goods awaiting sale, the goods in the course of production, and the goods to be consumed directly or indirectly in production. Recording inventory transactions involves both the inventory account on the balance sheet as well as the "Cost of Goods Sold" account in the income statement. For most manufacturing and merchandising firms, Cost of Goods Sold is the single largest expense in the income statement. Therefore, in order to comply with the matching principle, an important objective of recording inventory transactions is the proper pairing of expenses with revenues. As you will see later in the chapter, because of the different methods and the assumptions that must be made, this process is quite complex and requires significant analysis of company operations and production processes. There are four basic issues that must be considered when recording transactions affecting inventory.

1. What types of purchases are included in inventory?

2. How often do you compute "Ending Inventory" and calculate Cost of Goods Sold?

3. What cost flow assumption should be used to cost "Ending Inventory"?

4. At what value should Ending Inventory be presented in the balance sheet?

The most difficult and complex of these issues is the third — determining and applying the cost flow assumption to be used. In this chapter we will consider these four issues individually, with a primary focus on answering the third question. However, we must first acquire an understanding of the basic inventory equation.

Chapter 5: Inventory

Concepts

The Basic Inventory Equation

Understanding the basic inventory equation will help us to consider the fundamental inventory questions described above. The basic inventory equation is:

| Beginning inventory | + | Additions (purchases) | − | Withdrawals (cost of goods sold) | = | Ending inventory |

Any purchases of inventory will increase the total goods available for sale. Therefore, we can say that:

| Beginning inventory | + | Purchases | = | Cost of goods available for sale |

For example, if we started with $20,000 in inventory at the beginning of the year and purchased an additional $36,000 during the year, we would have a total of $56,000 goods available for sale. Withdrawals from inventory are made when the goods are actually sold (giving us the term "cost of goods sold"). For example, suppose we sold $40,000 of the $56,000 of goods available for sale at a sale price of $65,000. Total cost of goods sold for the year would be $40,000 and ending inventory would be $16,000. By manipulating the basic equation, we can see that at any given point in time, total goods available for sale equals ending inventory plus total goods sold and unsold goods:

| Beginning Inventory | + | Purchases | = | Cost of goods sold | + | Ending inventory |
| $20,000 | + | $36,000 | = | $40,000 | + | $16,000 |

Determining beginning inventory is easy; it is the ending inventory from the prior period. In the next section, we will consider what types of purchases are considered inventory and what should be included in the acquisition cost of inventory.

Chapter 5: Inventory

What to Include in Inventory

The components of inventory costs include all expenses incurred to acquire the goods and prepare them for sale. The types of costs that fit into this category vary depending on the type of company. In this section we will cover the different inventory costs for both manufacturing and merchandising firms. However, the remainder of the chapter will focus solely upon the inventory issues faced by merchandising firms.

MERCHANDISING FIRMS

For merchandising firms, the acquisition cost of inventory includes the cost of the good plus any transportation, receiving, unpacking, inspecting, and storage costs. Inventory costs also include **goods in transit,** which are goods for which ownership has been passed but which have not been received yet by the company. The most common example of goods in transit are goods that have been shipped **FOB shipping point.** FOB shipping point is a term used for goods for which ownership is transferred at the point of shipment, normally the seller's place of business. Therefore, although the goods have not been received, the ownership has transferred and they are included as a part of inventory costs. Conversely, goods shipped **FOB destination point** are not included in inventory. FOB destination point is a term used for goods whose ownership does not pass until the buyer actually receives them.

In the purchase transaction, goods are ordered, received, inspected, and recorded. When the invoice for the good is received, the good is then paid for. However, the supplier often provides discounts to customers who pay by a certain date. **Purchase discounts** are stated in the invoice in terms such as "2/10, net/30," which means that the customer will receive a 2% discount if the invoice is paid within 10 days and that the full amount is due within 30 days. In addition to adjustments for discounts, all of the goods received may not pass inspection and may be returned or an allowance may be given.

The acquisition cost of inventory must be adjusted to reflect any discounts, returns or allowances. These adjustments can either be made directly to the "merchandise inventory" account or to a separate "purchase discount" or "purchase returns" and allowance accounts. Purchase discounts, returns and allowances accounts can either be contra accounts (accounts on the balance sheet that reduce another account) or **adjunct accounts** (accounts on the balance sheet that increase another account). The contra or adjunct account is presented in the balance sheet directly after merchandise inventory. In this chapter, we will assume that any discounts, returns, and/or allowances are recorded directly in the Merchandise Inventory account. As an illustration, consider the following example:

CHAPTER 5: INVENTORY

On May 5, Year 3, Iron Retailers purchased goods from Ready Supply, Inc. for a total cost of $56,000. The goods were received one week later on May 12. Upon receipt, it was determined that $6,000 of the goods were damaged, and they were returned to Ready Supply on May 13. On May 19, an invoice was received for payment of the $56,000 with payment terms "2/10, net/30." On May 21, a debit memo was received from Ready Supply, indicating that Iron Retailers had been given credit for the $6,000 of damaged goods. On May 26, Iron Retailers paid Ready Supply in full for the goods purchased. What is the total acquisition cost of the goods purchased from Ready Supply?

To answer this question, let's record the journal entries in this transaction.

1. **Record the purchase on May 5 at the original cost.** We do this by increasing inventory and accounts payable because Iron Retailers has received an asset and now owes money to the supplier.

Merchandise Inventory	56,000	
Accounts Payable		56,000

2. **Reduce inventory by the amount of goods returned on May 21.** Credit Merchandise Inventory for the cost of the goods returned and debit Accounts Payable.

Accounts Payable	6,000	
Merchandise Iinventory		6,000

3. **Record the payment for the goods on May 26.** The balance in the Accounts Payable account is now 50,000 (56,000 - 6,000). However, since Iron Retailers is paying within 10 days, it has to pay only 45,000 [(50,000 - (50,000 x 2%)]. The entry for the payments is as follows:

Accounts Payable	45,000	
Cash		45,000

4. **Record the discount taken for making the payment within 10 days.** The balance in Accounts Payable is now $5,000 (50,000 - 45,000), which represents the 2% discount taken. Since this amount does not have to be paid, we can remove the payable from the books and reduce the cost of our inventory.

Accounts Payable	5,000	
Merchandise Inventory		5,000

Thus, while it may initially appear that the acquisition cost of the inventory is $56,000, it is actually $45,000, which is the total cash paid.

Original Cost	$56,000
Less: Goods Returned	(6,000)
Less: 2% Discount	(5,000)
	45,000

MANUFACTURING FIRMS

For manufacturing firms, inventory costs include direct materials, direct labor (employees' wages), and manufacturing overhead. Manufacturing overhead costs are indirect costs that are related to the production of the product. Common items appearing in a company's manufacturing overhead include indirect materials, indirect labor (such as the salary of the factory supervisor), depreciation of the factory building, and rent and electricity for the factory. Manufacturing firms normally utilize three inventory accounts instead of just one:

- **Raw Materials:** This account includes purchases of direct materials, minus any discounts, including transportation costs.

- **Work in Process:** This account includes direct materials placed into production, direct labor, and any manufacturing overhead used during the period.

- **Finished Goods:** This account includes goods that are completed and ready for sale.

Instead of using one inventory account like most merchandising firms, manufacturing firms use three different accounts to monitor how its goods are distributed across the stages of production. If everything were included in finished goods, it would be difficult to determine what goods can really be sold. Therefore, direct materials are purchased and initially recorded in the "Raw Materials" account. When they are put into production, they are transferred to the "Work in Process" account. During this stage, labor costs are incurred (direct and indirect labor), other materials are used (indirect materials), and expenses to operate the factory are incurred (depreciation, rent, and utilities). When the product is finally finished, it is transferred to the "Finished Goods" account at the total cost to make the good. The following T-accounts summarize the flow of inventory from a direct material to a finished good.

Chapter 5: Inventory

Raw Materials		Work In Process		Finished Goods	

Raw materials	Direct materials used in production	Direct materials used in production
		Direct labor
		Manufacturing overhead
		  Indirect materials
		  Indirect labor
		  Rent
		  Utilities
		  Depreciation
			Completed product	Completed product	Cost of goods sold

Accounting for Inventory

For both merchandising and manufacturing firms, the cost of goods sold is generally the single largest expense that appears on the income statement. The correct calculation of cost of goods sold is critical to ensure that expenses associated with the cost of the goods sold are correctly matched with the revenues earned from sale. There are two basic systems for accounting for ending inventory and calculating cost of goods sold:

- the periodic inventory system
- the perpetual inventory system

Periodic Inventory System

Under the **periodic inventory system,** the physical quantity of goods on hand is counted and priced once a year, and the total cost of goods sold is calculated based on ending inventory. The most common type of company that uses this system is the seller of large quantities of similar, relatively inexpensive goods (e.g. a clothing retailer). Once inventory is purchased, a transaction is recorded to list the item as an asset as it awaits resale. However, all purchases are not made at the same time for the same price. In fact, merchandising firms make purchases of the same good throughout the year from different suppliers at different prices. For this reason, it is very difficult for these types of companies to determine the cost of a good sold on a given day. To do this, they would have to tag every good with the acquisition cost and record a transaction every time a good is sold. Imagine how timely and costly this process would be if a company had 500,000 units of the same good in its inventory and completed an average of 2,000 sales per day. Instead of spending this time

Chapter 5: Inventory

and money, these companies make no entry at the time of sale. Instead, they perform a physical count of inventory once a year and compute the ending inventory. Then, using the basic inventory equation, they compute cost of goods sold. The justification for using this approach is that the goods being counted are the same or similar and are within the same price range. Recall the basic inventory accounting equation:

$$\underbrace{\text{Beginning inventory} + \text{Purchases}}_{\text{(cost of goods available for sale)}} - \text{Cost of goods sold} = \text{Ending inventory}$$

Manipulating this equation, we arrive at:

$$\underbrace{\underset{\text{(known)}}{\text{Beginning inventory}} + \underset{\text{(known)}}{\text{Purchases}}}_{\text{(cost of goods available for sale)}} - \underset{\substack{\text{(physically count} \\ \text{and price)}}}{\text{Ending inventory}} = \underset{\text{(solve for)}}{\text{Cost of goods sold}}$$

Beginning inventory is known, because it is the ending inventory from the prior period. Purchases are known, because they were recorded at acquisition cost when they were received. Knowing these two items, we know what goods are available for sale. If we count and price all of the goods we have at the end of the year, we know that this is what is available for sale but remains unsold in ending inventory. By subtracting what we still have from what was available, we arrive at what we sold, or cost of goods sold.

Application: A Comprehensive Example of the Periodic Inventory System

To illustrate the calculation of ending inventory and costs of goods sold under this method, we'll work through an example.

Home Appliances, Inc. began the year with $20,000 of inventory on hand. During the year, it made purchases of $110,000 and had sales of $175,000. Through a physical count of inventory made at the end of the year, it was determined that $15,000 of goods remained unsold at year end. What was the cost of the goods sold during the year?

Beginning inventory	$20,000
Plus: Purchases	+110,000
Cost of goods available for sale	130,000
Less: Ending inventory	-15,000
Cost of Goods Sold	115,000

We calculate the cost of goods sold to arrive at an answer of $115,000.

Chapter 5: Inventory

This reconciliation is simply the basic inventory equation, which can also be used to compute other unknowns. If you were given cost of goods available for sale as $400,000 and beginning inventory as $60,000, you could determine that $340,000 of goods were purchased during the year.

The entry to record the sales for the year would be made at the time of sale as follows:

	Debit	Credit
Accounts Receivable (or cash)	175,000	
Sales Revenue		175,000

At the end of the year, the entry to record the cost of goods sold would be as follows:

	Debit	Credit
Cost of Goods Sold	115,000	
Merchandise Inventory		115,000

Don't confuse the sales price of the goods ($175,000) with the cost of the goods ($115,000).

Under the periodic system of accounting for inventory, this entry is considered an adjusting entry. Recall that in Chapter 3, we adjusted the inventory account of Just Toys Manufacturing Company for $147,000 under cost of goods sold after all transactions for the year had been recorded and the trial balance was prepared. You will see in the next section on perpetual inventory systems that the entry to record cost of goods sold is made before the trial balance is prepared.

Perpetual Inventory System

Under the **perpetual inventory system**, cost of goods sold is recorded at the time of sale every time a sale is made. Using this system, the inventory account on the balance sheet is always current and no adjusting entry is necessary at the end of the year to determine the cost of goods sold. The most common types of companies that use this system are those that sell a small quantity of unique, high-value goods (e.g. an antique shop or a diamond retailer). For these types of companies, recording a transaction every time a good is sold is not timely and costly. In fact, this approach may be an even more effective method of matching expenses with revenues than the periodic inventory system.

CHAPTER 5: INVENTORY

Application: A Comprehensive Example of the Perpetual Inventory System

Suppose that Unbelievable Antiques made the following purchases on January 5.

Item	Cost (each)	Total Cost	Sales Price
2 Jewelry boxes	$ 160	$ 320	$ 220
3 English chairs	450	1,350	600
1 Chaise lounge	1,000	1,000	1,600
5 Old-fashioned pocket watches	50	250	70
		$2,920	

This is the first year of operation for Unbelievable Antiques and the beginning inventory is zero. The following items were sold in January.

1. **January 12: Sold one jewelry box and one pocket watch for cash.**

Journal Entries	Debit	Credit	
a) Record the revenue from the sale			
Cash	290		(220 + 70)
Sales Revenue		290	
b) Record the cost of goods sold			
Cost of Goods Sold	210		(160 + 50)
Merchandise inventory		210	

2. **January 23: Sold the chaise lounge for cash.**

Journal Entries	Debit	Credit
a) Record the revenue from the sale		
Cash	1,600	
Sales Revenue		1,600
a) Record the cost of the goods sold		
Cost of Goods Sold	1,000	
Merchandise Inventory		1,000

Total cost of goods sold at the end of the month is $1,210 (210 + 1,000). To calculate ending inventory, use the following basic inventory equation:

Chapter 5: Inventory

Beginning inventory	$ 0	(known)
Plus: purchases	+2,920	(known)
Costs of goods available for sale	2,290	
Less: costs of goods sold	-1,210	(known)
Ending inventory	1,710	

Note that under the perpetual inventory system, the cost of goods sold is used to calculated ending inventory. In contrast, under the periodic inventory system, ending inventory is used to calculate the cost of goods sold.

Using the perpetual inventory system does not eliminate the need to perform a physical count of inventory at the end of the year. This is because **shrinkage**, or theft, may occur. For example, based on the calculation above, ending inventory is comprised of the following items.

Item	Cost (each)	Total Cost
1 Jewelry box	$ 160	$ 160
3 English chairs	450	1,350
4 Old-fashioned pocket watches	50	200
		$1,710

However, suppose a physical count of the inventory on hand reveals that only 3 old-fashioned pocket watches remain, making the true ending inventory balance $1,660. Unbelievable Antiques would then record and expense the loss; it would reduce inventory by $50 with the entry below.

	Debit	Credit
Loss from Inventory Shrinkage (IS)	50	
Merchandise Inventory		50

The physical count of inventory under the perpetual inventory system serves as a reconciliation between the physical quantity of inventory in stock and the amount reflected in the accounting records.

Which method to use for inventory

Which inventory processing system a company uses essentially depends on the cost and benefits of each approach to the individual company. In some cases, the periodic system is less timely and less costly — by using it, a company will save money on accounting costs.

Chapter 5: Inventory

However, a company that checks inventory on the periodic system will not know for the entire year (or however long the inventory accounting period is) whether its accounting records actually match what is physically on hand. Being "out of stock" of goods which, according to accounting records are still on hand, may lead to downturns in the production process (not to mention dissatisfaction). In addition, the periodic inventory system provides no information on shrinkage; when the ending inventory is counted to arrive at the cost of goods sold, there is no way to differentiate between what was sold and what was stolen or accidentally destroyed. The perpetual inventory system is more costly and more timely, but it provides a company with a much better idea of the physical quantity of goods on hand throughout the year and the size of losses from shrinkage.

The periodic inventory system is more commonly tested on accounting examinations than the perpetual inventory system because, as you will see in the next sections, the time it takes to calculate the cost of inventory under the perpetual inventory system can take too much time on an exam.

Cost Flow Asumptions

Let's return to our basic inventory equation, in which beginning inventory and purchases are always known values. Beginning inventory is simply the ending inventory from the prior period; a company records purchases as it receives them. We determine the quantity of goods on hand (ending inventory) under the periodic inventory system. Under the perpetual inventory system, we know the quantity of good sold because we record the transactions as sales are made. In both cases, however, we do not know the dollar amount to assign to the known quantity of goods. Ending inventory in the periodic inventory system goods sold in the perpetual inventory system.

Do we compute the dollar value of the units remaining in ending inventory (under the periodic system) or the units sold (under the perpetual system) based on the actual costs, the oldest costs, the most recent costs, or on an average basis? In our previous example of a periodic inventory system (home appliances), the dollar amount in ending inventory was given to you. In the example on perpetual inventory systems, all of the purchases at the antique store made on the same day for the same price for each item. These two scenarios were simplifications of real world situations. In the next section, we will learn the different ways to measure ending inventory and the cost of goods sold.

The physical flow of goods relates to the actual flow of goods from purchase to production (in manufacturing companies) to sale. **Cost flow assumptions** are assumptions that

Chapter 5: Inventory

companies make about the physical flow of their goods. These assumptions may or may not coincide with the actual flow. There are four basic methods of measuring the cost of (or **costing**) inventory.

1. **Specific Identification:** Under this method, the actual cost of a good is assigned to both the units remaining in ending inventory and to those in the "Cost of Goods Sold" account.. No cost flow assumption is necessary. This method is the same under the perpetual inventory system as it is under the periodic inventory system. It is also the most accurate method of allocating the costs of goods between the balance sheet and the income statement. The perpetual inventory system facilitates the use of the specific identification method because of the detailed records required to record cost of goods sold at the time of every sale. However, even if this system is used, it is still very difficult and impractical to keep track of the purchase and sale of individual items within a particular group (e.g. the cost of 3 of 25 pocket watches, all of which were acquired at different times). For this reason, most companies use cost flow assumptions.

2. **First-In, First-Out (FIFO):** Under this method, the assumption is made that goods flow on a first-in, first-out basis, meaning that the first goods purchased are the first to be sold. Working from this assumption, the cost of goods in ending inventory is based on the most recent cost, while the cost of goods sold presented in the income statement are based on the oldest costs (which are often lower than the most recent costs). Because the oldest costs are reflected in the income statement, this assumption yields the highest net income of the four inventory costing methods. FIFO is acceptable under the Generally Acceptable Accounting Principles for use by any business and most closely approximates the actual flow of goods in most businesses. However, this method is often criticized because it distorts figures appearing in the income statement.

3. **Last-In, First-Out (LIFO):** Under this method, the assumptions is made that goods flow on a last-in, first-out basis, meaning that the last goods purchased are the first to be sold. By using this assumption, the cost of goods in ending inventory is based on the oldest costs, while the cost of goods sold presented in the income statement is based on the most recent costs. This method results in a lower net income than the income reported under the FIFO assumption. This assumption is acceptable under the Generally Acceptable Accounting Principles and is preferred over FIFO, although it does not accurately describe the actual physical movement of goods in most businesses. Supporters of this assumption believe that income is more fairly presented and more useful to financial statement users if the current cost of the goods is matched with the current sales prices of the goods. In addition, since the most recent prices are reflected in the income statement, changes due to inflation or deflation, are reflected in net income. A disadvantage of this assumption is that the valuation of ending inventory in

Chapter 5: Inventory

the balance sheet may not reflect the true value of the goods. This is because in contrast to FIFO, the LIFO assumption does not coinicide with the physical flow of goods.

4. **Weighted Average:** Under this method, costs are assumed to flow on an "average basis." The units in ending inventory and the cost of goods sold are based on the weighted average cost of all goods available for sale. The average cost is computed by dividing the total cost of goods available for sale by the total units available for sale. By using an average cost assumption instead of a LIFO or FIFO assumption, the effects of increases and decreases in prices are leveled. As a result, neither the income statement nor the balance sheet reflects the "oldest" or "newest", but rather an average of the two. Critics of this cost flow assumption argue that this method also distorts net income, because the most recent costs are not reflected in the income statement with the most recent sales prices.

The weighted average method is the easiest to apply, but it is the least often tested for this reason. You should probably know both LIFO and FIFO for any exam that covers inventory.

To illustrate the four methods of costing inventory under both processing systems, we will look at one month's operations for Iron Retailers, Inc.

IRON RETAILERS, INC.
Inventory data for the month of August

August			
1	Beginning Inventory	35 units @ $2.00	$ 70
8	Purchase	60 units @ $2.20	132
15	Purchase	120 units @ $2.40	288
22	Purchase	150 units @ $2.50	375
29	Purchase	100 units @ $2.55	255
	Total Goods Available For Sale	465	$ 1,120
18	Sale	160 units @ 3.00	480
30	Sale	135 units @ 3.00	405
31	Ending Inventory	170 units	

Costing Inventory Under Periodic Inventory Systems

Specific Identification

Under the specific identification method, it is assumed that the goods in ending inventory can be specifically identified as relating to a particular purchase. In this example, assume that of

Chapter 5: Inventory

the 170 units on hand at the end of the month, 60 relate to the August 29 purchase, 90 relate to the August 22 purchase, and 20 relate to the August 8 purchase. Using this information, ending inventory at August 31 would be costed as shown in the table on the next page.

SPECIAL IDENTIFICATION METHOD
– Periodic Inventory System

60 units @ $2.55	$ 153
90 units @ $2.50	225
20 units @ $2.20	46
170 units	$ 424

Manipulating the basic inventory equation, we get cost of goods sold of $696:

Goods Available for Sale	$ 1,120 (beginning inventory plus purchases)
Less: Ending Inventory	424
Costs of Goods Sold	$ 696

First-In, First-Out (FIFO)

Under FIFO, the first goods to be purchased are the first assumed to be sold; the goods purchased last are assumed to remain in ending inventory. In our example, of the 170 units on hand at the end of the month, 100 relate to the August 29 purchase and 70 relate to the August 22 purchase. Using this information, the ending inventory at August 31 would be costed in the following manner:

First-In, First-Out (FIFO)
– Periodic Inventory System

100 units @ $2.55	$ 255
70 units @ $2.50	175
170 units	$ 430

Manipulating the basic inventory equation, we get cost of goods sold of $690:

Goods Available for Sale	$ 1,120
Less: Ending Inventory	430
Cost of Goods Sold	$ 690

Chapter 5: Inventory

Last-In, First-Out (LIFO)

Under LIFO, the last goods to be purchased are assumed to be the first sold; therefore, in our example, of the 170 units on hand at the end of the month, 35 relate to the units in beginning inventory, 60 relate to the August 8 purchase, and 75 relate to the August 15 purchase. Using this information, the ending inventory at August 31 would be costed as follows:

Last-In, First-Out (LIFO)
– Periodic Inventory System

35 units @ $2.00	$ 70
60 units @ $2.20	132
75 units @ $2.40	180
170 units	$ 382

Manipulating the basic inventory equation, we get cost of goods sold of $738:

Goods Available for Sale	$ 1,120
Less: Ending Inventory	382
Cost of Goods Sold	$ 738

Note that the LIFO cost of goods sold is higher than the amount calculated under FIFO ($738 versus $690), and the LIFO ending inventory is lower than the amount calculated under FIFO ($382 versus $430). As you will see in the next section, ending inventory and cost of goods sold under the weighted average method will fall between these two numbers.

Weighted Average

To compute the inventory cost under the weighted average method, first calculate the average cost of the goods available for sale. Then apply this amount to the units in ending inventory. In our example, ending inventory will be costed as follows:

Weighted Average
Periodic Inventory System

Total Cost of Goods Available for Sale / Units Available for Sale = Average Unit Cost

$1,120 / 465 = $2.41

Ending Inventory $410   (170 units @ $2.41)

Chapter 5: Inventory

Manipulating the basic inventory equation, we get cost of goods sold of $710:

Goods Available for Sale	$ 1,120
Less: Ending Inventory	410
Cost of Goods Sold	$ 710

Costing Inventory Under Perpetual Inventory Systems

Under the perpetual inventory system, the cost of goods sold is calculated every time a sale is made. The units in ending inventory are then costed by deducting the total cost of goods sold from cost of goods available for sale. As we have discussed, the specific identification method of costing inventory is the same under both the perpetual and the periodic inventory system, because the goods are specifically identified as goods sold or goods remaining in ending inventory. However, the calculation under the other three inventory costing methods are different. The following illustrations demonstrate inventory costing under the FIFO, LIFO, and weighted average methods. When costing inventory under the perpetual inventory system, it is important to remember that you can only use the cost of goods that you have available at the time of sale.

First-In, First-Out (FIFO)

August 18 sale of 160 units

On a first-in, first-out basis, the units in beginning inventory are assumed to be the first to be sold. Thus, the cost of the goods sold on August 18 comes to $358, calculated as follows:

35 units @ $2	$ 70	
60 units @ $2.20	132	
65 units @ $2.40	156	
160	$ 358	Cost of goods sold on Aug. 18

Because only 65 units of the 120 purchased on August 15 were sold and all of the units purchased on previous dates were sold, the remaining inventory at the end of the day on August 18 is calculated as follows:

55 units @ $2.40	132	Remaining inventory after Sale

August 30 sale of 135 units

The cost of the goods sold on August 30 is $322, calculated as follows. Since we are using FIFO, the remaining 55 units from the August 15 purchase will be used first.

55 units @ $2.40	132	
80 units @ $2.50	200	
135	322	Cost of goods sold on Aug. 30

Chapter 5: Inventory

Because all 55 units remaining were sold, only 80 units of the 150 purchased on August 22 were sold, and none of the 100 units purchased on August 29 were sold, the remaining inventory at the end of the day on August 30 is calculated as follows. This is also the ending inventory on August 31 since no additional purchases or sales were made.

70 units @ $2.50	175	
100 units @ $2.55	255	
170 units	430	Ending inventory
	$690	Total cost of goods sold for the month (358 + 332)

Note that ending inventory of $430 and total cost of goods sold of $690 is the same under the periodic inventory system. This will always be the case, as ending inventory will always consist of the last items purchased no matter what method is used.

Last-In, First-Out (LIFO)

August 18 sale of 160 units

On a last-in, first-out basis, the last units purchased BEFORE THE DATE OF SALE are assumed be the first to be sold. Thus, the cost of the goods sold on August 18 is $376, calculated as follows:

120 units @ $2.40	$280	
40 units @ $2.20	88	
160 units	$376	Cost of goods sold on Aug. 18

Since none of the units in beginning inventory were sold, only 40 units of the 60 purchased on August 15 were sold, and all of the units purchased on August 15 were sold, the remaining inventory at the end of the day on August 18 is calculated as follows:

35 units @ $2	70	
20 units @ $2.20	44	
55 units	$114	Remaining inventory after sale

August 30 sale of 135 units

The cost of the goods sold on August 30 is $343, calculated as follows. Since we are using LIFO, the last goods purchased are used first, not the remaining 55 units calculated above.

100 units @ $2.55	255	
35 units @ $2.50	88	
135 units	$343	Cost of goods sold on Aug. 30

Chapter 5: Inventory

Since only 135 of the 250 purchases made after August 18 were used, the 55 units remaining in inventory on that date sill remain unsold as of August 30. Additionally, 115 of the 150 units purchased on August 22 also remain unsold as of August 30.

55	114
115 units @ $2.50	288
170	$ 402 Ending inventory

$ 719 Total cost of goods sold for the month
(376 + 343)

Weighted Average

Under the periodic method, the average cost of goods available for sale is computed at the end of the month to calculate ending inventory. Under the perpetual system, the average cost of goods available for sale is computed every time a purchase is made.

The following table summarizes the calculation of the weighted average cost of goods sold on August 18 and August 30 for Iron Retailers. As shown below, ending inventory is just the remaining units at the end of month multiplied by the average cost calculated at the time of the last purchase.

August				
	1 Beginning Inventory	35 units @ $2.00	$ 70
	8 Purchase	60 units @ $2.20	132
	8 **Balance**	95 units @ $2.13	202
	15 Purchase	120 units @ $2.40	288
	15 **Balance**	215 units @ $2.28	490
	18 Sale	160 units @ $2.28	(365)
	18 **Balance**	55 units @ $2.28	125
	22 Purchase	150 units @ $2.50	375
	22 **Balance**	205 units @ $2.44	500
	29 Purchase	100 units @ $2.55	255
	29 **Balance**	305 units @ $2,48	755
	30 Sale	135 units @ $2.48	(355)
	30 **Balance**	170 units @ $2.28	420

Total Goods Avaiable for Sale	1,120
Less: Cost of Goods Sold	
Aug. 18 Sales	(365)
Aug. 30 Sales	(335)
Total Cost of Good Sold	(700)
Ending Inventory	420

Chapter 5: Inventory

Other LIFO Issues: LIFO Layers

In our LIFO example under the periodic inventory system, total units in ending inventory consisted of the items shown in the table below.

35 units @ $2.00	$ 70
60 units @ $2.20	132
75 units @ $2.40	180
170	$ 382

Recall from our example that the total units purchased during the period (465) exceeded the total units sold (295). When this occurs, a **LIFO layer** is created. A LIFO layer is essentially the excess of total purchases over sales during a company's fiscal year (purchases - sales). In the example above, assuming that this is the company's second year of operations, Iron Retailers had one LIFO layer at the beginning of the year of 35 units. At the end of the year, the company added an additional LIFO layer of 135 units.

KEY CONCEPT

The problem with using the LIFO inventory method is that if total units purchased for the year always exceed total units sold, a company will add a LIFO layer to its inventory every year. Then, when the company actually begins to "dip into the layer" and apply the old unit costs to its ending inventory and cost of goods sold, there may be a distortion of current year income. For example, assume that in Year 4 all units purchased during the year have been sold and Iron Retailers begins to dip into its LIFO layers after the average cost of each unit has risen to $2.75. Because the company bought the units, the older, lower costs, net income is higher than if it had purchased enough goods to sell during the year. Conversely, net income would be lower if prices fell in Year 4 to $1.85. These effects on net income caused by dipping into LIFO layers lead to an increase (or a decrease, if prices fell) in the amount of income taxes to be paid. To avoid these effects, companies generally make purchases in excess of sales, so they won't have to apply any old costs to cost of goods sold. Moreover, dipping into layers defeats the justification for using the LIFO cost flow assumption that making such an assumption match current costs with current revenues. To avoid LIFO layers, companies try to match yearly purchases with sales for the year. This way, the company inventory account reflects items that management plans and "wants" to sell in the short term.

Chapter 5: Inventory

Inventory Valuation

After inventory is processed, counted, and costed, the proper valuation must be made for the ending inventory amount presented in the balance sheet. Recall that balance sheet items are normally presented in order of liquidity, with cash appearing first, followed by marketable securities and accounts receivable. Inventory is normally presented following accounts receivable in the current assets section of the balance sheet. Inventory is placed there is because this account is considered to be relatively — since financial statement users normally expect that the items included in inventory at the end of the year will be sold the following fiscal year. For this reason, inventory is presented at the lower of cost or market value (LCM) instead of on a historical cost basis. To apply the LCM rule, follow three steps.

1. Determine the cost of the goods using one of the three cost flow assumptions or the specific identification method.

2. Compare this amount to the market value of the goods (this is normally given to you in an exam).

3. Choose the lower figure of the two.

If the market value of the goods is lower than cost, the following entry must be recorded for a loss from the decline:

	Debit	Credit
Loss from Decline in Market Value of Inventory	XXXX	
Inventory		XXXX

Chapter 5: Inventory

Key Terms

adjunct accounts: accounts on the balance sheet that increase another account.

cost flow assumptions: assumptions that companies make about the physical flow of the goods that may or may not coincide with the actual flow. There are four basic methods of costing inventory: specific identification, FIFO, LIFO, and weighted average.

first-in, first-out (FIFO): an inventory costing method in which it is assumed that goods flow on a first-in, first-out basis, meaning that the first goods purchased are the first to be sold. With this method, the cost of goods in ending inventory is based on the most recent costs. Meanwhile, the cost of goods sold presented in the income statement is based on the oldest costs, which are often lower than the most recent costs. Because the oldest costs are reflected in the income statement, in a period of rising prices this assumption yields the highest net income of the four inventory costing methods.

last-in, first-out (LIFO): an inventory costing method in which it is assumed that goods flow on a last-in, first-out basis, meaning that the last goods purchased are the first to be sold. With this method, the cost of goods in ending inventory is based on the oldest costs, while the cost of goods sold presented in the income statement is based on the most recent costs. As a result, the current cost of the goods is matched with the current sales prices of the goods.

periodic inventory system: an inventory processing system by which the physical quantity of goods on hand is counted and priced once a year, and the cost of goods sold is calculated based on ending inventory. Companies that commonly use this system are those that sell a large quantity of similar, relatively low-value goods (e.g. a clothing retailer).

perpetual inventory system: an inventory processing system by which the cost of goods sold is recorded at the time of sale each time a sale is made. Using this system, the inventory account on the balance sheet is always current, and no adjusting entry is necessary at the end of the year to determine the cost of goods sold. Companies that commonly use this system are those that sell a small quantity of unique, high-value goods (e.g. an antique shop or diamond retailer).

Chapter 5: Inventory

purchase discounts: discounts given to customers who pay their outstanding bills within a certain number of days. Purchase discounts are stated in the invoice in terms such as "2/10, net/30," meaning that the customer will receive a 2% discount if paid within 10 days but the full amount is due within 30 days.

specific identification: an inventory costing method in which the actual cost of the good is assigned to the units remaining in ending inventory and those in cost of goods sold. No cost flow assumption is assumed under this method. This method is the same under a perpetual inventory system and a periodic inventory system; it is the most accurate method of allocating the costs of goods between balance sheet and the income statement.

weighted average: under this inventory costing method, costs are assumed to flow on an "average basis." The units in ending inventory and cost of goods sold are costed based on the weighted average cost of all goods available for sale.

Chapter 5: Inventory

Thrills, Chills and Drills

True or False

1. Raw Material, is included in the inventory of a merchandising corporation.

2. Inventory cost = purchase price + freight out - purchase discounts.

3. Specific identification is used by companies that deal in small volumes of high priced items.

4. Cost of Goods Sold is presented on the balance sheet as part of the Inventory account.

5. FOB shipping point means that ownership is transferred at the origination point.

6. Goods shipped FOB destination point are included in the inventory of the buyer.

7. An adjunct account on the balance sheet increases another balance sheet account.

8. An indirect cost that is related to the production of a product is called manufacturing overhead.

9. Goods available for sale = beginning inventory + purchases - ending inventory.

10. Perpetual inventory systems require an adjusting entry at the end of the period to determine the cost of goods sold.

11. The periodic inventory system does not account for shrinkage.

12. The perpetual inventory method is more timely and more costly than the periodic method.

13. The FIFO inventory valuation method means that the goods left in ending inventory are valued at the latest costs.

14. When inflation is high, FIFO will result in lower net income.

15. Manufacturing companies use three types of inventory categories.

16. The weighted average method of inventory valuation will result in ending inventory being valued at an amount between the result of the FIFO and LIFO methods for the same inventory.

17. The lower of cost or market inventory valuation is used because of the liquidity of inventory.

Chapter 5: Inventory

18. If cost of goods sold is understated, then net income is also understated.

19. LIFO usually produces lower income tax obligations.

20. A company that uses perpetual inventory valuation does not have to have a physical inventory taken at the end of the period.

Multiple Choice

1. Company ABC produced and sold the same amount of goods as Company XYZ. ABC uses LIFO, while XYZ uses FIFO. Which company will report higher net income?
    a) The answer is dependent on the change in inventory costs during the year and if more goods were produced than sold.
    b) XYZ
    c) ABC
    d) The answer is dependent on the price at which the goods were sold and the cost of those goods at the end of the period.

2. Which of the following statements is true about the LIFO method?
    a) Ending inventory is calculated based on the cost of the last goods purchased.
    b) Ending inventory is calculated based on the cost of the first goods purchased.
    c) Cost of goods sold is lower than it is with the FIFO method.
    d) Income is higher than it is with the FIFO method.

3. Which of the following statements is true about the FIFO method?
    a) Ending inventory is calculated based on the cost of the last goods purchased.
    b) Ending inventory is calculated based on the cost of the first goods purchased.
    c) Cost of goods sold is lower than with the LIFO method.
    d) a and b
    e) b and c
    f) a and c

4. Which method applies the actual cost of goods to both the units remaining in the inventory and the cost of goods sold?
    a) FIFO
    b) LIFO
    c) specific identification
    d) weighted average

Chapter 5: Inventory

5. T-Bone Steel Rule Die Company is a new business. It has purchased 10,000 strips of ruling die at $2.25 per strip, 50 pieces of plywood at $8.25 per sheet, and 1,000 pieces of mounting rubber at $.45 per piece. The owner also purchased a ruling bench for $1,000, a layout table for $400, and a bender for $600. The first week of the company's operations was pretty productive and they manufactured two dies for two different companies. The die for Scott, Inc. used 800 strips of steel, 8 pieces of plywood, and 1,000 strips of mounting rubber. The die for Dennis, Inc. used 1,000 strips of steel, 10 pieces of plywood, and 2,000 pieces of mounting rubber. The charge for these two dies was $500 and $800, respectively. What is the raw material inventory at the end of the first week?
   a) $23,362.50
   b) $5,548.50
   c) $28,911.00
   d) $17,814.00

6. The T-Bone Steel Rule Die Company will account for its finished goods inventory is
   a) FIFO
   b) LIFO
   c) specific identification
   d) weighted average

The information about Working Stiffs International applies to Questions #7 and #8:

Working Stiffs International conducted the following transactions:

1. On March 1, 1998, a beginning inventory of 130 cases of beer for $9.90 each
2. On March 15, 1998, purchased 100 cases for $10.15 each
3. On March 20, 1998, sold 40 cases for $13.20 each
4. On April 1, 1998, purchased 200 cases for $11.25 each
5. On April 5, 1998, sold 240 cases for $13.90 each
6. On April 20, 1998, purchased 100 cases for $11.00 each
7. On April 29, 1998, sold 200 cases for $13.90 each

7. Using the LIFO method of inventory valuation, what was the value of Working Stiffs International inventory on April 30, 1998?
   a) $2,227.50
   b) $1,089.00
   c) $4,563.00
   d) None of the above

Chapter 5: Inventory

8. Using the weighted average method of inventory, what is the cost of goods sold for Working Stiffs International?
    a) $4,411.58
    b) $4,563.00
    c) $1,155.41
    d) none of the above

9. What is added to work in process inventory to move the inventory to finished goods?
    a) labor
    b) freight out
    c) overhead
    d) a and c
    e) a and b

10. What is the total of goods available for sale if the beginning inventory was $40,000, and $45,000 of purchases were made?
    a) $40,000
    b) $45,000
    c) $5,000
    d) $85,000

11. If the beginning balance of an inventory account is $45,000, purchases for $155,000 are made, and the ending inventory is $85,000, what was the cost of goods sold?
    a) $200,000
    b) $115,000
    c) $85,000
    d) $70,000

12. If the ending balance in the inventory account is $95,000, the cost of goods sold was $145,000, and the beginning balance was $15,000, what was the amount of total purchases?
    a) $240,000
    b) $130,000
    c) $75,000
    d) $225,000

CHAPTER 5: INVENTORY

13. If the ending inventory is $135,000, purchases were $300,000, and cost of goods sold is $275,000, what was the beginning inventory?
    a) $110,000
    b) $135,000
    c) $575,000
    d) $200,000

14. If, for a manufacturing firm, work in process beginning inventory was $45,000, ending inventory was $50,000, and $65,000 was transferred to finished goods. What was the amount of raw materials transferred to work in process?
    a) $95,000
    b) $20,000
    c) $70,000
    d) $5,000

15. Cost of goods sold was $25,000, beginning inventory was $85,000, and ending inventory was $110,000. What is the missing part of the finished goods inventory?
    a) Purchases of $50,000
    b) Sales of $50,000
    c) Transferred from WIP of $50,000
    d) None of the above

16. Shatner, Inc., a retailer of shirts, had a beginning inventory of $75,000, purchases of $200,000, and tallied up its ending inventory as $50,000. Where should the $225,000 be posted?
    a) Finished goods
    b) Work in process
    c) Cost of goods available for sale
    d) None of the above

17. Holly Green, Inc. had an ending inventory for 12/31/98 of $950,000. The company made purchases of $300,000 and had cost of goods sold totaling $650,000. The ending inventory for 6/30/99 is $600,000. What was the beginning inventory for Holly Green?
    a) $1,250,000
    b) $300,000
    c) $50,000
    d) $950,000

CHAPTER 5: INVENTORY

18. On January 15, 1999, Kaplan and Kaplan, LLP was hired to prepare the financial statements for Richie Read, Inc. When observing and then testing inventory, the auditor found the following
    1. $100,000 merchandise stored in the warehouse
    2. $600,000 merchandise ordered FOB shipping point
    3. $200,000 merchandise ordered FOB destination, shipped by UPS
    4. $300,000 merchandise in ending inventory at December 31, 1998

    What is the total of Richie Read's inventory for December 31, 1999?
    a) $1,200,000
    b) $1,000,000
    c) $400,000
    d) None of the above

19. Holly Green ordered merchandise totaling $400,000 that was received on January 5, 1998. The invoice was dated January 8, 1998 and received January 11, 1998 with the terms of 2%/10, net 30. What does this mean?
    a) Holly Green should pay $320,000 by January 15, 1998 or $400,000 by February 20, 1998.
    b) Holly Green should pay $400,000 by January 18, 1998.
    c) Holly Green should pay $80,000 by January 15, 1998.
    d) Holly Green should pay $320,000 by January 18, 1998 or $400,000 by February 23, 1998.

20. In a perpetual inventory system, the cost of goods sold is calculated:
    a) at the end of the period
    b) every time a sale is made
    c) at the beginning of the period
    d) any of the above, depending on the company's choice

CHAPTER 5: INVENTORY

Short Essays

1. When George's Clothing Outlet released its financial statements at the end of 1995. It reported $8 million of inventory on a FIFO basis. During 1996, the company purchased $30 million of inventory. It reported $10 million of inventory at the end of 1996 on a FIFO basis. If the company had used LIFO, it would have reported $6 million of inventory at the end of 1995 and $7 million at the end of 1996.

    a. What would the difference have been in George's net income if it had used LIFO instead of FIFO in 1996?

    b. Show the tax benefit and the effect on net income. (Tax Rate is 34%.)

2. Billy's Baseball Manufacturing Company had a beginning raw materials inventory of $900,000, $1,400,000 of work in process inventory, and $700,000 of finished goods inventory. During the year, the company purchased $4,550,000 of raw materials, and it used $3,990,000 of raw materials in production. Labor used in production for the year was $2,660,000. Overhead was $1,480,000. Cost of goods sold for the year was $7,500,000. The ending balance of the finished goods inventory was $640,000.

    Show the effect of these events given above on Billy's inventory accounts for the year. (Hint: use T-accounts.)

3. Tony's Athletic Supplies had the following inventory information available at the end of a recent accounting period

Date	Transaction	Units	Unit Cost	Total Cost
Jan 1	Beginning Inventory	5	$ 20	$ 100
Mar 31	Purchase	6	22	132
July 2	Purchase	10	24	240
Oct 31	Purchase	10	27	270
	Cost of Goods Available for Sale			$ 742

    Total units available for sale during the year   31

    Total units sold during the year   26

    Total units in ending inventory at end of year   5

    Determine the ending inventory and the cost of goods sold assuming the FIFO, LIFO, and weighted average methods. Show your computations.

CHAPTER 5: INVENTORY

4. When reviewing the inventory account for Slippery Steve, Inc. an auditor noticed that the company's bookkeeper had made the following entry:

Loss from Inventory Shrinkage (IS)	$50	
Merchandise Inventory		$50

   From this entry, tell what kind of inventory system Slippery Steve, Inc. probably uses. Explain how you can determine this.

5. When preparing to account for its inventory, On The Move, Inc. realized that it had several inventory items housed off-site. These items included $3,000 of merchandise stored in a warehouse on 5th Street, a shipment of $60,000 worth of merchandise FOB shipping point, and $100,000 worth of merchandise FOB destination. Which of the above merchandise should be included in On The Move's inventory account? Explain why.

6. On January 22, 1997, Holy Smoke, Inc. received 4,000 smoke alarms at a cost of $100 each. At that time it was determined that one box that contained 25 smoke alarms was damaged. The damaged goods were returned on January 25, 1997. The invoice dated January 27, 1997 arrived on February 1, 1997. The terms were 2%/10, net 30. Prepare all necessary journal entries.

7. Michael's Lawn Supplies is a provider of garden supplies. As of December 31, 1996, the company had 300 bags of grass seed in its inventory. The value of the inventory was $9 per bag. During January, February, and March of 1997, the company made the following transactions.

   1. Purchased 800 bags on January 5, 1997 at $9.25 per bag
   2. Sold 1,000 bags during January
   3. Purchased 2,000 on February 3, 1997 at $9.50 per bag
   4. Sold 1,400 bags during February
   5. Purchased 1,600 bags during March at $10.00 per bag
   6. Sold 1,375 bags during March

   What amount of inventory will be reported in the March 31, 1997 balance sheet? What would the cost of goods sold be under the FIFO method? Under the LIFO method? What about under the weighted average method? Show layers.

Chapter 5: Inventory

Answers

True or False

1. **False.** A merchandising company does not manufacturer and therefore would not have a raw materials inventory.
2. **False.** Freight in is part of raw materials inventory not freight out.
3. **True.** Specific identification is used with unique items that are easily identified.
4. **False.** Cost of goods sold is part of the income statement.
5. **True.** FOB shipping point means that ownership transfers at the shipping point when the items are shipped by common carrier. FOB destination means that ownership is transferred at the buyers loading dock.
6. **False.** Goods shipped FOB destination are not included in the buyers inventory until received.
7. **True.** An adjunct account increases another account while a contra-account decreases another account.
8. **True.** Manufacturing overhead relates to those expenses indirectly related to the production of a product such as indirect material, indirect labor, rent, utilities, depreciation, factory supervisor's salary.
9. **False.** Goods Available for Sale = Beginning Inventory + Purchases. Cost of Goods Sold = Beginning Inventory + Purchases - Ending Inventory.
10. **False.** Perpetual inventory systems are adjusted continually during the year when a sale is made and therefore does not require an adjusting entry at the end of the period to determine cost of goods sold.
11. **True.** The perpetual inventory system only adjusts inventory at the point of sale therefore it does not account for theft or shrinkage this must be accomplished by a physical inventory at the end of the period. Whereas, the periodic method is a physical count at the end of the period which will find the shrinkage.
12. **False.** The periodic system is more timely and more costly but at the expense of not knowing about any shrinkage until the count is taken.
13. **True.** FIFO stands for first in first out meaning that the first items purchased would be the first items sold. Leaving the ending inventory to be valued at the cost of the last items purchased.
14. **True.** For the same reasons as in question # 13.
15. **True.** Manufacturing companies use a raw materials inventory, a work in process inventory and a finished goods inventory.
16. **True.** Weighted average uses an average cost to account for the inventory values. This will result in a value between FIFO and LIFO.
17. **True.** Inventory is considered relatively liquid because financial statement users expect that the inventory will be turned to cash in the near future.
18. **False.** If the cost of goods sold is understated, then net income will be overstated because net income = total income - total expenses and if cost of goods sold is lower than it should be, than net income would be higher.
19. **True.** LIFO the result depends on the situation. If the company has a continuing increase to cost of goods sold and the sales are more or less equal, LIFO will result in lower income tax obligations due lower net income. Whereas, if the cost and sales are both unstable, FIFO will result in a lower tax obligation.
20. **False.** A physical inventory must be taken to account for shrinkage, such as, theft.

Chapter 5: Inventory

Multiple Choice Answers

1. **(a)** Not b, unless this period was a time of inflation (see explanation below). Not c, unless this was a time of no inflation (see explanation below). Not d, because this is the formula for gross profit or gross loss. LIFO (last in first out) would in inflationary times cause the cost of goods sold to be higher, thereby lowering the net income; FIFO would have the opposite effect. Therefore, the answer would depend on the change in the inventory cost and on whether more items were produced than sold.

2. **(b)** Not a; LIFO leaves the cost of ending inventory based on the first goods purchased. Not c; cost of goods sold may be higher if purchasing price is down. Not d, because income may be lower or higher depending on cost of goods sold. Therefore, B is the correct answer.

3. **(a)** See the explanation for Question #2, above.

4. **(c)** Not a, because FIFO bases the cost of inventory and the cost of goods sold on the last items purchased, which may or may not be in the inventory. Not b, because LIFO bases the cost of inventory and cost of goods sold on the first items purchased, which may or may not be in the inventory. Not d, because weighted average uses an average cost to value inventory and cost of goods sold. Therefore, c, is the correct answer. Specific identification uses the cost of the specific item to value the inventory and the cost of goods sold.

5. **(d)**

Raw Material Inventory

Beginning Balance	$23,362.50		10,000	@ $2.25	$22,500.00
Cost of Goods Sold	5,548.50		50	@ 8.25	412.50
End Balance	$17,814.00		1,000	@ .45	450.00
					$23,362.50

Scott	Dennis				
800	1,000	strips	1800	@ $2.25	$4,050.00
8	10	pieces	18	@ 8.25	148.50
1,000	2,000	pieces	3,000	@ .45	1,350.00
					$5,548.50

6. **(c)** The products that T-Bone makes are unique and easily identified.

7. **(b)**

Cases	Price	Cost of Goods	Date				
						Inventory	
130	9.9	1,287	3/1	Beginning Inventory		1,287	
100	10.15	1,015	3/15	Purchases		1,015	
-40	10.15	-406	3/20	Sales			-406
200	11.25	2,250	4/1	Purchases		2,250	
-200	11.25	-2,250	4/5	Sales			-2,656
-40	10.15	-406	4/20	Purchases		1,100	
100	11	1,100	4/29	Sales			-1,501
-100	11	-1,100				5,652	-4,563
-20	10.15	-203				1,089	
-20	9.9	-198					
110		1,089					

Chapter 5: Inventory

8. (a)

	WEIGHTED AVERAGE		
	Cases	Price	Cost of Goods
	130	9.9	1,287.00
	100	10.15	1,015.00
	200	11.25	2,250.00
	100	10.15	1,015.00
Total Purchases	530		5,567.00
Costs of Goods Sold	420	10.50377	4,411.58
Ending Inventory	110	10.50377	1,155.41

$$\text{Average Cost} = \frac{5,567}{530} = 10.50377$$

9. (d) Not a, because labor is not the only thing added. Not b nor e, because freight out is not part of inventory. Not c, because labor is also part of the equation. Therefore, the answer must be d -both labor and overhead.

10. (d)
Beginning Balance	40,000
Purchases	45,000
Goods available	**85,000**

11. (b)
Beginning Inventory	45,000
Purchases	155,000
Cost of Goods Sold	**-115,000**
Ending Inventory	85,000

12. (d)
Beginning Inventory	15,000
Purchases	**225,000**
Cost of Goods Sold	-145,000
Ending Inventory	95,000

13. (a)
Beginning Inventory	**110,000**
Purchases	300,000
Cost of Goods Sold	-275,000
Ending Inventory	135,000

14. (c)
Beginning Inventory	45,000
Transferred from Raw Materials	**70,000**
Transferred to Finished Goods	-65,000
Ending Inventory	50,000

15. (c)
Beginning Inventory	85,000
Transferred from Work-in-Process	**50,000**
Cost of Goods Sold	-25,000
Ending Inventory	110,000

16. (d) Not a or b, because a retailer does not have a work-in-process or finished goods inventory. Not c, because the cost of goods available for sale = beginning inventory plus purchase, which in this case equals $275,000.

17. (d) The beginning balance of one period is the ending balance of the next.

Chapter 5: Inventory

18. **(b)** Not a, because title to purchases shipped FOB destination does not change hands until it reaches the destination. Not c, because title to purchases shipped FOB shipping point changes hands when it leaves the sellers, if shipped by common carrier. B is the correct answer.

19. **(d)** Not a, because the terms are 2%/10 days or the full amount in 30 days from the date of the invoice, not the date the merchandise was received. Not b, because the full price would be due February 23 or 30 days after the invoice date. Not c, this amount is the amount of the discount available to Holly Green. Therefore, d is the correct answer.

20. **(b)** Not a; this is the answer for a periodic inventory system. Not c; the cost of goods sold is calculated at the end of the period. Not d, because the calculation is made at the end of the period to adjust the net income.

Short Essay Answers

1.

	FIFO	LIFO
Beginning Balance	8,000,000	6,000,000
Purchases	30,000,000	30,000,000
Available for Sale	38,000,000	36,000,000
Cost of Goods Sold	-28,000,000	-29,000,000
Ending Inventory	10,000,000	7,000,000
Tax Benefit	-3,400,000	-2,380,000
Effect on Income	6,600,000	4,620,000

2.

Raw Material Inventory

	Debit	Credit
Beginning Balance	900,000	
Purchases	4,550,000	
Raw Materials Used		3,990,000
	5,450,000	3,990,000

Work-in-Process

	Debit	Credit
Beginning Balance	1,400,000	
Transferred from R/M	3,990,000	
Labor	2,660,000	
Overhead	1,480,000	
Finished Products		7,440,000
	9,530,000	7,440,000

Finished Goods

	Debit	Credit
Beginning Balance	700,000	
		7,500,000
Transferred from W-I-P	7,440,000	
	8,140,000	7,500,000
	640,000	

Chapter 5: Inventory

3.

LIFO			
Ending Inventory	5	20	100
Costs of Goods Sold	10	27	270
	10	24	240
	6	22	132
			642

FIFO			
Ending Inventory	5	27	135
Costs of Goods Sold	5	20	100
	6	22	132
	10	24	240
	5	27	135
			607

Weighted Average			
Ending Inventory	5	23.94	119.7
Costs of Goods Sold	26	23.94	622.44
Weighted Average	742	31	23.93548

4. Slippery Steve, Inc. uses a perpetual inventory system. We can tell this because a perpetual inventory is adjusted at the time of the sale, which does not take into account shrinkage or theft. These situations are adjusted at the end of the period by a physical inventory count, and an adjusting entry is made at this time.

5. Merchandise worth $63,000 should be included in the inventory for On The Move, Inc. The $3,000 stored in the warehouse on 5th Street is included in inventory because it is the company's merchandise stored off-site. The $60,000 worth of merchandise shipped FOB shipping point is included in inventory, because the ownership of the merchandise changes hands when the merchandise is delivered to a common carrier. The merchandise shipped FOB destination should continue be included in the inventory of the seller until it reaches its destination, the buyer's loading dock.

6.
```
Merchandise Inventory        400,000
    Accounts Payable                    400,000
To record the purchase on January 22, 1997.
```

```
Accounts Payable             2,500
    Merchandise Inventory               2,500
To record the amount of returned goods on January 25, 1997.
```

```
Accounts Payable             357,750
    Cash                                357,750
To record cash paid on February 5, 1997.
```

```
Accounts Payable             39,750
    Merchandise Inventory               39,750
To record discount taken on merchandise for making
payment within 10 days from date of invoice.
```

Chapter 5: Inventory

7.

FIFO

Beginning Inventory Balance	+	Purchases	−	Sales	=	Ending Inventory
300 bags @ 9.00 = 2,700		800 bags @ 9.25 = 7,400				
				300 bags @ 9.00 = 2,700		
				700 bags @ 9.25 = 6,545		
		2,000 bags @ 9.50 = 19,000				
				100 bags @ 9.25 = 925		
				1,300 bags @ 9.50 = 12,350		
		1,600 bags @ 10.00 = 16,000				
				700 bags @ 9.50 = 6,650		
				675 bags @ 10.00 = 6,750		
				Ending Inventory		925 bags @ 10.00 = 9,250
				Cost of Goods Sold		3,775 bags = 35,920

LIFO

Beginning Inventory Balance	+	Purchases	−	Sales	=	Ending Inventory
300 bags @ 9.00 = 2,700		800 bags @ 9.25 = 7,400				
				800 bags @ 9.25 = 7,400		
				200 bags @ 9.00 = 1,800		
		2,000 bags @ 9.50 = 19,000				
				1,400 bags @ 9.50 = 13,300		
		1,600 bags @ 10.00 = 16,000				
				1,375 bags @ 10.00 = 13,750		
						100 bags @ 9.00 = 900
						600 bags @ 9.50 = 5,700
						225 bags @ 10.00 = 2,250
				Ending Inventory		925 bags = 8,850
				Cost of Goods Sold		3,775 bags = 36,250

Weighted Average

300 bags @ 9.00 =	2,700
800 bags @ 9.25 =	7,400
2,000 bags @ 9.50 =	19,000
1,600 bags @ 10.00 =	16,000
4,700 (Total bags)	45,100 (Total Cost)

9.595744681 (Average Cost)

Ending Inventory   925 bags @ 9.60 =   8,880
Cost of Goods Sold   3,775 bags @ 9.60 =   36,240

Calculations

FIFO		LIFO		Weighted Average
Cost of Goods Sold	Ending Inventory	Cost of Goods Sold	Ending Inventory	Ending Inventory
$2,700	300	$800	300	4,700
$6,545	800	$200	800	−3,775
$925	−300	$1,400	−800	Total bags 925
$12,350	−700	$1,375	−200	
$6,650	−100	Total Cost $3,775	2,000	
$6,750	−1,300		−1,400	
Total Cost $35,920	−700		1,600	
	−675		−1,375	
	Total bags 925		Total bags 925	

Chapter

Long Term Assets and Depreciation

6

Chapter 6: Long-term Assets and Depreciation

Overview

Every year companies spend thousands, millions, sometimes billions of dollars on purchases of long-term assets. In fact, for many companies, especially manufacturing companies, the cost of long-term assets has the largest dollar value on the balance sheet. **Long-term assets** are assets acquired for use in the company's operations that have a useful life of more than one year and appear in the non-current section of the balance sheet. In addition, to be classified as a long-term asset, an asset cannot be intended for resale to customers. Long-term assets are either tangible or intangible in nature, and the costs are normally allocated over the useful life of the asset. By the end of this chapter you should be able to:

- understand the basic types of tangible and intangible assets
- determine what costs to include in the acquisition cost of a long-term asset
- understand and apply acceptable methods of allocating the cost of long-term assets
- record transactions when an asset is sold or disposed
- calculate depreciation/amortization when there is a change in an estimate
- distinguish between repair/maintenance expenses and improvements

Of these topics, determining the acquisition costs of a long-term asset and calculating the annual depreciation/amortization when there is a change in an estimate are the most complex. However, all of these topics will be covered on any examination covering long-term assets.

Chapter 6: Long-term Assets and Depreciation

Concepts

Capitalized Asset Costs

Purchases of property, plant, and equipment for use in a company's operations often cost large amounts and are expected to provide benefits for longer than one accounting period. These types of expenditures are considered **capital expenditures** and are initially recorded as long-term assets (capitalized) on the balance sheet according to historical cost. In Chapter 5, we defined inventory costs as all expenses incurred to acquire goods and to prepare them for sale. Similarly, the acquisition cost of long term asstes includes all the expenses incurred to acquire the assets and make them ready and available for use. Among the most common capitalizable costs (aside from the actual cost of the asset) are transportation, insurance, and installation costs. However, there are a variety of additional costs often included as part of the acquisition cost of the asset. The following chart summarizes acceptable capitalizable costs for the four basic categories of **tangible assets,** which are long term assets having a physical substance.

Fixed Asset Type	Capitalizable Costs
Land	• Purchase price • Title search fees • Commissions paid to real estate agents • Brokerage and legal fees • Excavation, draining, clearing, grading costs to prepare the land for building • **Cost of tearing down the old building less any salvage value received** • Landscaping • Accrued taxes paid
Buildings	• Purchase price • Title and legal fees • Any repairs and expenses required to put it in "usable condition"
Self-Constructed Assets	• Cost of materials, labor, and overhead • Architects fees for designs • Insurance paid during construction • Interest paid on loans • Lawyers fees • Building Permits
Equipment	• Purchase price less any discounts • Transportation/ freight costs • Installation Costs • Insurance Costs • Excise taxes and tariffs • **Cost of test runs BEFORE the equipment is put into operation**

Pay Attention
Note that the costs of tearing down the building is classified in the land instead of the building account.

Pay Attention
Any test runs included as a capital cost must take place BEFORE the asset was put into operation.

Chapter 6: Long-term Assets and Depreciation

Depreciation Defined

As we have discussed, purchases of tangible assets are recorded as assets because they provide benefits over more than one accounting period. After the asset is recorded at acquisition cost, the cost is allocated over the accounting periods benefited by the asset. To do this, depreciation is recorded based on the matching principle. The tangible assets purchased are expected to generate revenues for a company over a number of years. Therefore, it is logical that the expenses associated with the purchase of the asset should be matched with the revenues that are generated over that long period.

The following entry is the standard entry to record depreciation:

	Debit	Credit
Depreciation Expense	XXXX	
Accumulated Depreciation		XXXX

As an asset is depreciated, the expense is recorded in the income statement at the end of each accounting period and accumulated in a **contra asset** account. The contra asset account is shown in the balance sheet, below the related long-term asset account. The original cost of the asset less the accumulated depreciation is the **net book value** of the asset. It is crucial to understand that depreciation is a method of allocation and not valuation. The net book value of an asset is not the same as the market value of the asset. Long-term assets are presented in the balance sheet based on the historical cost principle and are not valued at their market value unless they are significantly impaired. Recording transactions for the impairment of long term assets is beyond the scope of this guide. For now, just remember to record assets at acquisition cost and without adjusting for market value, even at the time of sale or disposal.

In the next section we will cover the five basic depreciation methods. However, we should first define a few key terms:

- **useful (service) life:** The useful life of an asset is the period (either in years or in units) over which the asset is expected to provide benefits or generate revenues. As you will see in the next section, determining the useful life of an asset is critical to determining the annual depreciation of an asset.

- **salvage value:** When companies purchase a long-term asset, sometimes it is determined that the asset will have some value at the end of its useful life. The salvage value of an asset is the estimated scrap value or trade-in value of an asset at the end of its useful life.

Chapter 6: Long-term Assets and Depreciation

Salvage value is also referred to as **residual value** or **disposal value**.

- **depreciable basis:** The depreciable basis of an asset is simply the cost less any estimated salvage value. Salvage value is deducted from the original cost when determining depreciation under the assumption that part of the cost of the asset (the amount equal to the estimated salvage value) will be returned at the time of disposal, so there is no need to allocate those costs over the life of the asset. With the exception of the MACRS and declining balance depreciation methods (which will be discussed in the next section), tangible assets are always depreciated using their depreciable basis.

Each of the depreciation methods discussed in the following sections can be applied to capital expenditures for buildings, self-constructed assets, machinery, and equipment. However, land is never depreciated, because there is no limited useful life over which to allocate the acquisition costs.

Depreciation Methods

There are five different methods of allocating asset costs over time. These depreciation methods are summarized in the following chart:

Method	Annual Depreciation Calculation	Accounting for Salvage Value
Straight-line	$\dfrac{\text{Cost less estimated salvage value}}{\text{Estimated useful life in years}}$	Depreciate asset to salvage value and remove asset when sold.
Production or Use	$\dfrac{\text{Cost Less Estimated SalvageValue}}{\text{Estimated Number of Units}}$ x Number of units produced/ used in the current year	Depreciate asset to salvage value and remove asset when sold.
Sum-of-the-years digits	Cost less estimated salvagevalue x $\dfrac{\text{Remaining useful life in years at the beginning of the year}}{\text{Sum of the useful life in years}}$	Depreciate asset to salvage value and remove asset when sold.
Declining balance	Net Book Value (Cost less accumulated depreciation) x $\dfrac{1}{\text{Estimated useful life in years}}$ x Declining factors	Depreciate until straight-line provide higher depreciation charges; then apply straight-line method.
Modified Accelerated Cost Recovery System (MACRS)	Cost x MACRS percentage	Depreciate asset to zero and record gain for salvage value.

Chapter 6: Long-term Assets and Depreciation

Straight-line Method

The **straight-line method** of depreciation is the method most commonly used for financial reporting purposes. It is also the easiest method to apply. Under this method, costs are allocated evenly over the useful life of the asset based upon the assumption that cost allocation depends only on the passage of time. For example, suppose that a delivery truck is purchased for $27,000. The estimated useful life of the truck is 5 years, and the truck has a salvage value of $2,000. The annual depreciation under the straight-line method would be calculated as follows:

$$\frac{\text{Cost less estimated salvage value}}{\text{Estimated useful life in years}} = \frac{\$27,000 - \$2,000}{5} = \$5,000/\text{year}$$

The annual depreciation would be $5,000/year or 20% (1/5) of the depreciable basis per year. At the time of purchase, the following entry is made:

Cash	27,000	
Equipment – Trucks		27,000

Then, depreciation expense of $5,000 is recorded every year, beginning in the first year as follows:

Depreciation Expense	5,000	
Accumulated Depreciation		5,000

At the end of the fifth year, the asset will have been depreciated down to its salvage value, which will equal the net book value of the asset, or $2,000. The net book value of the truck is presented on the balance sheet as follows:

Equipment – Trucks	27,000	
Accumulated Depreciation	(25,000)	$5,000 annual depreciation x 5 years
Net book Value	2,000	

When the asset is disposed of and the salvage value is received, the following entry is recorded to remove the asset from the books:

Cash	2,000	
Accumulated Depreciation	25,000	
Equipment – Trucks		27,000

Chapter 6: Long-term Assets and Depreciation

Production or Use Method

KEY CONCEPT

The **production or use method** is similar to the straight-line method, except that instead of basing the cost allocation assumption on the passage of time, the allocation of cost is based on the production or use of the assets. Therefore, to calculate the annual depreciation, the denominator will be the estimated useful life in terms of the number of units produced or used, instead of the estimated useful life in years. Continuing with our truck example from above, suppose that the estimated useful life of the truck is 100,000 miles. Based on this calculation, the annual depreciation is calculated as follows:

$$\frac{\text{Cost less estimated salvage value}}{\text{Estimated useful life in years}} = \frac{\$27,000 - \$2,000}{100,000} = \$.25/\text{mile}$$

This per mile rate would be applied to the number of miles driven per year. Thus, the depreciation expense recognized every year will be different if the total miles driven for the year are different. If 10,000 miles are driven in the first year, 20,000 in the second and third year, 35,000 in the fourth year, and 15,000 in the fifth year, depreciation will be recorded year according to the following schedule:

Year	Miles Driven		Deprciation Rate		Depreciation Expense	Net Book Value
						$27,000 ← Original Cost
1	10,000	x	$0.25	=	2,500	24,500
2	20,000	x	$0.25	=	5,000	19,500
3	20,000	x	$0.25	=	5,000	14,500
4	35,000	x	$0.25	=	8,750	5,750
5	15,000	x	$0.25	=	3,750	**2,000**
	100,000				25,000	

Notice that the asset is still depreciated down to its salvage value of $2,000. Therefore, the same entry is made to write the asset off when it is disposed of or sold at the end of Year 5 as is made under the straight-line method.

Cash	2,000	
Accumulated Depreciation	25,000	
Equipment – Trucks		27,000

Chapter 6: Long-term Assets and Depreciation

Sum-of-the-Years-Digits Method

The **sum-of-the-years digits-method** is an accelerated method by which most of the cost of an asset is allocated to the earlier years of its useful life. **Accelerated methods** of depreciation are based on the assumption that a long-term asset generates greater revenue in the earlier stages of its useful life than in the later stages. Equipment and buildings naturally deteriorate with time and generally require more repair and maintenance as they become older. As a result, there may be more frequent shutdowns or machines may operate slower, generating additional expenses and less revenue. Thus, it can be argued that to better match expenses with revenues, an accelerated approach should be taken to record depreciation charges on an asset. Because accelerated methods provide higher expenses in the earlier years of the asset and thus a lower net income, many companies use accelerated methods for income tax purposes, even though they may simultaneously use the straight-line or production/use method for financial reporting purposes.

Under the sum-of-the-years-digits method, a fraction of the cost of the asset, which decreases every year, is depreciated based on the sum of its useful life in years. For example, for a $20,000 asset with a useful life of 7 years and no salvage value, the annual depreciation would be recorded every year based on the schedule given below.

Formula	Cost less estimated salvage value	x	Remaining Useful life in years at the BEGINNING of the year / Sum of the useful life in years	=	Annual Depreciation
Year 1	20,000	x	7/28	=	5,000
Year 2	20,000	x	6/28	=	4,286
Year 3	20,000	x	5/28	=	3,571
Year 4	20,000	x	4/28	=	2,857
Year 5	20,000	x	3/28	=	2,143
Year 6	20,000	x	2/28	=	1,429
Year 7	20,000	x	1/28	=	714
				Total	20,000

Quick Formula for Calcultating Sum of Years Digits ➔ $\frac{n(n+1)}{2}$ $\frac{7(7+1)}{2} = 28$

Remember to use the years remaining at the BEGINNING of the year.

Chapter 6: Long-term Assets and Depreciation

Declining Balance Method

The **declining balance method** is the most common type of accelerated method used for financial reporting purposes. Under this method, the assumption is made that the costs allocable to each period over the useful life of the asset decreases faster than the straight-line method by a certain percentage. For example, a double declining balance assumption means that the assets decrease twice as fast as in the straight-line method, or by 200%. Look carefully at the formula for calculating annual depreciation under this method:

$$\text{Net Book Value (Cost less accumulated depreciation)} \times \frac{1}{\text{Estimated useful life in years}} \times \text{Declining factor}$$

Let's analyze each segment of this equation. Under a double declining balance assumption, since the allocable costs are assumed to decrease twice as fast, the declining factor is 2. If a 150% declining balance is assumed, then the declining factor is 1.5. The rate of depreciation is calculated by applying this factor to the depreciation rate under the straight-line method. In our example of the straight-line method above, we determined that an asset with a useful life of 5 years will be depreciated at a rate of 20% per year. Using double declining balance, to depreciate twice as fast we apply a rate of 40% per year [(1/5) x 2], or double the 20% rate. The depreciation rate is then applied to the net book value of the asset instead of the depreciable basis. Therefore, the salvage value is not initially considered when determining the annual depreciation.

- The net book value is the only part of the declining balance equation that changes every year because the net book value of the asset decreases as depreciation is recognized every year. Therefore, remember to use the net book value at the beginning of each year to determine the annual depreciation for the year.

- When comparing the annual depreciation under the declining balance method with the amount calculated using the straight-line method, remember to calculate the straight-line depreciation using the formula below.

$$\frac{\text{net book value - salvage value}}{\textbf{remaining} \text{ useful life of the asset at the } \textbf{beginning} \text{ of each year}}$$

Chapter 6: Long-term Assets and Depreciation

The following schedule summarizes the annual depreciation for an asset with a cost of $37,000, a salvage value of $2,000, and a useful life of 7 years, using a 200% declining balance assumption for depreciation.

Acquisition Cost: $37,000
Useful life: 7 years
Salvage Value: $2,000
Depreciation: 200% Declining Balance
Declining Factor: 28.75%   ($1/7 \times 2$)

Year	Acquisition Cost	Net Book Value	200% Declining Balance	Straight-Line	Annual Depreciation
1	$37,000	$37,000	$10,751	$5,000	$10,751
2	37,000	26,429	7,551	4,071	7,551
3	37,000	18,878	5,394	3,376	5,394
4	37,000	13,484	3,853	2,871	3,853
5	37,000	9,631	2,752	2,544	2,752
6	37,000	6,880	1,966	2,440	2,440
7	37,000	4,440	1,269	2,440	2,440
					$35,000

Note that in Year 6, a switch is made to straight-line depreciation, because the annual depreciation charges are higher that year under the straight-line method than under the doubld declining balance assumption ($2,440 versus $1,966). Note also that the asset has only been depreciated down to the depreciable basis of the asset.

Sample calculation of 200% declining balance depreciation for Year 2 and Year 3:

Year 2   26,429 x 28.57% = 7,551

Year 3   18,878 x 28.57% = 5,394

Sample calculation of straight-line depreciation for Year 2 and Year 3:

Year 2 $\dfrac{26,429 - 2,000}{6}$ = 4,071

Year 3 $\dfrac{18,878 - 2,000}{5}$ = 3,376

Because a percentage is always applied to the remaining balance, the formula used to calculate the annual depreciation under this method will never depreciate the asset down to zero. Therefore, companies must switch to the straight-line method at some point during the life of the asset, normally when the straight-line method results in higher depreciation charges. When the switch is made to the straight-line method, the depreciable basis of the asset is used to determine the annual depreciation. The depreciable basis is calculated by deducting the salvage value from the net book value of the asset at the time of the switch. The asset is then depreciated down to its salvage value over the remaining useful life.

MODIFIED ACCELERATED COST RECOVERY SYSTEM (MACRS)

The modified accelerated cost recovery system (MACRS) of depreciation is the method used by companies for tax purposes and generally results in the highest amount of depreciation in the second year of the **tax life** of the asset. The tax life of an asset is its life as determined by the federal tax laws and is generally shorter than the asset's useful life. Under MACRS, the assumption is made that the asset is acquired in the middle of the year, so only a half-year of depreciation is taken in the first year. To use MACRS, assets are grouped into classes based on the span of the tax life and depreciated using percentages determined by the Internal Revenue Code. Salvage value is not deducted from the cost of the asset when determining the annual depreciation. Instead, the asset is depreciated down to zero and a gain is recorded for the amount of the salvage value at the time of disposal. Note that this is the only method of depreciation under which salvage value is not considered when calculating annual depreciation. The following entry would be recorded if a fully depreciated machine with an acquisition cost of $14,000 were sold for $2,000 at the end of its economic life.

Cash	2,000	
Accumulated Depreciation	14,000	
Machinery & Equipment		14,000
Gain on Disposal of ‹Machinery		2,000

Generally, if you are given a MACRS question on an exam, you will be provided with a depreciation schedule similar to the one listed below. Just apply the acquisition cost of the asset to each of the percentages to determine the depreciation for a given year. Remember, don't subtract salvage value before applying the percentage. Also, remember to use the economic life, not the useful life. It's generally the lower of the two.

Chapter 6: Long-term Assets and Depreciation

Sale or Disposal of Property, Plants, and Equipment

In our example of using the MACRS method of depreciation, we demonstrated that the gain on a disposal of a fully depreciated asset for the amount of the salvage value is recorded as follows:

Cash	2,000	
Accumulated Depreciation	14,000	
Machinery & Equipment		14,000
Gain on Disposal of Machinery		2,000

Sometimes expenses are actually incurred to dispose of an asset and the estimated salvage value is not received. Suppose that instead of receiving $2,000, the company in this example had to pay $3,000 to dispose of the assets. Under the MACRS depreciation method, the following entry would be made to record the loss on disposal:

Loss on Disposal of Machinery	3,000	
Accumulated Depreciation	14,000	
Machinery & Equipment		14,000
Cash		3,000

If the straight-line method had been used and the asset was depreciated down to its salvage value of $2,000, the following entry would be made to record the loss on disposal:

Loss on Disposal of Machinery	5,000		
Accumulated Depreciation	12,000		Net Book Value =
Machinery & Equipment		14,000	14,000 - 12,000 = 2,000
Cash		3,000	

In this case, the loss on disposal is $5,000, since the company expected to receive $2,000 and ended up paying $3,000.

Sometimes assets are sold before they become fully depreciated, because the company determines that it is more profitable to sell an asset than to keep it to use in its normal operations. Companies also sell assets to obtain additional cash flow that may be used to pay off current expenses. When an asset is sold that has not been fully depreciated, the company often realizes a gain on the sale that is different from the cash received. For example suppose that equipment with an acquisition cost of $55,000 was sold for $40,000,

Chapter 6: Long-term Assets and Depreciation

had accumulated depreciation of $25,000, and an estimated salvage value of $5,000. The following entry would be recorded at the time of sale.

Cash	40,000		
Accumulated Depreciation	25,000		Do not deduct salvage
Machinery & Equipment		55,000	value here!
Gain on Sale of Equipment		10,000	

A similar entry would be made if the asset were sold at a loss with a debit to loss on sale of equipment instead of a credit to gain on sale of equipment. Note that the salvage value of $5,000 is not taken into consideration. This is because the asset was sold for a profit before it could be disposed. Don't make the mistake of deducting the salvage value from the acquisition cost of the asset when the credit is made to write the asset off the books. Note also that the gain is considered a gain on **sale** and not a gain on disposal. Be careful not to lose points for writing the incorrect description of the transaction.

Changes in Depreciation Estimates

Once you have mastered the formulas, calculating depreciation under any of the methods described above becomes relatively easy. The real difficulty in calculating depreciation arises when one of the estimates changes. There are two basic estimates that can change:

- useful life
- salvage value

The key to mastering problems with changes in depreciation estimates is recognizing that any change is considered **prospective** in nature and not retroactive. Therefore, the changes will only affect the annual depreciation charges for future accounting periods. Since only future periods are adjusted, the new depreciable basis is calculated as the net book value of the asset at the time of the change less the estimated salvage value (use the new salvage value if this is revised). Consider the following example about AutoRotors, Inc..

AutoRotors, Inc. purchased a new machine in Year 5 with an acquisition cost of $200,000 and an expected salvage value of $10,000. The machine will be depreciated according to a straight-line basis over a period of 10 years. The annual depreciation for the new machine is $19,000, calculated as shown on the next page.

Chapter 6: Long-term Assets and Depreciation

$$\frac{\text{Cost less estimated salvage value}}{\text{Estimated useful life in years}} = \frac{\$200,000 - \$10,000}{10} = \$19,000/\text{ year}$$

At the end of Year 9, the balance sheet of AutoRotors, Inc. would contain the following information related to the new machine:

Non-Current Assets		
Machinery & Equipment	200,000	
Accumulated Depreciation	(95,000)	19,000/year x 5 years
Net Book Value	105,000	

At the beginning of Year 10, the remaining useful life of the asset is five years. During Year 10, AutoRotors determines that the asset is expected to have a salvage value of $9,000 instead of $10,000. In addition, the estimate of the useful life of the asset is extended by an additional three years. What is depreciation expense for Year 10? (An exam question might also state that "AutoRotors determined that the useful life of the asset is really 13 years instead of 10 years.") The formula for this problem is shown below.

$$\frac{\textit{Net book value} \text{ less } \textit{revised} \text{ estimated salvage value}}{\text{Remaining useful life in years}} = \frac{\$105,000 - \$9,000}{13 \text{ years} - 5 \text{ years}} = \$12,000/\text{ year}$$

The annual depreciation for Year 10 would be $12,000 / year.

Recording Depreciation for Mid-Year Purchases

In the examples that we have considered so far (except the MACRS method), the assumption has been made that the asset was acquired at the beginning of the year and a full year of depreciation is taken in the first year. However, most companies begin depreciating tangible assets in the month of acquisition, which is not always the beginning of the fiscal year. In addition, some companies use **half-year conventions,** in which a half-year of depreciation is taken in the year of acquisition no matter when the asset was acquired. Other companies used **mid-quarter conventions,** in which the depreciation for the first year is calculated starting from the middle of the three-month period that the asset was acquired.

Exam questions on depreciation normally require you to calculate depreciation in the first year of acquisition when the asset is acquired some time during the year (e.g. March or

Chapter 6: Long-term Assets and Depreciation

September for a company with a fiscal year that is the same as the calendar year). The simplest approach to take in answering these types of questions is to first determine the annual depreciation for the whole year, then multiply this result by the appropriate fraction, depending on when the asset was acquired and the depreciation convention that the company is using. Suppose a company's depreciation policy is to depreciate all tangible assets on a straight-line basis beginning in the month of acquisition. If an asset is acquired on May 31, the depreciation expense for the first year would be 8 / 12, or ⅓, of the total annual depreciation. In the second year, depreciation expense is calculated as discussed earlier for full years.

Repairs & Maintenance versus Improvements

Not all expenditures made related to tangible assets are capitalizable costs; they do not all provide benefits that extend beyond more than one accounting period. These types of expenditures are typically repair and maintenance expenses, they are considered revenue expenditures. A common example is the cost of yearly maintenance to tune-up major equipment used in a company's business. The following series of questions can be used to distinguish between capital expenditures and regular expenditures.:

1. Is the expenditure required to make the asset readily available for use?

    If yes, then capitalize as part of the acquisition cost of the asset. If no, then ask the question:

2. Does the expenditure:

    a. Extend the useful life of the asset?

    b. Increase the number of units produced by the asset?

    c. Increase the quality of the units produced?

    d. Increase the efficiency of the asset?

    If the answer to any of these questions is yes, then capitalize the expenditure as an improvement. If no, then expense it in the current period.

Improvements are expenses incurred after an asset is purchased that provide additional economic benefits that span more than one accounting period. Land improvements are recorded in a separate account (commonly named Land Improvements). Although land is never depreciated, improvements such as repaving or building a new parking lot have limited

Chapter 6: Long-term Assets and Depreciation

useful lives and are recorded in a separate account so that they can be appropriately depreciated. All other improvements are recorded in the long-term asset account of the asset that was improved.

The following table provides examples of the different types of repairs and improvements. This table can serve as a useful list of examples to look for in an exam. Remember, this table is not intended to be all-inclusive; if your exam does not list any of the items shown below, simply apply the two-step thought process described above.

Category	Expense or Capitalize?	Examples	Fixed Asset Account
Betterments Improvements that do not add to the physical layout of the asset	Capitalize	• New roof on a building • Resurfacing a driveway or parking lot	Building Land Improvement
Additions, extensions, & enlargements Improvements that add to the physical layout of the asset	Capitalize	• New fence around a building • An additional parking lot • New wing on a building • Installing an air-conditioning system	Land Improvement Land Improvement Building Building
Extraordinary Repairs that affect the estimated useful life or salvage value of the asset	Capitalize	• Machine overhauls • Replacement of major parts in a machine (e.g. motors, etc.)	Machinery & Equipment Machinery & Equipment
Ordinary repairs Repairs NECESSARY to keep the asset in working condition	Expense	• Replacement of minor parts in a machine (e.g. gears, bolts, etc.) • Painting a building • Replacing woodwork or small fixtures in an office building • Tune-ups, tires, and batteries • Normal maintenance, lubrication, cleaning, and inspection	None – Expense None – Expense None – Expense None – Expense None – Expense

The appropriate capitalization and depreciation of improvements varies depending on the type of improvement. Costs for betterments, additions, extensions, and enlargements are added to the original costs of the asset and depreciated over the useful life of the **improvement** — not the useful life of the asset. If these costs do not have their own useful life but instead increase the useful life or change the salvage value of the original asset, simply add the total costs of the improvement to the net book value of the asset. Then treat the improvement as a change in the depreciation estimate.

Costs for extraordinary repairs are not added to the original cost of the asset. Instead, they are deducted from accumulated depreciation (by debiting the account), thereby increasing the net book value of the asset. The new net book value is then depreciated prospectively over the remaining useful life of the asset, taking into consideration any changes in estimates. To see how this works, let's return to our example of AutoRotors, Inc.

Chapter 6: Long-term Assets and Depreciation

AutoRotors, Inc. purchased a new machine in Year 5 with an acquisition cost of $200,000 and an expected salvage value of $10,000. The machine is to be depreciated on a straight-line basis over a period of 10 years. Based on these facts, we determined that the annual depreciation for the new machine is $19,000. We also calculated that at the end of Year 9, the asset had an accumulated depreciation of $95,000, making the net book value $105,000. Now suppose that at the end of Year 10, AutoRotors decided to do a complete overhaul of the machine. The overhaul costs $40,000 and extends the useful life of the asset for three additional years. What is the depreciation expense for Year 10?

First, let's calculate the new net book value of the asset by recording the entry for the cost of the overhaul.

Accumulated Depreciation	40,000	
Cash		40,000

Total accumulated depreciation is now $55,000 (95,000 - 40,000), increasing the net book value of the asset from $105,000 to $145,000 (200,000 - 55,000). Based on this net book value, we can calculate the annual depreciation.

$$\frac{\text{Net book value less } revised \text{ estimated salvage value}}{\text{Remaining useful life in years}} = \frac{\$145,000 - \$10,000}{5 \text{ years} + 3 \text{ years}} = \$16,875/\text{year}$$

The annual depreciation for Year 10 is $16,875/year.

Intangible Assets

So far we have discussed depreciation methods for tangible assets. **Intangible assets** are long-term assets without any physical substance that are expected to provide some future rights or advantages to a company over a period that extends beyond one year. Some examples of intangible assets include goodwill, patents, copyrights, trademarks and brand names, franchises, leaseholds, and leasehold improvements. All intangible assets have a limited useful life and, therefore, the costs of the intangible asset must be allocated over its useful life. Most intangible assets are allocated on a straight-line basis over the reasonable life of the asset (not to exceed 40 years under GAAP). Instead of using the term depreciation to denote the process of allocating the cost of assets over the relevant, the term amortization is used. **Amortization** is the process of writing off the costs of intangible assets over their useful lives. Amortization expense is credited directly to the intangible asset account

Chapter 6: Long-term Assets and Depreciation

instead of a separate contra account. For example, to record $15,000 of amortization expense for patents owned, the following entry is made:

Amortization Expense	15,000	
Patent		15,000

Intangible assets less their accumulated amortization are presented in the non-current asset section of the balance sheet, normally after tangible assets. The chart below summarizes some of the most common types of intangible assets.

Intangible Asset	Definition	Amortization Period
Goodwill	Arises when one company decides to acquire another. It is the excess of the cost over the fair market value of the net assets of the acquired. (To record goodwill it must be paid for in connection with the purchase of the business.)	Amortize over the useful life, not to exceed 40 years.
Patents	A right granted by the government that permits exclusive rights to manufacture or use a particular product. Patents can only be amortized if purchased from an outside party. If the patent is developed internally the total costs of development are expensed in the period incurred. Capitalize all legal fees associated with the purchase of a patent or the defense of a patent infringement.	Amortize over the shorter of the useful life or the legal life (20 years).
Trademarks, Brand Names	A registered symbol or name that can only be used by one company to identify a particular product (e.g. Rollerblades).	Amortize over the legal life, not to exceed 40 years
Franchises	A right granted by the government that permits exclusive rights to a particular territory.	Amortize over the useful life, not to exceed 40 years.
Leaseholds	A right to use land or office space owned by another party.	Capitalize the right and amortize over the useful life, not to exceed 40 years. Expense actual rental payment.
Leaseholds Improvements	Improvements made to leased property by the party leasing the property (leasee) that will revert to owner of the property at the end of the lease.	Amortize over the remaining life of the lease.

Chapter 6: Long-term Assets and Depreciation

Key Terms

accelerated depreciation methods: depreciation methods based on the assumption that the long-term asset generates more revenues in the earlier stages of its useful life than the later stages. Examples include the double declining balance method and the sum-of-the-years digits method.

amortization: the process of writing off the costs of intangible assets over their useful lives.

capital expenditures: purchases of long-term assets that are expected to provide benefits to more than one accounting period.

depreciable basis: the acquisition cost of an asset less any estimated salvage value.

depreciation: the process of allocating the cost of the long-term tangible assets (property, buildings, and equipment) over the periods of future benefit.

improvements: expenses incurred after an asset is purchased which provide additional economic benefits that span more than one accounting period.

intangible assets: long-term assets without any physical substance that are expected to provide some future rights or advantages to a company over a period extending beyond one year.

long-term assets: assets that 1) are acquired for use in the company's operations, 2) have a useful life of more than one year, and 3) are not intended for resale to customers.

net book value: the original cost of an asset less the related accumulated depreciation.

revenue expenditures: expenditures made related to long-term assets that do not provide benefits extending beyond more than one accounting period. The most common examples are repair and maintenance expenses.

salvage value: the estimated scrap value or trade-in value of an asset at the end of its useful life. Salvage value is also referred to as residual value or disposal value.

Chapter 6: Long-term Assets and Depreciation

straight-line method: the most commonly used depreciation method for financial reporting purposes. Under this method, costs are allocated evenly over the useful life of the asset, based on the assumption that cost allocation depends only upon the passage of time.

tangible assets: long-term assets that have a physical substance and that are expected to provide future benefits to a company over a period extending beyond one year.

useful (service) life: the period (either in years or in units) over which the asset is expected to provide benefits or generate revenues.

Chapter 6: Long-term Assets and Depreciation

Thrills, Chills and Drills

True or False

1. Long-term assets are assets acquired for use in the company's operations that have a useful life of less than one year. They appear in the current section of the balance sheet.

2. In order to be classified as long-term, assets cannot be intended for resale to customers.

3. The most difficult long-term asset transactions to record require determining the acquisition costs and annual cost recovery when there is a change in an estimate.

4. Purchases of property, plants, and equipment for use in operations are considered capital expenditures.

5. Capitalizing asset costs means recording them on the balance sheet as long-term assets at historical cost.

6. The acquisition cost of property, plants, and equipment includes all expenses incurred to acquire the assets, as well as costs necessary to make them ready and available for use.

7. By recording depreciation expense, the company is allocating the cost over the periods benefited.

8. Contra assets normally maintain debit balances.

9. Depreciation is a method of valuation.

10. Salvage value is the value at the end of an asset's useful life.

11. The useful life of an asset is the period (years or units) over which the asset is expected to provide benefits or generate revenues.

12. The depreciable basis of an asset is its acquisition cost.

13. Land is never depreciated.

14. All depreciation methods except the declining balance method depreciate the asset to salvage value.

15. Under the declining balance method, a company deducts more from the value of an asset than under the straight-line method.

Chapter 6: Long-term Assets and Depreciation

16. In order to apply the MACRS percentage, the company must first reduce the acquisition cost by the depreciation taken.

17. When equipment is sold before being fully depreciated, the company recognizes a gain or loss upon disposal.

18. There is no difference between a repair and an improvement.

19. All repairs are recorded as expenses.

20. Intangible assets can be touched and felt.

Multiple Choice

1. Long-term assets are
    a) tangible
    b) intangible
    c) acquired for use in the company's operations
    d) all of the above
    e) none of the above

2. Long-term assets do not
    a) have the largest dollar value on the balance sheet
    b) have a useful life over one year
    c) appear in the non-current balance sheet section
    d) get resold to customers

3. Capital expenditures are
    a) the purchases of property, plants, and equipment
    b) used in the company's operations
    c) expected to provide benefits to more than one accounting period
    d) all of the above
    e) none of the above

Chapter 6: Long-term Assets and Depreciation

4. The acquisition cost of property, plants, and equipment include
   I. installation costs
   II. insurance
   III. transportation
   IV. the manufacturer's cost
   a) I and IV
   b) I, II and IV
   c) II, III and IV
   d) I, III and IV
   e) all four of the above
   f) none of the above

5. Capitalized costs for land include all of the following except
   a) title search fees
   b) excavation costs
   c) demolition costs
   d) landscaping costs
   e) none of the above

6. Identify the contra asset.
   a) building
   b) depreciation expense
   c) accumulated depreciation
   d) long-term asset

7. Identify the correct statement.
   a) net book value = market value
   b) net book value > market value
   c) net book value < market value
   d) none of these are true statements

Use the following information to answer questions 8-14.

Cotter Company purchased $500,000 worth of equipment in Year 5 of its operations. The salvage value is given as $50,000. The estimated useful life of the equipment is 10 years.

8. Using straight-line depreciation, what is the depreciation expense in Year 10?
   a) $45,000
   b) $40,500
   c) $36,000
   d) $31,500

Chapter 6: Long-term Assets and Depreciation

9. If the equipment produced 100,000 units a year, what would the depreciation be for 30,000 units?
    a) $120,000
    b) $150,000
    c) $135,000
    d) $100,000

10. If the equipment produced 100,000 units a year, what would the depreciation be for 50,000 units?
    a) $135,000
    b) $225,000
    c) $250,000
    d) $360,000

11. Using the sum-of-years digits method in the year of acquisition, the depreciation would be
    a) $100,000
    b) $90,000
    c) $81,818
    d) $73,636

12. Using the double-declining balance method in the year of acquisition, the depreciation would be
    a) $100,000
    b) $90,000
    c) $80,000
    d) none of the above

13. Using the double-declining balance method, the depreciation in Year 6 would be
    a) $100,000
    b) $90,000
    c) $80,000
    d) none of the above

Chapter 6: Long-term Assets and Depreciation

14. Using MACRS, what would the depreciation be in Year 5? Use the table below.

Year	5-Year	10-Year
1	20%	10%
2	32%	18%
3	19.2%	14.4%
4	11.5%	11.5%
5	11.5%	9.2%

a) $50,000
b) $46,000
c) $45,500
d) $100,000

15. What is the journal entry to record the sale of a fully depreciated machine with an acquisition cost of $20,000 for its salvage value of $4,000?

a)
Cash	$4,000	
Accumulated Depreciation	$20,000	
Machinery & Equipment		$20,000
Gain on Disposal of the Machinery		$4,000

b)
Cash	$4,000	
Accumulated Depreciation	$20,000	
Machinery & Equipment		$20,000
Gain on Sale of the Machinery		$4,000

c) either a or b is acceptable
d) neither a nor b is acceptable

16. What is the journal entry to record the disposal of equipment with an acquisition cost of $25,000, a book value of $2,000, and expenses incurred to dispose of the asset of $3,000?

a)
Loss on Disposal of Equipment	$3,000	
Accumulated Depreciation	$25,000	
Equipment		$23,000
Cash		$3,000
Gain on sale of the equipment		$2,000

b)
Loss on Disposal of Equipment	$3,000	
Accumulated Depreciation	$25,000	
Equipment		$25,000
Cash		$3,000

Chapter 6: Long-term Assets and Depreciation

c)
Loss on Disposal of Equipment	$5,000	
Accumulated Depreciation	$23,000	
Equipment		$25,000
Cash		$3,000

d) none of the above.

17. What is the journal entry to record the sale of machinery for $50,000 if the machinery has a book value of $25,000 and was acquired for $100,000 ten years ago?

a)
Cash	$50,000	
Accumulated Depreciation	$75,000	
Machinery		$100,000
Gain on Sale of the Machinery		$25,000

b)
Cash	$50,000	
Accumulated Depreciation	$25,000	
Loss on Sale of the Machinery	$25,000	
Machinery		$100,000

c)
Cash	$50,000	
Accumulated Depreciation	$75,000	
Machinery		$100,000
Gain on Disposal of the Machinery		$25,000

d) none of the above

18. Robbins Company purchased a new machine with an acquisition cost of $120,000, an expected salvage value of $20,000, and a useful life of 10 years. At the beginning of the year, the useful life of the asset was extended for an additional five years. What is the depreciation expense for the fifth year?
   a) $12,000
   b) $10,000
   c) $6,000
   d) $5,454

19. Which is not a test for capitalization as an improvement?
   a) The asset must extend the useful life.
   b) The asset must increase production.
   c) The asset must increase the quality.
   d) The asset must increase the efficiency.
   e) All of the above are tests.
   f) None of the above are tests.

Chapter 6: Long-term Assets and Depreciation

20. Which is not an intangible cost?
    a) betterment
    b) goodwill
    c) leasehold improvement
    d) brand name

Short Essays

1. Prepare the appropriate journal entries for each of the following events:

    a. Purchased a patent for $500,000 with an economic life of 10 years and a legal life of 17 years. Legal fees associated with the purchase cost $25,000.

    b. The use of the patent for the first year.

    c. The company developed a patent internally with an economic life of 10 years and a legal life of 17 years at a cost of $275,000.

    d. The use of this second patent for the first year.

2. Match the following definitions with the appropriate terms

    a. goodwill, patents, and trademarks
    b. long-term assets that have a physical substance
    c. excess of cost over fair market value
    d. exclusive right to manufacture or use
    e. long-term assets having no physical substance
    f. property, plants, and equipment
    g. right to use land owned by another

       1) tangible assets
       2) intangible assets
       3) goodwill
       4) franchise
       5) trademark
       6) patent
       7) leasehold

Chapter 6: Long-term Assets and Depreciation

3. For the following fixed assets, identify at least four capitalizable costs

   a. land

   b. building

   c. equipment

   d. self-constructed assets

4. Differentiate between the following terms and give examples (if appropriate).

   a. asset

   b. contra asset

   c. net book value

   d. market value

   e. useful life

   f. salvage value

   g. depreciable basis

   h. acquisition cost

5. Capital Company acquired machinery for $20,000 with a salvage value of $2,000. The estimated useful life of the machinery is 5 years. Figure the first and last year's depreciation with each of the following methods.

   a. straight-line

   b. sum of years digits

   c. MACRS (20%; 5.8%)

Chapter 6: Long-term Assets and Depreciation

6. For $6,000, the Waldo Corporation disposed of machinery with a salvage value of $4,000, a book value of $0, and an acquisition cost of $40,000. The accountant for the company prepared the following entry to record the sale.

Cash	$6,000	
A/D	$40,000	
Machinery		$40,000
Gain on Disposal		$6,000

Is this journal entry correct? Justify your answer.

7. Using the outline below, finish the chart.

	Example	Category	Expense or Capitalize	Account
	new roof	betterment	capitalize	Building
a.	paint a building			
b.	machine overhaul			
c.	adding a fence			
d.	resurfacing a driveway			
e.	normal maintenance			
f.	new wing			
g.	replacing a motor			

Chapter 6: Long-term Assets and Depreciation

Answers

True or False

1. **False.** Long-term assets have a useful life of more than one year and appear in the non-current section of the balance sheet.
2. **True.**
3. **True.** Determine cost recovery through depreciation/amortization.
4. **True.**
5. **True.**
6. **True.**
7. **True.**
8. **False.** Contra assets normally maintain credit balances. They offset assets to determine net book value.
9. **False.** Depreciation is a method of allocation.
10. **True.**
11. **True.**
12. **False.** It is the acquisition cost less estimated salvage value, if any.
13. **True.** Because there is no limited useful life over which to allocate the acquisiton cost.
14. **False.** MACRS depreciates the asset of zero and then records a gain for the salvage value, if any.
15. **True.** Under the declining balance method, we deduct more than straight-line in early years, then switch to straight-line when straight-line provides higher depreciation deduction.
16. **False.** Under MACRS, the percentage is applied to the acquisition cost.
17. **False.** The company recognizes a gain or loss upon sale.
18. **False.** Repairs are necessary to keep the asset in working condition. Improvements extend the useful life, the number of units produced, the quality of units produced, or the efficiency of assets.
19. **False.** Extraordinary repairs that affect the estimated useful life or salvage value are capitalized.
20. **False.** Intangible assets have no physical substance.

Multiple Choice Answers

1. **(d)** All of the above.
2. **(d)** Long-term assets are not intended for re-sale and are used in operations.
3. **(d)** All of the above.
4. **(e)** The cost includes at least these items.
5. **(e)** All of these are capitalized costs for land.

Chapter 6: Long-term Assets and Depreciation

6. **(c)** A building is an asset; Accumulated depreciation is a contra asset. It offsets an asset account and keeps track of all depreciation taken.

7. **(c)** Net book value = original cost - accumulated depreciation. However, long-term assets are not valued at market value unless they are significantly impaired.

8. **(a)** 500 - 50 = 450 / 10 = 45 (for all 10 years)

9. **(c)** 500 - 50 = 450 / 100 = $4.50 per unit x 30,000 units

10. **(b)** $4.50 x 50,000

11. **(c)** 500 - 50 = 450,000 x 10 / 55

12. **(a)** 500 x 1/10 x 2

13. **(c)** The asset is acquired in year 5 and in year 6 is in its second year as a held asset.
    500 x 1/10 x 2 = 100
    500 - 100 = 400
    400 x 0.20 = 80

14. **(a)** Year 5 is the year of acquisition. $500,000 at 10 years is 10%. $500,000 x 10% = $50,000.

15. **(a)**

Cost	$20,000	So sold for	$4,000, Salvage Value
Less A/D	$20,000	Sales Price	$4,000
Equals Book Value	0	Less Book Value	0
		Gain/Loss	$4,000

    There has been a gain on disposal at the end of the economic life of the asset.

16. **(c)** Cost less book value equals A/D. Cost less A/D equals book value. If the company paid $3,000 and did not receive salvage value of $2,000, then it must record a loss of $5,000.

17. **(a)** Cost less book value equals A/D, sales price less book value equals a gain on sale.

18. **(d)** 120-20 = 100 / 10 = 10 year for 10 years. At the beginning of year 5, the asset has 6 years left + 5 years = 11 years. Cost $120,000 less A/D ($10,000 per year for 4 years or $40,000) equals book value of $80,000. Book value less salvage value $20,000 equals $60,000/11 years equals $5,454.54

19. **(f)** All are tests.

20. **(a)** A betterment is an improvement that does not add to the physical layout of the asset.

Chapter 6: Long-term Assets and Depreciation

Short Essay Answers

1. a.
Patent	500,000	
Legal Fees	25,000	
Acquisition Cost	$525,000	
Patent	525,000	
Cash		525,000

   b.
   525000 / 10 = 52,500
   (shorter period of time)

Amortization Expense	52,500	
Accum. Amort. Patent		52,500

   c.
Patent Expense	275,000	
Cash		275,000

   d. Not applicable: patents developed internally are expensed in the period incurred.

2. a. (2)
   b. (1)
   c. (3)
   d. (6)
   e. (2)
   f. (1)
   g. (7)

3. a. Capitalizable costs for land include: the land's cost, title search, real estate commissions, brokerage/legal fees, accrued taxes paid, costs to prepare land to build on (excavation, draining, clearing, grading), costs of tearing down the old building less the old building's salvage value.

   b. Capitalizable costs for a building include: the cost of the building, title fees, legal fees, and repairs and other expenses required to put the building in usable condition.

   c. Capitalizable costs for equipment include: the cost of the equipment, transportation, installation, insurance, excise taxes, tarrifs, and equipment tests needed prior to using the equipment.

   d. Capitalizable costs for self-constructed assets include: the cost of materials used in the self-constructed assets, labor, overhead, architect fees for design, insurance paid during construction, interest paid on loans, legal fees, and building permits.

4. a. Example: property, plant, and equipment. Maintains a normal debit balance on balance sheet.

   b. Example: accumulated depreciation. Maintains a normal credit balance on balance sheet and reduces asset for depreciation taken.

   c. Equals the original acquisition cost less accumulated depreciation.

Chapter 6: Long-term Assets and Depreciation

    d. Equals the value of asset in market (experiences fluctuations).

    e. This is service life; the period it provides benefits or generate revenues.

    f. The scrap value or trade-in value. The value at end of useful life.

    g. The cost less salvage value.

    h. The costs incurred to acquire assets and make ready and available for use.

5 a. 20 - 2 = 18 / 5 = $3,600 every year

    b. 20 x 5 / 5 x (5 + 1) / 2 = $6,666.67 and 20 x 1 / 5 x (5 + 1) x 2 = $1333.33

    c. 20 x 20% = $4,000 and 20 x 5.8% = $1,160

6. Acquisition cost ($40,000) less book value ($0) equals A/D $40

   Acquisition cost ($40,000) less A/D ($40,000) equals book value $0

   Sales Price ($6,000) less book value ($0) equals gain $6,000

   However, the book value cannot be zero if the salvage value equals $4,000. So, the book value must be $4,000, the same as the salvage value. Therefore, depreciable basis is $36,000 and A/D is $36,000. If it is sold for $6,000 when book value is $4,000, gain is $2,000, and the journal entry should be:

Cash	6,000	
A/D	36,000	
Machinery		40,000
Gain on Disposal		2,000

7.

	Example	Category	Expense or Capitalize	Account
	new roof	betterment	capitalize	Building
a.	paint a building	ordinary repair	expense	maintenance expense
b.	machine overhaul	extraordinary repair	capitalize	machinery & equipment
c.	adding a fence	addition	capitalize	land improvement
d.	resurfacing a driveway	betterment	capitalize	land improvement
e.	normal maintenance	ordinary repair	expense	maintenance expense
f.	new wing	addition	capitalize	building
g.	replacing a motor	extraordinary repair	capitalize	machinery & equipment

Chapter

Liabilities and the Time Value of Money

7

Chapter 7: Liabilities and the Time Value of Money

Overview

In Chapters 4 through 6, we described how to record transactions that affect the most common current and non-current assets of a company. In particular, we focused on the proper presentation and valuation of the economic resources of a company. It is necessary to focus on presentation and valuation because of the risk that companies may overstate the value of their assets in order to present their financial positions in the best light. Companies have incentive not only to overstate their assets, but also to understate their liabilities. As a result, the accounting principles relating to asset accounts include established standards of reporting to ensure that financial statements are accurate. Accountants use two basic standards when deciding which transactions that affect non-owners' claims on a company's resources should be recorded as liabilities:

- **completeness**: ensuring that all the obligations of a company are accounted for in the accounting records and reflected in the financial statements

- **valuation**: ensuring that all debt obligations accounted for are presented at the present value of all expected future payments

In our overview of the accounting process, we recorded transactions affecting the most common current liabilities, including accounts payable, accrued expenses, and advances from customers. Other current liabilities include deferred income taxes and taxes payable. Taxes and the related liabilities will be covered in Chapter 9.

The purpose of the next two chapters is to explore the complexities of recording transactions that deal with some of the non-current liabilities that appear on a company's balance sheet. In this chapter we will focus on time value of money concepts and recording note payable transactions. By the end of the chapter you should be able to:

- understand and apply the requirements for liability recognition

- understand the concepts of interest payments and implicit interest

- perform present value calculations on future lump sum payments and payment streams

- record note payable transactions from both the borrower's and the lender's perspective

Chapter 7: Liabilities and the Time Value of Money

Concepts

Liability Recognition: The Continuum

Liabilities are the claims of creditors upon a company's economic resources, or its assets. What gives creditors the right to have a claim on these resources? Essentially, they have provided some service or good to the company under the agreement that they will be compensated for it. In other words, a **liability** is an obligation payable for past transactions or events that have already occurred. The recognition of a liability depends both on the timing of the event and the certainty of the obligation. In fact, the timing of the event often determines the certainty of the transaction. To ensure the completeness of the liabilities presented in the balance sheet, all "certain" obligations relating to "past transactions or events" must be recorded. However, the certainty of an obligation is not always easily discernible.

The following chart provides a summary of different types of liabilities based on the certainty of each transaction. Use it as a guideline for determining which obligations must be recognized as liabilities. However, the two elements of liability recognition — completeness and valuation — can also be applied to any obligation.

Most Certain ── Least Certain

Bonds payable	Accounts payable	Warranties payable	Advance from	Purchase	Pending lawsuits
Notes payable	Salaries payable	Vacation pay	customers	commitments	Off-Balance sheet items
Interest payable	Wages payable				Other contingencies
	Taxes payable				

Recognize as liabilities ──────────────────────→ Do not recognize as liabilities ──────→

As this chart shows, bonds payable, notes payable, and the related interest are the most certain, because they have a fixed payment amount and date. Accounts payable and accrued liabilities follow these obligations; although the amount is fixed in such cases, the payment date has been estimated.

On the other hand, purchase commitments, pending lawsuits and other contingencies are the least certain types of obligations. **Commitments** are agreements between at least two mutually consenting parties to execute a specific transaction in the future. The most common type of commitments are **purchase commitments**, which state that a company will make a commitment to purchase a specific number of supplies from a vendor over a specified period of time. At the time a commitment is made, however, neither party has fulfilled the terms of the agreement. While commitments are certain, and even though they have specific

Chapter 7: Liabilities and the Time Value of Money

amounts and dates, no transaction or event has actually occurred. Therefore, a liability is not recognized in the balance sheet. **Contingencies** are potential liabilities that relate to some past transaction or event but are contingent on the occurrence of some future event. A contingent liability cannot be certain, because there is no certainty about what may occur in the future. Because commitments and contingencies do not meet both requirements for recognition of a liability, these potential liabilities are often disclosed in the footnotes rather than in the main body of financial statements.

The Time Value of Money: Basic Terminology

Liabilities are valued in the balance sheet at the present value of all expected future payments, normally the amount borrowed or loaned. The amount borrowed or loaned is called the **principal** on the debt outstanding. The **present value** of an expected future payment or series of payments is the cash that someone would pay now to receive the future payments later. Using present value to record liabilities takes into consideration the time value of money. The **time value of money** is a concept meaning that cash received later has a lesser value than cash received now because of the risk associated with time and the unpredictability of the future.

For current liabilities, the present value is usually the actual amount owed, because they are normally paid within a short timeframe. However, since non-current liabilities extend beyond one year, the value of the liability must be **discounted** to its present value to take into consideration the length of time the money is owed and the risk associated with owing the money for that length of time. We can do this by discounting the expected future cash flows at an appropriate **discount rate**, or interest rate. **Interest** is the payment for the use of the cash. Therefore, the higher the risk and the longer the debt is outstanding, the higher the interest rate. For example, treasury bonds are considered by many investors to be the safest types of debt obligations for investment, because of the perceived stability (an indicator of low risk) of the government. Therefore, the interest paid on a treasury bond would be lower than the interest paid on a corporate bond of a public company that just released a new product. A corporate bond maturing tomorrow will have a lower discount rate than a corporate bond (of a similar company) maturing in 5 years.

Chapter 7: Liabilities and the Time Value of Money

The Time Value of Money: Simple v. Compound Interest

Now that we have reviewed the basic terminology surrounding present value concepts, we are ready to discuss the calculation of interest on outstanding debt obligations. Interest rates are normally stated on a per year basis (e.g. 12 percent per year). If the description does not include the unit of time, assume that the rate applies to a year.

There are two basic methods of calculating interest payments on debt outstanding:

- **simple interest method:** Interest is calculated on the outstanding principal only during the life of the loan, based on the applicable interest rate

- **compound interest method:** Interest is calculated on the outstanding principal and the prior period's interest during the life of the loan, based on the applicable interest rate

To illustrate the two methods, consider the following example:

You deposit $20,000 on January 1 into a savings account that earns 6% per year. Interest is paid on a monthly basis at the end of each month (meaning that the monthly interest rate is 6% divided by 12 months or 0.5%). You make no additional deposits and no additional withdrawals on the principal or the interest during the entire year. What is the interest paid on your account on June 30?

Simple Interest Method

Since no deposits or withdrawals were made during the year, the principal outstanding in the account on June 30 is $20,000. Applying the interest rate to the principal only, the bank will pay you $20,000 x 0.5% = $100 for the month of June. Under the simple interest method, you would earn $100 every month on the account for the entire year, so that the total interest earned as of June 30 would be $100 x 6 months = $600.

Compound Interest Method

Using the compound interest method, you would apply the interest rate on the principal and the interest earned to date on the account. Therefore, the interest paid on June 30 would be $102.53, calculated as shown in the table below.

Month	Principal & Interest (at beginning of month)		Interest Rate		Monthly Interest Payment	Principal & Interest (at end of month)
January	20,000.00	x	0.5%	=	100.00	20,100.00
February	20,100.00	x	0.5%	=	100.50	20,200.50
March	20,200.50	x	0.5%	=	101.00	20,301.50
April	20,301.50	x	0.5%	=	101.51	20,403.01
May	20,403.01	x	0.5%	=	102.02	20,505.03
June	20,505.03	x	0.5%	=	102.53	20,607.55
				Total Interest	607.55	

Chapter 7: Liabilities and the Time Value of Money

The total interest paid as of June 30 would be $607.55. Notice that this figure is $7.55 higher than the amount calculated using the simple interest method. This difference represents the total interest earned on the interest received during the previous months.

A note on compounding periods:

In the example above, the annual interest rate was 6% but was paid on a monthly basis, meaning that is was compounded monthly at a rate of .5% (6% divided by 12 months) per month. Many times you will be given an annual interest rate followed by the compounding period. Remember to re-compute the interest rate based on the compounded periods and calculate the interest for the number of periods specified. The following formulas offer some examples:

12% compounded annually	= 12% per year; calculated once per year
12% compounded semi-annually	= 6% twice a year calculated every 6 months
12% compounded quarterly	= 3% four times a year; calculated every 3 months
12% monthly	= 1% twelve times a year; calculated monthly

The Time Value of Money: Present Value Concepts

Now that you have a basic understanding of the methods of calculating interest payments on outstanding debt, we will consider the three important present value concepts applicable to recording transactions affecting non-current liabilities.

1. **present value of a lump sum payment:** The value of a lump sum payment received at some specified point in the future discounted at the appropriate discount rate.
2. **present value of an ordinary annuity:** An ordinary annuity (sometimes referred to as an annuity in arrears) is a stream of cash flows to be received or paid over a specified number of periods, with the first payment to be received or paid at the end of the first period. For example, a life insurance policy that pays $600/month at the end of each month for 10 years would be considered an ordinary annuity. The present value of an ordinary annuity is simply the total value today of the future payment streams.
3. **present value of an annuity due:** An annuity due is a stream of cash flows to be received or paid over a specified number of periods, with the first payment to be received or paid at the beginning of the first period. If the terms of the life insurance policy described above dictate that the monthly payments are to be received at the beginning of each month, then the stream of payments would be considered an annuity due.

Chapter 7: Liabilities and the Time Value of Money

The following chart lists the formulas for calculating the present value for each of these three different situations:

Type of Liability	Theoretical Formula	Accounting Formula
Present Value of a Lump Sum Payment	$\dfrac{F_n}{(1+r)^n}$	Lump Sum Payment × Present Value Factor
Present Value of an Ordinary Annuity	$\dfrac{[1-(1+r)^{-n}] \times P}{r}$	Annuity Factor × Periodic Payment
Present Value of an Annuity Due	$P_1 + \left[\dfrac{(1-(1+r)^{-(n-1)})}{r}\right] \times P$	First Payment + [Annuity Factor × Periodic Payment]

F = future value
n = number of periods (not necessarily years)
r = discount rate
P = periodic payment
P_1 = periodic payment

Recall that the value of a non-current liability must be discounted to its present value to take into consideration the length of time the money is owed and the risk associated with owing the money for that length of time. In the formulas above, "n" represents the length of time the money is owed, and "r" represents the appropriate discount rate based on the risk associated with the liability.

To calculate the present value of a lump sum payment, the future value is divided by a present value factor that will discount the payment based on the discount rate and the number of periods. The first part of the theoretical formula for calculating the present value of an ordinary annuity is the annuity factor. Multiplying the annuity factor by the periodic payment will yield the present value of the stream of payments to be received or paid. Normally, you will be provided with a present value table and an annuity table that will give you the factor, providing that you know the discount rate and the number of periods the payment is outstanding. Otherwise, using the theoretical formula and a calculator will provide the same answer.

Note that n defines the number of periods, which is not necessarily the number of years. In the life insurance example above, monthly payments for ten years gives us 120 periods.

Implicit Interest Rates (Internal Rate of Return)

The present value formulas defined above assume that the interest rates, or discount rates, are known and explicitly stated. However, sometimes a company may loan out a sum of

Chapter 7: Liabilities and the Time Value of Money

money under an agreement that some future sum of money will be paid back, without stating an interest rate. In other words, we know the present value, the future value, and the number of periods, but the discount rate is **implicit.** The implicit interest rate is known as the **internal rate of return (IRR)** and must be calculated based on the other known factors. For example, suppose that you borrow $1,000 today from a friend and agree to pay her back $1,200 in two years. To solve for the implicit interest rate, recall the formula for calculating the present value of a lump sum payment:

$$PV = \frac{F_n}{(1+r)^n}$$

where PV = present value

By inserting the known values into the equation, we get:

$$1000 = \frac{1200}{(1+r)^2}$$

This problem can be solved mathematically because n is only 2 periods. However, many calculators can calculate the IRR simply by using the known values. To solve for r without a calculator, use the **trial rate method**. The trial rate method involves selecting an interest rate and, using the appropriate factor from the table based on that rate, calculating the present value of future payment. If you come close of $1000, then you have arrived at the implicit interest rate. Solved mathematically, the implicit rate is 9.54% per period (which is, in this case, per year).

You may be asked on an exam to calculate the IRR on a series of cash flows that a company plans to earn over a specified number of years. To answer such a question, assume that the present value is zero and apply the trial rate method using the annuity table, if a mathematical approach cannot be used. In the following sections, we will combine the present value concepts and the interest calculation methods to record transactions affecting notes payable.

Notes Payable Transactions

Notes payable are obligations in the form of promissory notes that are used by companies to obtain bank loans, materials from vendors, or machinery and equipment for use in the companies operations. To illustrate the accounting for notes payable transactions, we will use an example involving a company called Decal Corp.

CHAPTER 7: LIABILITIES AND THE TIME VALUE OF MONEY

On April 1, Year 1, Decal Corp. receives cash from Society Bank in return for a $100,000 note, promising to repay the loan in four equal installments of $30,000 over the next 2 years. Interest on any unpaid principal balance will accrue at a rate of 12% per year and is to be compounded semi-annually. Decal Corp. operates on a calendar year and the first payment is due on October 1, Year 1.

Using this example, we will walk through the steps for solving problems involving note payable transactions.

1. **Document the knowns.** The first thing to do when given a noncurrent liability problem is to document what you know.

Face value of note:	$100,000
Monthly payments:	$30,000
Interest rate:	12%
Compound period:	semiannual
Discount rate:	6% (12% / 2 because the compound period is semi-annual)
Life of note:	2 years

2. **Ask yourself what you have to find out.** After you document the known, you need to determine what the question is so you can determine what information you need to answer the question. In our case, we are going to record transactions to solve for any potential questions that could be asked on a note payable problem. Some of the more common questions asked are given in the chart below.

IF THE QUESTION ASKS FOR:	YOU WILL NEED TO KNOW:
the cash received at the time the loan is made	monthly payments, discount rate, compound period, and life of note
total interest paid over the life of the note	cash received at the time the loan is made, total monthly payments
the preparation of an interest amorization schedule	cash received at the time the loan is made, discount rate compound period, monthly payments, life of note, and unpaid principal balance at the beginning of each payment period
the interest/principal portion of a given payment	unpaid principal balance at the time of the last interest payment, discount rate
total interest expense for a given time period	the interest portion of a given payment, number of months between the last interest payment date and accrual date
current/non-current portion of long term debt	unpaid principal balance at the end of the period, total principal reduction for the next current period

CHAPTER 7: LIABILITIES AND THE TIME VALUE OF MONEY

Note that some of the questions build on each other. You cannot determine the interest paid over the life of the note without knowing the cash received at the time the loan is made. Also, you cannot accrue interest between interest payments without knowing the interest portion of a given payment. Note also that the "need to know" information never mentions usage of the face value of the note. Normally, the face value of the note is not necessary to solve a note payable question. You will, however, use the face value of a bond when recorded bond payable transactions.

3. **Solve for the unknowns.** Based on the question being asked and what you know from the information given to you, solve the question by solving for all appropriate unknowns. We will solve for each of the five questions in the table on the previous page.

   a. <u>Cash received at the time the loan is made</u>. Recall that all noncurrent liabilities are presented in the balance sheet at the present value of all expected future payments, which is normally the amount borrowed or loaned. Thus, the cash received is equal to the amount borrowed, which is equal to the present value of the expected future payments. In this problem, the expected future payments are in the form of an annuity in arrears, because it is a fixed payment stream over a specified number of periods with the first payment due at the end of the first period. Recall the formula to calculate present value of an annuity:

   periodic payments x annuity factor (based on discount rate, r, and number of periods, n)

   = $30,000 x 3.46511 (taken from annuity in arrears table where r = 6% and n = 4)
   = $103,953

   Thus, the total cash received at the time the loan is made is $103,953. It is recorded as follows:

	Debit	Credit
Cash	$103,953	
Note Payable		$103,953

   Sometimes the present value of the expected future payments may be given to you. In this case you will be asked to calculate the payments. This can be done by simple manipulation of the formula above.

   Don't be intimidated by unequal loan payments $20,000 in the first year, $30,000 in the second year, etc.). Although the payment stream cannot be treated as an annuity the same method of answering the questions will apply. Instead of treating the

Chapter 7: Liabilities and the Time Value of Money

payment stream as an annuity, pn you must calculate the present value of each individual payment separately using the present value table (instead of the annuity table) and add them together to arrive at the total present value of the expected future payments.

b. <u>Total interest paid over the life of the note</u>. Calculating the present value of a payment stream discounts the payment to determine the value of those payments today. Thus, any payment made in excess of the value today must be the interest on the note. Therefore, the total interest paid over the life of a note is:

total expected payments - the present value of the expected future payments
- = ($30,000 x 4) - $103,953 (as calculated above)
- = $120,000 - $103,953
- = $16,047

c. <u>Prepare an interest amortization schedule</u>. In our problem, the interest on the note is not paid separately but is included in the four equal semiannual installments. The total interest paid must be amortized over the life of the loan and recognized as interest expense. To amortize the total interest on the loan, each period interest expense is calculated on the unpaid principal balance. This amount is subtracted from the cash payment, with the remainder of the payment being applied to the outstanding principal on the loan. Although the interest on the note is included in the cash payments, the interest rate is explicit, not implicit, because it was used to calculate the present value. An interest amortization schedule summarizes the payment activity of a note over its life and is similar to the depreciation schedules used in Chapter 6. As listed in the table, to prepare an amortization schedule you will need to know the cash received at the time the loan is made, the interest rate, the compound period, the monthly payments, the life of note, and the unpaid principal balance at the beginning of each payment period. The following is an amortization schedule for Decal Corp. This table format is common and can be applied to any note payable/bond payable problem.

Period	Date	Balance beg of period	Loan Payment	=	Interest Expense	+	Principal Reduction	Balance end of period
0	4/2/Year 1							103,953
1	10/1/Year 1	103,953	30,000		6,237		23,763	80,190
2	4/1/Year 2	80,190	30,000		4,811		25,189	55,001
3	10/1/Year 2	55,001	30,000		3,300		26,700	28,301
4	4/1/Year 3	28,301	30,000		1,698		28,301	0
			120,000		16,047		103,952	

CHAPTER 7: LIABILITIES AND THE TIME VALUE OF MONEY

Always start with period zero, making this period the day the cash is received. Input the amount of cash as the balance at the end of the period. Note that the portion of the payment allocable to interest expense decreases over the life of the note. This is due to the corresponding decrease in the unpaid principal balance over the life of the note. Preparing an amortization schedule is can sometimes be very time consuming, especially when the life of the note covers several time periods. However, as you will see, this amortization schdedule will be helpful in answering the last three questions from our table.

d. The interest/principal portion of a given payment. Once you have prepared an amortization schedule, these numbers will come directly from the "interest expense" and "prinicipal reduction" column. Thus, the total interest portion of the 10/1/Year 1 payment is $6,237 and the total principal reduction on the 4/1/Year 3 payment is $28,301 (in this case, also the remaining balance). These numbers can be calculated without preparing an amortization table as long as you know the unpaid principal balance at the time of the last interest payment and the discount rate. For example, based only on the information originally given, to calculate the principal reduction on the 4/1/Year 2 loan payment of $25,189, you would do the following:

Unpaid principal 10/1/Year 1 (first payment)	$103,953	
x discount rate	6%	
Interest portion of 10/1/Year 1 payment	6,237	= (103,953 x 6%)
Total payment	30,000	
Interest Portion of 10/1/Year 1 payment	- 6,237	
Principal portion of 10/1/Year 1 payment	23,763	= (30,000 - 6,237)
Unpaid principal 4/1/Year 2	$80,190	= (103,953 - 23,763)
x discount rate	6%	
Interest portion of 4/1/Year 2 payment	4,811	= (80,190 x 6%)
Total payment	30,000	
Principal portion of 4/1/Year 2 payment	**25,189**	=(30,000 - 4,811)

e. Total interest expense for a given time period. Suppose you were asked to calculate the total interest expense for Year 1. The $6,237 interest portion of the 10/1/Year 1 payment covers the period from the time the cash is received to the first payment (4/1/Year 1 through 10/1/Year 1) and is allocable evenly over that period. Likewise, the $4,811 interest portion of the 4/1/Year 2 payment covers the period beginning from the last payment date (10/1/Year 1 through 4/1/Year 2) and is allocable evenly over that

Chapter 7: Liabilities and the Time Value of Money

period. Recall from our original example that Decal Corp. operates on a calendar year basis, meaning that financial statements for the year are prepared as of December 31. Therefore, total interest expense for Year 1 cannot be $6,237 + $ 4,811 ($11,048) because part of the $4,811 interest expense from the 4/1/Year 2 payment is allocable to the first three months of Year 2. To calculate the total interest expense for year one, we must **accrue** the portion of the 4/1/Year 2 interest payment at the end of the year as follows:

Total interest expense 10/1/Year 1 through 4/1/Year 2	(6 months)	$4,811
Total portion allocable to Year 1 (3 months / 6 months)		50%
Total interest expense allocable to Year 1		$2,405
Total interest expense 4/1/Year 1 through 10/1/Year 1		+ $6,237
(all of which is allocable to Year 1)		
Total Year 1 interest expense		**$8,642**

Using our amortization schedule, on 10/1/Year 1 the following entry would be made to record the loan payment and the related interest expense and principal reduction:

Interest Expense	6,237	
Note Payable	23,763	
Cash		30,000

(Note: A similar entry with different amounts would be made for the 10/1/Year 2 loan payment.)

On 12/31/Year 1 the following entry would be recorded to accrue for the additional interest expense:

Interest Expense	2,405	
Interest Payable		2,405

(Note: A similar entry with different amounts would be made at the end of the year on 12/31/Year 2.)

At the end of the year after these two entries are recorded, the total interest expense on the books is $8,642 (6,237 + 2,405). On 4/1/Year 2, when the entry for the second payment is made, the interest accrued at the end of the year is paid out and the payable is removed from the books as follows:

Chapter 7: Liabilities and the Time Value of Money

Interest Expense	2,406	($4,811 - $2,405 recognized in Year 1)
Interest Payable	2,405	
Notes Payable	25,189	
Cash		30,000

(Note: A similar entry with different amounts would be made for the 4/1/Year 3 loan payment.)

f. <u>The current/noncurrent portion of long term debt</u>. Recall that non-current liabilities are obligations not payable within one year (or operating cycle, whichever is shorter). However, some portions of a non-current liability will be due within a year if payments are being made throughout the life of the note. The current portion of any long term debt is presented in the current liability section of the balance sheet and the remainder is presented in the non-current liability section of balance sheet. In our example, the current portion of the note is the total principal reduction for Year 2. Using our amortization schedule, at the end of Year 1 the unpaid principal on the note of $80,190 ($51,889 current; $28,301 non-current) would be reflected in the balance sheet as shown below.

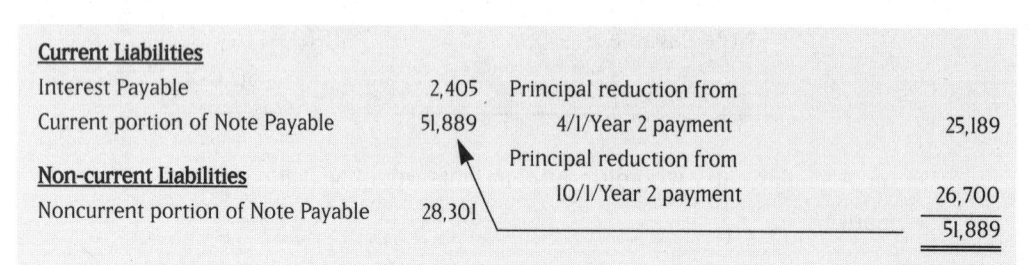

<u>**Current Liabilities**</u>
Interest Payable	2,405	Principal reduction from		
Current portion of Note Payable	51,889	4/1/Year 2 payment		25,189
<u>**Non-current Liabilities**</u>		Principal reduction from		
Noncurrent portion of Note Payable	28,301	10/1/Year 2 payment		26,700
				51,889

Note that the interest accrued at the end of Year 1 is also presented in the current liabilities section of the balance sheet because it will be paid out in the following year when the 4/1/Year 2 loan payment is made.

Chapter 7: Liabilities and the Time Value of Money

Key Terms

annuity due: a stream of cash flows to be received or paid over a specified number of periods with the first payment to be received or paid at the beginning of the first period.

commitments: agreements between at least two mutually consenting parties to execute a specific transaction in the future.

compound interest method: interest computation method where interest is calculated on the outstanding principal and the prior periods interest during the life of the loan based on the applicable interest rate.

contingencies: potential liabilities that relate to some past transaction or event but are contingent on the occurrence of some future event.

internal rate of return (IRR): the implicit interest rate on future cash flows.

liability: an obligation payable for past transactions or events that have already occurred. To ensure the completeness of the liabilities presented in the balance sheet, all "certain" obligations relating to "past transactions or events" must be recorded.

notes payable: obligations in the form of promissory notes often used by companies to obtain bank loans, materials from vendors, or machinery and equipment for use in the companies operations.

ordinary annuity: a stream of cash flows to be received or paid over a specified number of periods with the first payment to be received or paid at the end of the first period.

present value: the discounted value of expected future cash flows.

principal: the amount of debt borrowed or loaned.

simple interest method: interest computation method where interest is calculated on the outstanding principal only during the life of the loan based on the applicable interest rate.

Chapter 7: Liabilities and the Time Value of Money

Thrills, Chills and Drills

True or False

1. To ensure proper valuation of liabilities, both the interest charged and the time value of money must be accounted for and reflected in the financial statements.

2. Liabilities are creditors' claims on a company's economic resources.

3. The recognition of a liability depends on either the timing of the event or the certainty of the obligation.

4. To ensure the completeness of the liabilities presented in the balance sheet, all "certain" obligations relating to "past transactions or events" must be recorded.

5. Recognition of liabilities is determined by the certainty of payment amount and date.

6. Commitments are potential liabilities that relate to some past transaction or event contingent on the occurrence of some future event.

7. Neither commitments nor contingencies meet both requirements for recognition of a liability.

8. Liabilities are valued at the future value of all expected payments.

9. The present value of an expected future payment or series of payments is the cash that someone would pay now to receive payments in the future.

10. Due to the time value of money principle, cash received today is worth more than cash received in the future.

11. The present value of current liabilities is the amount actually owed.

12. Non-current liabilities are discounted to their present value.

13. The simple interest rate is calculated on the outstanding principal and the prior period's interest.

14. If interest is calculated at 10% compounded semi-annually, then the interest is calculated at 5% twice a year.

Chapter 7: Liabilities and the Time Value of Money

15. The present value of an annuity due is a stream of cash flows to be received or paid over a specified number of periods with the first payment to be received or paid at the end of the first period.

16. The present value and future value formulas are the inverse of each other.

17. In order to calculate the amount of cash received upon the issuance of a note, multiply the periodic payment by the annuity factor according to the discount rate and number of periods.

18. Interest rates are considered explicit when used to calculate present value.

19. When interest owed is accrued, the journal entry is:

Interest Expense	XXXXXX	
Cash		XXXXXX

20. The current portion of a long-term debt remains classified as a non-current liability.

Multiple Choice

1. Current liabilities include
    a) accounts payable
    b) accrued expenses
    c) advance from customers
    d) deferred income taxes
    e) all of the above
    f) a, b, and c

2. Which of the following liabilities is least likely to be recognized?
    a) vacation payable
    b) salaries payable
    c) bonds payable
    d) pending lawsuits

3. Which of the following liabilities is most likely to be recognized?
    a) off-balance sheet items
    b) purchase commitments
    c) pending law suits
    d) advances from customers

Chapter 7: Liabilities and the Time Value of Money

4. Identify the false statement.
    a) Commitments are agreements between at least two mutually consenting parties to execute a specific transaction in the future.
    b) Commitments are certain because they have specific amounts and dates.
    c) Contingencies are potential liabilities.
    d) Commitments and contingencies both meet the requirements for recognition of a liability.

5. Contingencies are
    a) liabilities that relate to transactions or events in the past
    b) able to meet the certainty test
    c) recorded in the financial statements
    d) potential liabilities that relate to some past transaction or event but depend on the occurrence of some future event

6. According to purchase commitments,
    a) companies make commitments to purchase a specific number of supplies from a vendor
    b) neither party has exchanged performance of the agreement at the time the commitment is made
    c) a liability is not recognized in the balance sheet
    d) All of the above are true.
    e) None of the above is true

7. Which of the following statements is incorrect?
    a) The higher the risk and the longer the period of time the debt is outstanding, the higher the interest rate.
    b) The shorter the period of time the debt is outstanding, the lower the interest rate.
    c) The lower the risk and the shorter the period of time the debt is outstanding, the lower the interest rate.
    d) None of the above.

8. You deposit $2,000 into a savings account that earns 3% per year on January 1. The account pays the interest semi-annually. Using the simple interest method, what is the interest for the first six months?
    a) $30
    b) $60
    c) $90
    d) $15

Chapter 7: Liabilities and the Time Value of Money

9. Using the same information from Question #8, compute the annual interest using the compound interest method.
    a) $30
    b) $60
    c) $60.45
    d) none of the above

10. If you invest $100,000 for two years at 12% compounded quarterly, what is the amount of interest that you would receive at the end of two years?
    a) $25,440
    b) $26,247.69
    c) $26,677.01
    d) can't determine with the given information

11. The formula for present value of an annuity due is:
    a) future value / present value annuity
    b) first payment x (annuity factor x periodic payment)
    c) annuity factor x periodic payment
    d) none of the above

12. Which statement is not true regarding an ordinary annuity?
    a) It is a stream of cash flows to be received or paid over a specified number of periods.
    b) The first payment to be received or paid is at the end of the first period.
    c) It is sometimes referred to as an annuity in arrears.
    d) None of the above.

13. When an interest rate is known and stated on the face of the instrument, it is called
    a) implicit
    b) an internal rate of return
    c) explicit
    d) none of the above

14. Notes payable are
    a) obligations in the form of promissory notes
    b) used to obtain bank loans
    c) used to obtain materials from vendors
    d) none of the above
    e) all of the above

Chapter 7: Liabilities and the Time Value of Money

15. If period payments are $50,000, the discount rate is 6%, and the number of periods is 4, how much total cash was received at the time the loan was made? (Annuity factor for r = 6, n = 4 is 3.46511.)
    a) $14,429.56
    b) $173,255.50
    c) cannot be determined
    d) none of the above

16. Given the facts in Question #15, the total interest paid over the life of the loan is
    a) $14,429.56
    b) $185,570.74
    c) $26,744.50
    d) $126,744.50

17. In order to prepare an amortization schedule, you need to know
    I. the cash received at the time the loan is made
    II. the interest rate
    III. the compound period
    IV. the monthly payments
    V. the life of the note
    VI. the unpaid balance at the beginning of each payment period

    a) I through V
    b) II through VI
    c) I, III, IV, V, VI
    d) I through VI

18. In order to calculate the unpaid principal on a loan, in which sequence should you make the following calculations?

    I. Multiply the unpaid principal by the discount rate.
    II. Subtract the principal portion from the unpaid principal.
    III. Subtract the interest portion from the total payment.

    a) I, II then III
    b) I, III, then II
    c) II, I, then III
    d) none of the above

Chapter 7: Liabilities and the Time Value of Money

19. If the interest for October 1 through April 1 is $4,900, what is the amount of interest that must be accrued at the end of the year, December 31?

    a) $4,900
    b) 0
    c) $2,450
    d) cannot be determined

20. When a company has accumulated interest of $2,500 over three months, and makes a semi-annual payment of $40,000 on the note payable, what is the correct journal entry?

    a)
Interest Expense	$2,500	
Interest Payable	$2,500	
Notes Payable	$35,000	
Cash		$40,000

    b)
Interest Expense	$2,500	
Notes Payable	$37,500	
Cash		$40,000

    c)
Interest Expense	$2,500	
Interest Payable	$2,500	
Notes payable	$40,000	
Cash		$45,000

    d) none of the above

Short Essays

1. Place each of the following items along this continuum for liability recognition:

    Most Certain   1   2   3   4   5   6   Least Certain
    Recognize as Liability   Do Not Recognize

    a. pending lawsuits

    b. advances from customers

    c. accounts payable

    d. purchase commitments

    e. notes payable

    f. warranties payable

CHAPTER 7: LIABILITIES AND THE TIME VALUE OF MONEY

2. The unpaid balance on a note is $90,500, as of December 31, 1998. According to the amortization schedule, the principal reduction from the January 1, 1999 payment is $24,200 and the principal reduction from the July 1, 1999 payment is $26,400. Prepare the balance sheet portion affected by the above information.

3. Themy Company issued ten $100,000 bonds with 6% interest paid quarterly on October 1. What would the journal entry be on December 31, the company's year-end? Would your answer change if the bonds paid interest semi-annually?

4. Prepare an amortization schedule given the following information:

Face of note	$100,000
Periodic payment	$40,000
Interest rate	12%
Compound period	semi-annual
Life of note	2 years

5. Explain the difference between an ordinary annuity and an annuity due. Does the same present value formula apply to both types of annuity? Explain.

6. Explain why a dollar today is worth more than a dollar in the future.

7. Why does the compounding interest method yield more interest than the simple interest method?

Chapter 7: Liabilities and the Time Value of Money

Answers

True or False

1. True.
2. True.
3. False. Recognition depends on both.
4. True.
5. False. Recognition is determined by the timing of the event, the certainty of the obligation, and the performance of the agreement.
6. False. Contingencies are potential liabilities.
7. True.
8. False. They are valued at the present value of all expected future payments.
9. True.
10. True.
11. True.
12. True.
13. False. The compound interest method is calculated this way.
14. True.
15. False. This is the definition of an ordinary annuity.
16. True.
17. True.
18. True.
19. False. This is the entry for interest paid. For interest accrued, credit interest payable.
20. False. The current portion of long-term debt is classified as a current liability.

Multiple Choice Answers

1. (e) All of these are current liabilities.
2. (d) Pending lawsuits are so uncertain that they are not recognized.
3. (d) All of the others are not recognized, but usually disclosed in footnotes.
4. (d) Neither meet the requirements.
5. (d) This is the definition of a contingency.
6. (d) All of the above.
7. (b) The time could be short, but the risk could be extremely high, which would raise the interest rate.
8. (a) 3% / 2 = 1.5% every six months, so $2,000 x 1.5% = $30.

Chapter 7: Liabilities and the Time Value of Money

9. (c) 3% / 2 = 1.5%
   2000 x 1.5% = 30
   2030 x 1.5% = 30.45
   30.45 + 30.00 = $60.45

10. (c)

	Year 1	Year 2
($100,000 + prior interest) x (12% / 4) =	3000	3376.53
	3090	3477.82
	3182.7	3582.16
	3278.18	3689.62
	12550.88 +	14126.13 = 26677.01

11. (b) This is the correct formula.

12. (d) All of the statements about an ordinary annuity are true.

13. (c) An implicit or internal rate of return is not given, and must be calculated from other known factors.

14. (e) All of the statements about notes payable are true.

15. (b) 50,000 x 3.46511

16. (c) 50,000 x 4 minus 173255.5 = $26,744.50

17. (d) All of this information is necessary.

18. (b) I, III, II

19. (c) 4900 x 50% or $2,450 for three months

20. (a) We must record interest expense, so b cannot be correct. The company only paid 40,000, so c is not correct. If three months interest equals $2,500, then six months' interest equals $5,000. If, the company paid $40,000, note payable is reduced by ($40,000 - $5,000 = $35,000).

Short Essay Answers

1.
   a. pending lawsuit   6
   b. advances from customers 4
   c. accounts payable   2
   d. purchase commitments   5
   e. notes payable   1
   f. warranties payable   3

2.

XYZ Company
Balance Sheet
As of December 31, 1998

Current Liability
Current portion of Note Payable $50,600
($24,200 + 26,400)

Non-current Liability
Noncurrent portion of Note Payable $39,900
($90,500 - (24,200 + 26,400))

Chapter 7: Liabilities and the Time Value of Money

3.
```
When Issued:
    1-Oct.   Cash                    $1,000,000
                 Bonds Payable              $1,000,000
    31-Dec.  Interest Expense        $15,000
                 Cash                       $15,000
             (10 x 100,000 x (6% / 4))

If the bonds paid interest semi-annually, then interest
would be paid in April and October, and the journal entry
would be as follows:

    31-Dec.  Interest Expense        $15,000
                 Interest Payable           $15,000
             (10 x 100,000 x (6% / 2))
```

4.

Period	Begin Balance	Lease Payment	Interest Expense	Principle Reduction	End Balance
1	138604	40000	8316	31684	106920
2	106920	40000	6415	33585	73335
3	73335	40000	4400	35600	37735
4	37735	40000	2265	37735	0
		160000	21396	138604	

* 2 years with semi-annual compound interest equals four periods.
12% / 2 = 6% every six months.
The present value of an annuity = 40,000 x 3.46511 = $138,604.
Total interest paid over the life of the note = (40,000 x 4) - 138,604 = 21,396

* Due to rounding, you may have to adjust these numbers

5. An ordinary annuity (a.k.a. annuity in arrears) is a stream of cash flows to be received or paid over a specified number of periods, with the first payment to be received or paid at the end of the first period.

   An annuity due is a stream of cash flows to be received or paid over a specified number of periods, with the first payment to be received or paid at the beginning of the first period. The present value formulas for each type of annuity are different:

   Present Value of an Annuity = annuity factor x periodic payment

   Present Value of an Annuity Due = first payment x (annuity factor x periodic payment)

6. A dollar today is worth more because of the risk associated with time and the unpredictability of the future - i.e., the time value of money concept.

7. Under the simple interest method, interest is calculated on the outstanding principal only during the life of the loan, based on the applicable interest rate. Under the compound interest method, interest is calculated on the outstanding principal plus the prior periods interest during the life of the loan, based on the applicable interest rate.

Chapter

Bonds Payable and Leases

8

Chapter 8: Bonds Payable and Leases

Overview

Chapter 7 introduced you to transactions affecting non-current liabilities, including note payable accounts. This chapter uses the present value concepts that you have now learned to teach you how to record transactions affecting bonds payable and leases. By the end of this chapter, you should be able to:

- calculate the present value of a bond
- understand bond discounts and premiums
- record debt issuance transactions from the borrower's perspective
- understand the accounting for early retirement of bonds
- distinguish between operating and capital leases
- record lease transactions from both the lessee's and the lessor's perspective

The two non-current liabilities covered in this chapter — bonds payable and leases — are frequently tested subjects. By mastering a few crucial concepts, you can take a major step toward preparing yourself for examinations that cover the liability side of the balance sheet.

Chapter 8: Bonds Payable and Leases

Concepts

Bonds Payable: Application of Present Value Concepts

A **bond** is a debt security representing the evidence of a loan. When a company borrows funds from one lender, the funds change hands in the form of notes. However, sometimes a company needs such a large amount of cash, often millions of dollars, that one lender is not willing to risk the loan. In such situations, a company has to borrow from investors by issuing debt securities (bonds) and making a promise to repay them. There are two key differences between calculating the present value of a bond and calculating the present value of a note.

1. **Bonds are normally paid off in two payment streams.** First, there is the principal on the bond, commonly called the face value or par value, that is paid off at the end of the life of the bond. Second, there is the interest paid on the principal, which is normally paid out over the life of the note. In the last chapter, we calculated the present value of a note based on one payment stream, which included both the interest and the principal. Because there are two different payment streams for repayment of a bond, there are two components to calculating its present value, as shown in the formula below.

$$\text{PV of a bond} = \text{PV of the principal} + \text{PV of the interest}$$

The repayment of the principal is made in one lump sum payment at the end of the life of the bond. Therefore, to calculate the present value of the principal, we use the formula below. Recall from Chapter 7 that the present value of a bond is based on a given number of periods and interest rate. The factor obtained from the table is then applied to the lump sum payment to be received.

$$PV = \frac{F_n}{(1+r)^n}$$

Similar to an annuity, the payment of the interest is made in fixed installments over the life of the bond. Therefore, to calculate the present value of the interest, we use the annuity table, or the following formula:

$$\frac{P \times [1 - (1+r)^n]}{r}$$

2. **The interest rate used to calculate the present value of the bond is not always the interest rate used to calculate the interest payments.** The interest rate used to calculate the

Chapter 8: Bonds Payable and Leases

periodic interest payment on a bond is called the **coupon rate.** The coupon rate is also referred to as the nominal or stated rate of interest. The interest rate used to calculate the present value of the bond is called the market rate of interest.

We can use this information to distinguish between three types of bonds:

- If the total proceeds from a bond equals its face value, then the bond is **issued at par,** and the coupon rate equals the market rate of interest.

- If the total proceeds from a bond is greater than its face value, then the bond is **issued above par** at a premium, and the coupon rate is greater than the market rate of interest. When a bond is issued at a premium, the company receives proceeds in some amount greater than the face value of the bond and agrees to repay the face value when the bond matures. The **premium** on a bond is the excess cash that an investor is willing to pay over and above the face value of the bond.

- If the total proceeds from a bond is less than its face value, then the bond is **issued below par** at a discount, and the coupon rate is less than the market rate of interest. When a bond is issued at a discount, the company receives proceeds at some amount less than the face value of the bond and agrees to repay the face value when the bond matures. The **discount** on a bond is the excess debt that a company is willing to assume at the time the bond is issued.

Premiums and discounts on bonds payable are recorded in the liabilities section of the balance sheet as either an adjuct or contra liability and amortized over the life of the bond. An **adjunct liability** is a liability that increases a specific liability account (in this case, bond payable). As discussed in Chapter 3, a **contra liability** decreases a specific liability account. The chart below describes the three types of bonds:

For a Bond Issued	Relationship of Interest Rates	Discount or Premium	Treatment of discount or premium
At Par	Coupon rate = Market rate	No discount or premium	No amortization necessary
Above Par	Coupon rate > Market rate	Issued at a premium	Record as an adjunct liability at the time of issuance and amortize over the life of the bond
Below Par	Coupon rate < Market rate	Issued at a discount	Record as a contra liability at the time of issuance and amortize over the life of the bond

Remember, debt issuances are not to be confused with equity issuances. By buying bonds, investors purchase a debt security from a company and are still considered creditors, because there is a fixed agreement to repay those investors back at a specified period of

Chapter 8: Bonds Payable and Leases

time. For equity holders, there is no specific repayment period. Equity holders (shareholders) are entitled only to a return on their capital, either through dividends or an increase in the value of the company.

Bonds Payable: Recording Transactions for Bonds Issued at Par

Let's use these concepts to work through an example of how to record transactions affecting bonds payable.

To raise money for expansion into global markets, Monarch, Inc. issues $100,000 face value, 5-year, 10% semi-annual coupon bonds on January 2, Year 1. Under the terms of the bonds, periodic interest payments are due on January 1 and July 1 of each year for the next 5 years. Assume that the market rate of interest is 10%.

The coupon rate on the bonds is 10% per year, or 5% every six months (10% / 2). Since the interest payments occur semi-annually, we will calculate the interest payments based on a coupon rate of 5% as follows:

Semiannual interest payment	=	Face Value of Bond	x	Coupon Rate
	=	$100,000	x	10%/2
	=	$100,000	x	5%
	=	$5,000		

Note: If the interest payments were quarterly, the coupon rate would be 2.5% (10% / 4). In addition, remember that the coupon rate is necessary only to calculate the periodic interest payment.

STEP 1: RECORD THE PROCEEDS FROM THE DEBT ISSUANCE.

To record the proceeds from the debt issuance, we must calculate the present value of the bond, because liabilities are always recorded at the present value of expected future payments. In our problem, n (number of periods) is 10 (5 years x 2 payments per year). The market rate of interest, r, is 5% (10% / 2). Since the market rate equals the coupon rate, then the present value of the bond equals its face value. To show this is true, let's calculate the present value of the bond issuance using the present value tables on the next page.

CHAPTER 8: BONDS PAYABLE AND LEASES

$$\begin{aligned}
\text{PV of a bond } (r = 5\%, n = 10) &= \text{PV of the principal} + \text{PV of the interest} \\
&= \left(\begin{array}{c}\text{Lump Sum} \times \text{Present Value} \\ \text{Payment} \quad \text{Factor}\end{array}\right) + \left(\begin{array}{c}\text{Periodic} \times \text{Annuity} \\ \text{Payment} \quad \text{Factor}\end{array}\right) \\
&= \$100{,}000 \times .61391 + \$5{,}000 \times 7.72173 \\
&= \$61{,}391 + \$38{,}609 \\
&= \$100{,}000
\end{aligned}$$

The entry made by Monarch, Inc. to record the proceeds received is:

Cash	100,000	
Bond Payable		100,000

STEP 2: RECORD THE PERIODIC INTEREST PAYMENTS.

KEY CONCEPT

The periodic interest payment on the bond as calculated above is equal to the coupon rate times the face value of the bond. However, the interest expense recognized is equal to *the market rate of interest times the book value of the bond at the beginning of each interest period.* Since the bond was issued at par, the market rate equals the coupon rate, and the present value equals the face value of the bond. Therefore, the interest expense recognized is equal to the actual interest payment. We record the interest expense as:

Interest Expense	5,000	
Cash		5,000

If Monarch operated on a calendar year (meaning that its year-end is December 31), the total accrued interest at the end of Year 1 would be $5,000, and we would record it as follows:

Interest Expense	5,000	
Interest Payable		5,000

Note: This entry will be the same at the end of each year for the January 1 interest payment.

On January 1, Year 2, when the semi-annual interest payment is made, the following entry will be recorded:

Interest Expense	5,000	
Cash		5,000

Chapter 8: Bonds Payable and Leases

DIFFICULT TERRAIN

In our example, the actual issuance date of the bonds coincides with one of the interest payment dates. However, this alignment seldom actually occurs. Nevertheless, when the interest payments are due, investors expect a payment equal to six months of interest. As a result, the investor pays the borrower for the accrued interest up to the date of issuance, and the full amount is repaid to the investor on the first interest payment date. Suppose that Monarch issues the bonds on April 1 instead of January 2. In this case, the investor would pay Monarch $2,500 for the interest for the three-month period January 2 through March 31. The following entry would be recorded at the time of issuance by Monarch:

Cash	102,500	
Bond Payable		100,000
Interest Payable		2,500

On July 1, when the first interest payment is made, the following entry would be made to reverse the interest payable:

Interest Payable	2,500	
Interest Expense	2,500	
Cash		5,000

By recording interest payable at the time of issuance, Monarch only recognizes an interest expense of $2,500 for the three months that the debt is owed, instead of the full six-month payment period.

STEP 3: RECORD THE REPAYMENT OF THE PRINCIPAL.

In addition to the last $5,000 interest payment, the following entry is recorded on January 1, Year 5, when Monarch repays the principal on the bond:

Bond Payable	100,000	
Cash		100,000

Bonds Payable: Recording Transactions for Bonds Issued Above Par

Now we will work through the same example; this time, however, we will assume that the market rate of interest is 8%.

Chapter 8: Bonds Payable and Leases

STEP 1: RECORD THE PROCEEDS FROM THE DEBT ISSUANCE.

Since the coupon rate of 5% is greater than the market rate of 4% (8% / 2), the present value of the bond is greater than the face value. We calculate it using the following equation:

$$
\begin{aligned}
\text{PV of a bond } (r = 4\%, n = 10) &= \text{PV of the principal} + \text{PV of the interest} \\
&= \left(\begin{array}{c} \text{Lump Sum} \\ \text{Payment} \end{array} \times \begin{array}{c} \text{Present Value} \\ \text{Factor} \end{array} \right) + \left(\begin{array}{c} \text{Periodic} \\ \text{Payment} \end{array} \times \begin{array}{c} \text{Annuity} \\ \text{Factor} \end{array} \right) \\
&= \$100{,}000 \times 0.67556 + \$5{,}000 \times 8.1109 \\
&= \$67{,}556 + \$40{,}555 \\
&= \$108{,}111
\end{aligned}
$$

KEY CONCEPT

The total premium on the bond issuance is $8,111 ($108,111 - $100,000). When the proceeds are recorded, we record the premium as an adjunct liability:

Cash	108,111	
Bonds Payable		100,000
Premium on Bond Payable		8,111

After this entry is made, the total liability related to the bond (the book value) is $108,111 (principal + premium). However, Monarch is obligated to pay back only $100,000 when the bond matures in 5 years. As we will see in the next step, the book value of the bond is therefore amortized to its face value of $100,000, while the premium is simultaneously amortized to zero over the life of the bond.

STEP 2: RECORD THE PERIODIC INTEREST PAYMENTS.

Although the bond is issued above par, the periodic interest payment of $5,000 remains the same because the coupon rate and the face value of the bond are unchanged. However, the interest expense recognized at the time of the first interest payment on July 1, Year 1 — based on the market rate and the book value of the bond — is $4,324 (4% x $108,111). Based on these calculations, we make the following entry to record the July 1, Year 1, interest payment:

Interest Expense	4,324	
Premium on Bond Payable	676	
Cash		5,000

The difference between the interest expense recognized and the cash payment made is equal to the amortization of the premium. After this entry is made, the premium on the bond is reduced to $7,435, making the book value of the bond $107,345. The interest expense

Chapter 8: Bonds Payable and Leases

recognized at the time of the January 1, Year 2, interest payment will be calculated based on this new book value. The following amortization table shows the total interest expense and related premium reduction that will be recognized at the time of each interest payment.

Amortization Table 1

Period	Date	Book Value beg of period	Interest Payment	=	Interest Expense	+	Premium Amortization	Book Value end of period
0	1/2/Year 1							108,111
1	7/1/Year 1	108,111	5,000		4,324		676	107,435
2	1/1/Year 2	107,435	5,000		4,297		703	106,733
3	7/1/Year 2	106,733	5,000		4,269		731	106,002
4	1/1/Year 3	106,002	5,000		4,240		760	105,242
5	7/1/Year 3	105,242	5,000		4,210		790	104,452
6	1/1/Year 4	104,452	5,000		4,178		822	103,630
7	7/1/Year 4	103,630	5,000		4,145		855	102,775
8	1/1/Year 5	102,775	5,000		4,111		889	101,886
9	7/1/Year 5	101,886	5,000		4,075		925	100,962
10	1/1/Year 6	100,962	5,000		4,038		962	**100,000**
			50,000		41,889		8,111	

KEY CONCEPT: Note that the premium amortization increases over the life of the bond. This is because the interest expense decreases as the book value decreases down to $100,000 over the life of the bond.

Step 3: Record the repayment of the principal.

At maturity, the book value of the bond has been amortized to its principal amount. The entry to record the repayment of principal will be the same as that of a bond issued at par. The following entries will be made on January 1, Year 6, to record the last interest payment and the repayment of the principal:

Interest Payment		
Interest Expense	4,038	
Premium on Bond Payable	962	
Cash		5,000
Principal Payment		
Bond Payable	100,000	
Cash		100,000

Chapter 8: Bonds Payable and Leases

Bonds Payable: Recording Transactions for Bonds Issued Below Par

Finally, we will work through our example assuming that the market rate of interest is 12%.

Step 1: Record the proceeds from the debt issuance.

Now the coupon rate of 5% is less than the market rate of 6% (12% / 2). Therefore, the present value of the bond is less than the face value. We calculate the present value using the equation:

$$\text{PV of a bond } (r = 5\%, n = 10) = \text{PV of the principal} + \text{PV of the interest (annuity)}$$

$$= \left(\begin{array}{c} \text{Lump Sum} \\ \text{Payment} \end{array} \times \begin{array}{c} \text{Present Value} \\ \text{Factor} \end{array} \right) + \left(\begin{array}{c} \text{Periodic} \\ \text{Payment} \end{array} \times \begin{array}{c} \text{Annuity} \\ \text{Factor} \end{array} \right)$$

$$= \$100{,}000 \times 0.55840 + \$5{,}000 \times 7.36009$$

$$= \$55{,}840 + \$36{,}800$$

$$= \$92{,}640$$

The total discount on the bond issuance is $7,360 ($100,000 - $92,640). When the proceeds are recorded, we record the discount as a contra liability:

Cash	92,640	
Discount on Bonds Payable	7,360	
Bonds Payable		100,000

After this entry is made, the total liability related to the bond (the book value) is $92,640 (principal - discount). However, Monarch is obligated to pay back $100,000 when the bond matures in 5 years. Therefore, as we will see in the next step, the book value of the bond is amortized up to its face value of $100,000, while the discount is amortized down to zero over the life of the bond.

Step 2: Record the periodic interest payments.

The periodic interest payment of $5,000 remains the same, because the coupon rate and the face value of the bond is unchanged. However, the interest expense recognized at the time of the first interest payment on July 1, Year 1 — based on the market rate and the book value

Chapter 8: Bonds Payable and Leases

of the bond – is $5,558 (6% x $92,640). Based on these calculations, the following entry made to record the July 1, Year 1, interest payment:

Interest Expense	5,558	
Discount on Bonds Payable		558
Cash		5,000

The difference between the interest expense recognized and the cash payment made is equal to the amortization of the discount. After this entry is made, the discount on the bond is reduced to $6,802 (7,360 - 558), making the book value of the bond $93,198 (100,000 - 6,802). The interest expense recognized at the time of the January 1, Year 2, interest payment will be calculated based on this new book value. The following amortization table shows the total interest expense and related discount amortization that will be recognized at the time of each interest payment.

Amortization Table 2

		Book Value Beg of period	Interest Payment	=	Interest Expense	+	Discount Amortization	Book Value End of period
0	1/2/Year 1							92,640
1	7/1/Year 1	92,640	5,000		5,558		558	93,198
2	1/1/Year 2	93,198	5,000		5,592		592	93,790
3	7/1/Year 2	93,790	5,000		5,627		627	94,418
4	1/1/Year 3	94,418	5,000		5,665		665	95,083
5	7/1/Year 3	95,083	5,000		5,705		705	95,788
6	1/1/Year 4	95,788	5,000		5,747		747	96,535
7	7/1/Year 4	96,535	5,000		5,792		792	97,327
8	1/1/Year 5	97,327	5,000		5,840		840	98,167
9	7/1/Year 5	98,167	5,000		5,890		890	99,057
10	1/1/Year 6	99,057	5,000		5,943		943	**100,000**
			50,000		57,360		7,360	

KEY CONCEPT

Note that the discount amortization increases over the life of the bond, as we saw, also happens with a premium amortization. However, the interest expense increases as the book value increases up to $100,000 over the life of the bond.

Step 3: Record the repayment of the principal.

At maturity, the book value of the bond has been amortized to its principal amount. The entry to record the repayment of principal will be the same as a bond issued at par. The following entries are made on January 1, Year 6, to record the last interest payment and the repayment of the principal:

<u>Interest Payment</u>
Interest Expense	5,943	
Discount on Bond Payable		943
Cash		5,000

<u>Principal Payment</u>
Bond Payable	100,000	
Cash		100,000

Bonds Payable: Early Retirement

Bond retirement occurs when a company repays the outstanding principal on the bond at maturity (step 3 in our examples). However, sometimes a company may buy back its bonds from investors before they mature in order to pay off all or some of the debt early. Companies often take this action if the market rate of a bond increases because, as you will see, they can realize gains on early retirement of bonds. Let's return to our example for bonds issued at a discount with a market interest rate of 12% (6% semi-annually). Suppose that on January 1, Year 4, Monarch decides to retire all of its bonds early, and that the market rate of interest is now 14% (7% semi-annually). Because there are 2 years, or 4 periods left, the present value of the bond is calculated based on an r of 7% and an n of 4:

$$\text{PV of a bond } (r = 7\%, n = 4) = \text{PV of the principal} + \text{PV of the interest}$$

$$= \left(\begin{array}{c} \text{Lump Sum} \\ \text{Payment} \end{array} \times \begin{array}{c} \text{Present Value} \\ \text{Factor} \end{array} \right) + \left(\begin{array}{c} \text{Periodic} \\ \text{Payment} \end{array} \times \begin{array}{c} \text{Annuity} \\ \text{Factor} \end{array} \right)$$

$$= \$100{,}000 \times .76290 \;+\; \$5{,}000 \times 3.38721$$

$$= \$76{,}290 \;+\; \$16{,}936$$

$$= \$93{,}226$$

Looking at amortization table 2, we find that the book value of the bond on January 1, Year 4, (after the interest payment) is $96,535. Based on this information, we record the following entry to retire the bonds early:

Chapter 8: Bonds Payable and Leases

```
Interest Payment
Interest Expense                    5,747
    Discount on Bond Payable                747
    Cash                                  5,000

Retirement of Bond
Bond Payable                      100,000
    Discount on Bond Payable              3,465   (100,000 - 3,465 = 96,535)
    Cash                                 93,226
    Gain on Retirement of Bond Payable    3,309
```

Remember to use the remaining interest periods and the current interest rate when calculating the current market value of a bond for early retirement. Also, don't forget to record the last interest payment on the date of retirement.

Leases: Capital Leases versus Operating Leases

A **lease** is a contract between two parties, a lessor and a lessee, by which the lessee agrees to pay the lessor for the use of an asset. Many companies choose the option of leasing assets instead of buying them, because it is in some cases a more cost efficient and practical alternative. For example, a company — especially small ones — may lease office space in an existing building instead of buying its own. There are two types of Leases:

- An **operating lease** is a cancelable contract between a lessor and lessee for the use of an asset. Under an operating lease, the lessor transfers the rights to use the property to the lessee for a specified period of time. In exchange, the lessee agrees to make a lease payments to the lessor over the life of the lease. For example, the rent that a tenant pays for an apartments is considered an operating lease. The lease can be canceled at any time, and the property is returned to the lessor at the end of the lease term.

- A **capital lease** is non-cancelable contract between a lessor and lessee for the use of an asset. Under the terms of a capital lease, the rights to use the property are transferred to the lessee for a specified period of time in exchange for a fixed number of lease payments. Because a capital lease is non-cancelable, the arrangement is considered a form of borrowing to purchase an asset. In addition, because of the uncertainty of receiving the future lease payments, the lessor normally charges the lessee interest in exchange for agreeing to accept the payments over time. The present value of the lease payments is

Chapter 8: Bonds Payable and Leases

recorded as a liability in the balance sheet of the lessee to represent the obligation for the lease payments. A corresponding asset is recorded in the asset section of the balance sheet to represent the purchase.

There are four basic criteria for determining when to treat a lease contract as a capital lease rather than an operating lease. If the asset meets any one of the four criteria, then the transaction must be treated as a capital lease.

1. **Transfer of Ownership:** The asset becomes the property of the lessee at the end of the lease.

2. **Bargain Purchase Option:** The lessee has an option to purchase the property at the end of the lease at a price significantly below its market value.

3. **75% of Economic Life:** The lease life is greater than or equal to 75% of the economic (useful) life of the asset.

4. **90% of Fair Market Value:** The present value of the minimum lease payments is greater than or equal to 90% of the fair market value of the asset.

In the next two sections, we will work through the process of recording operating and capital lease transactions.

Operating Leases: Recording Transactions

Let's work through the following example:

On January 1, Year 1, Fabrics, Inc. decides to lease a delivery truck from a local automobile dealer that has a cost of $50,000 and a four-year life. Fabrics, Inc. will lease the truck for three years, making equal lease payments at the end of each year. The truck must be returned to the dealer at the end of the lease term. The automobile dealer has determined that 12% is the appropriate market rate of interest.

For the moment, set aside the question of whether this is a capital lease and treat it as an operating lease. Given this assumption, no liability or asset is recorded in the balance sheet. Instead, rent expense equal to the yearly lease payments is recorded at the time of each lease payment. In this problem, we are given the present value of the lease payments as $50,000. Since the payments will be made over the life of the lease, the payment stream is considered an annuity. We will, therefore, use the annuity table to calculate the yearly lease payments. Manipulating our annuity formula from Chapter 7, we can calculate the yearly rental payments as follows:

Chapter 8: Bonds Payable and Leases

Present value of annuity ($n = 3$, $r = 12\%$) = Periodic Payment × Annuity Factor

Periodic Payment = $\dfrac{\text{Present value of an annuity}}{\text{Annuity factor}}$

Periodic Payment = $\dfrac{\$50{,}000}{2.40183}$

Periodic Payment = $20,817

The entry to record the annual lease payments is:

Rent Expense	20,817	
Cash		20,817

The lessor's interest rate is always used if it is both lower than the lessee's interest rate and known. Also, don't forget to use the lease life to calculate the present value, not the asset life.

Capital Leases: Recording Transactions

Now let's apply the four lease criteria to determine whether or not Fabrics, Inc. should record a capital lease on its books:

Criteria	Satisfied?
Transfer of Ownership	Not mentioned; therefore, not satisfied
Bargain Purchase Option	Not mentioned; therefore, not satisfied
75% of Economic Life	3 years / 4 years = 75%; therefore, satisfied
90% of Fair Market Value	present value of $50,000 = FMV of $50,000; therefore, satisfied

Since at least one of the four criteria has been satisfied, we must treat the lease transactions as belonging to a capital lease. Therefore, we will record a liability and a corresponding asset in the balance sheet at the present value of the lease payments. As you should recall from Chapter 6, when a capital expenditure is made, the acquisition cost of the asset is recorded on the books and depreciated over the useful life of the asset. Similarly, if a lease qualifies as a capital lease, an asset equal to the present value of the minimum lease payments must be recorded in the accounting records and depreciated over the life of the

Chapter 8: Bonds Payable and Leases

useful life of the asset. In addition, similar to the accounting for notes payable transactions, the liability on the books is reduced as payments are made over the life of the lease.

To summarize, there are three basic entries that are recorded when a lease contract is accounted for as a capital lease:

1. **Record the asset and the corresponding liability on the books at the time of signing.** In our example, we make the following entry on January 1, Year 1, to record the obligation at its present value:

Leased Asset	50,000	
Capital Lease Obligation		50,000

2. **Depreciate the asset over its economic life.** Assuming that Fabrics, Inc. uses the straight-line method of depreciation, the yearly depreciation of $16,666 ($50,000 divided by three) is recorded as:

Depreciation Expense	16,666	
Accumulated Depreciation		16,666

   Note: Because we have rounded down with our figure $16,666, the entry made on December 31, Year 3, is in the amount of $16,668.

   At the end of the lease term, the total accumulated depreciation will be $50,000, making the net book value of the asset have a value of 0. However, for accounting purposes, the following entry will be made to remove the asset from the books when it is returned to the lessor:

Accumulated Depreciation	50,000	
Leased Asset		50,000

3. **Record the interest expense and the related liability reduction.** Recall from Chapter 7 that the interest expense on a note is calculated based on the remaining principal outstanding at the time the interest payment is made. Applying that concept, the December 31, Year 1, lease payment of $20,817 is recorded as follows:

Interest Expense	6,000		($50,000 x 12%)
Capital Lease Obligation	14,817		($20,817 - $6,000)
Cash		20,817	

Chapter 8: Bonds Payable and Leases

On January 1, Year 2, the remaining principal balance on the capital lease obligation is $35,183 ($50,000 - 14,817). The following amortization schedule summarizes the remaining lease payments and the related principal reductions on the lease obligation. We can use these numbers to make entries for the lease payments in Year 2 and Year 3.

Period	Date	Balance beg of period	Loan Payment	=	Interest Expense	+	Principal Reduction	Balance end of period
0	1/1/Year 1							50,000
1	12/31/Year 1	50,000	20,817		6,000		14,817	35,183
2	12/31/Year 2	35,183	20,817		4,222		16,595	18,588
3	12/31/Year 2	18,588	20,817		2,231		18,588	0
			62,451		12,453		50,000	

Year 2

Interest Expense	4,222	
Capital Lease Obligation	16,595	
Cash		20,817

Year 3

Interest Expense	2,231	
Capital Lease Obligation	18,588	
Cash		20,817

Chapter 8: Bonds Payable and Leases

Key Terms

bond: a debt security representing the evidence of a loan.

capital lease: a non-cancelable contract between a lessor and lessee for the use of an asset. Because a capital lease is non-cancelable, the arrangement is considered a form of borrowing to purchase an asset.

coupon rate: the interest rate used to calculate the periodic interest payment on a bond. The coupon rate is also referred to as the nominal or stated rate of interest.

discount: the excess debt that a company is willing to assume at the time that a bond is issued.

market rate of interest: the interest rate used to calculate the present value of the bond. It is the prevailing rate at which investors are willing to lend money.

operating lease: a cancelable contract between a lessor and lessee for the use of an asset. Under an operating lease, the lessor transfers the rights to use the property to the lessee for a specified period of time.

premium: the excess cash that an investor is willing to pay over and above the face value of a bond.

Chapter 8: Bonds Payable and Leases

Thrills, Chills and Drills

True or False

1. There are two key differences between calculating the present value of a bond and calculating the present value of a note.

2. In order to calculate the present value of a bond, the company must calculate the present value of a single sum (the principal payment) and the present value of a series of payments (the interest).

3. To calculate the present value of the principal, multiply the annuity factor times the periodic payment.

4. When a bond is issued at a premium, the market rate of interest is greater than the coupon rate.

5. Another name for the nominal rate is the market rate.

6. When the coupon rate is less than the market rate, the bond is issued at a premium.

7. The entry to record a contra liability involves premiums.

8. Equity holders have specific repayment periods.

9. Equity holders are entitled only to a return on their capital either through dividends or the appreciation of the value of the company.

10. To record the entry for receiving the proceeds from a bond issuance, bonds payable is always credited for face value.

11. Upon paying the interest on a semi-annual basis, interest expense is always calculated multiplying the face value times the coupon rate.

12. When bonds are purchased between interest dates, the borrower pays the investor for the accrued interest up to the date of issuance.

13. When interest payments are due, all investors receive interest in the amount of principal times the coupon rate.

14. Both premium amortization and discount amortization increase over the life of the bond.

15. Companies sometimes buy back bonds from investors before they mature, if the market rate of the bond has increased.

Chapter 8: Bonds Payable and Leases

16. A capital lease is a cancelable contract between a lessor and lessee for use of an asset.

17. An operating lease is considered a form of borrowing to purchase an asset.

18. Companies with capital leases record the asset and corresponding liability on the books at the time of signing.

19. Depreciation expense is recorded for operating leases.

20. A bargain purchase option allows the lessee to purchase the property at the end of the lease at a price significantly below its market value.

Multiple Choice

1. Bonds are
    a) debt securities
    b) normally paid off in two payment streams
    c) valued by calculating the present value of the principal and interest
    d) all of the above
    e) none of the above

2. The interest rate used to calculate the periodic interest payment is called the
    a) market rate
    b) discount rate
    c) present value
    d) nominal rate

3. If a bond is issued when the coupon rate equals the market rate of interest, it is said to be issued
    a) above par
    b) below par
    c) at par
    d) none of the above

4. If bonds are issued when the market rate of interest is less than the coupon rate, they are said to be issued
    a) at par
    b) above par
    c) below par
    d) none of the above

Chapter 8: Bonds Payable and Leases

5. Bonds are issued at a discount when
   a) coupon rate = market rate
   b) coupon rate > market rate
   c) coupon rate < market rate
   d) none of the above

6. A contra liability is recorded at the time of issuance when bonds are issued
   a) at par
   b) above par
   c) below par
   d) none of the above

7. If interest is paid quarterly on a 12%, 5-year bond, interest is paid
   a) 20 times, at 6 %
   b) 20 times, at 3 %
   c) 10 times, at 3%
   d) 10 times, at 6%

8. To record the proceeds received from the issuance of a bond
   a) debit cash; credit bond payable
   b) debit bond payable; credit cash
   c) debit cash; credit interest payable
   d) none of the above

9. If a bond is issued for $100,000 for 5 years with semi-annual interest calculated to be 5%, and the market rate is 10%. The bond is issued
   a) at par
   b) below par
   c) above par
   d) none of the above

Chapter 8: Bonds Payable and Leases

10. When bonds are issued at par between interest dates, the entry to record the issuance includes
    I. a debit to cash
    II. a credit to cash
    III. a debit to bond payable
    IV. a credit to bond payable
    V. a debit to interest expense
    VI. a credit to interest expense
    VII. a debit to interest payable
    VIII. a credit to interest payable
    a) I, IV, VIII
    b) III, V, II
    c) I, V, IV
    d) none of the above

11. To record a premium on Bond Payable of $6,000 at issuance one should
    a) debit Cash $106,000, credit Bond Payable $100,000, and credit Interest Payable $6,000
    b) debit Cash $106,000, credit Bond Payable $100,000, and credit Premium on Bond Payable $6,000
    c) debit Cash $94,000, debit Premium $6,000, and credit Bond Payable $100,000
    d) none of the above

12. To record a discount of $4,500 at issuance
    a) debit Cash $96,000, discount on Bond Payable $4,000, and credit Bond Payable $100,000
    b) debit Cash $104,500, credit Bond Payable $100,000, and discount $4,500
    c) debit Cash $95,500, discount on Bond Payable $4,500, and credit Bond Payable $100,000
    d) none of the above

13. The final journal entry for Bond Payable includes
    a) a debit to Interest Payable
    b) a credit to Cash
    c) a debit to Bond Payable
    d) all of the above
    e) none of the above

Chapter 8: Bonds Payable and Leases

14. The journal entry to record the retirement of 5-year, 12% bonds, issued at a discount, when the market rate is 14% includes
    I. a debit to Interest Expense
    II. a credit to Bond Payable.
    III. a debit to Bond Payable.
    IV. a credit to Cash.
    V. a credit to Gain on Retirement of Bond Payable.
    VI. a debit to Discount on Bond Payable.
    a) I through VI
    b) I through V
    c) I, and III through VI
    d) I, and III through V

15. An operating lease is
    a) cancelable
    b) transfers rights to use the property
    c) requires that the property is returned to the lessor
    d) all of the above
    e) none of the above

16. Capital leases
    a) are cancelable
    b) do not transfer ownership
    c) offer no bargain purchase option
    d) are those in which the economic life of the asset is greater than 75% of the lease life
    e) all of the above
    f) none of the above

17. The 75% of economic life test means that
    a) the lease life is three years, and the economic life is five years
    b) the lease life is four years, and the economic life is six years
    c) the lease life is four years, and the economic life is eight years
    d) the lease life is four years, and economic life is five years
    e) all of the above
    f) none of the above

CHAPTER 8: BONDS PAYABLE AND LEASES

18. If, as part of a lease agreement, there is a requirement that property be returned to the lessor upon completion of the lease, the lease is classified as
    a) an operating lease
    b) a capital lease
    c) both a and b
    d) neither a nor b

19. If the fair market value of a truck is $50,000, the periodic payment is $20,817, and the annuity factor is 2.40183, is the 90% of fair market value test satisfied?
    a) no
    b) yes
    c) cannot be determined from this information

20. When a lease includes a statement that the truck can be purchased for $1,000 at the end of the term, then
    a) the lease is an operating lease
    b) the lease is a capital lease
    c) then the lease contains a bargain purchase option
    d) a and c
    e) b and c

Short Essays

1. An accounting professor states: "Once you know how to calculate the present value of a note, you know how to calculate the present value of a bond. There is no difference in the two." Do you agree?

2. What are discounts and premiums? How are they handled? What affect do they have on interest expense?

3. Global Marketing issued $100,000 5-year, 10% semi-annual coupon bonds on April 1. Periodic interest payments are made on January 1 and July 1. Make the entries to record the issuance of the bonds and the first interest payment, assuming that the semi-annual market rate of interest has been calculated to be 5%.

Chapter 8: Bonds Payable and Leases

4. On January 2, Captain Moren, Inc. issued $100,000 5-year, 10 % semi-annual coupon bonds when the market rate was 8%. Periodic interest payments are due on January 1 and July 1 of each year. What are the entries to record the issuance of the bonds and the first interest payment?

5. CJ Fisher Enterprises issued $100,000 5-year, 10% semi-annual coupon bonds on June 1, when the market rate was 12%. If periodic interest payments are due on January 1 and July 1, what are the entries to record the issuance of the bonds and the first interest payment?

6. Kelcey Corporation decided to retire all of its 6-year, 10% semi-annual bonds on January 1, Year 4, when the market rate was 14%. The book value on 1/1/Year 4, before interest payments, was $95,788. The bonds were originally issued when the market rate was 12%. What is the entry to retire the bonds early?

7. On the first of the year, NIBOR Corporation decided to lease a truck from a local dealer due to excess demand. The truck cost $75,000 and had a five-year life. NIBOR decided to lease the truck for three years making annual payments of $31,226. The first payment is due December 31. NIBOR's incremental borrowing rate is 13%. According to paperwork received by NIBOR, the dealer sets its annual rentals to yield a return on investment of 12%.

   a. What type of lease is this? Explain.

   b. Make the entry to record this transaction.

   c. NIBOR uses the straight-line method of depreciation. Make the entry to record depreciation.

   d. Make the entry to record the interest expense and related liability reduction.

   e. Make the entry to return the truck at the end of the lease.

Chapter 8: Bonds Payable and Leases

Answers

True or False

1. True.
2. True.
3. False. Multiply the face value times single-sum factor.
4. False. The market rate is less than the coupon rate.
5. False. Another name is the coupon rate or stated rate.
6. False. The bond is issued at a discount.
7. False. The entry involves discounts.
8. False. They have no specific repayment periods.
9. True.
10. True.
11. False. At par this is true. If the bonds are issued at greater than par, deduct premium. If the bonds are issued at less than par, add discount.
12. False. The investor pays the borrower.
13. True.
14. True.
15. True.
16. False. A capital lease is non-cancelable.
17. False. Capital leases meet this definition.
18. True.
19. False. It is recorded for capital leases.
20. True.

Multiple Choice Answers

1. (d) All of the above.
2. (d) Also called the coupon or stated rate.
3. (c) coupon rate = market rate, if issued at par
4. (b) coupon rate > market rate, if issued at premium
5. (c) They are issued below par
6. (c) A contra liability is recorded when bonds are issued at a discount
7. (b) 5 x 4 = 20 times at 12% / 4 = 3%
8. (a) increase cash; record liability incurred

Chapter 8: Bonds Payable and Leases

9. **(a)** market rate = 10%, coupon rate = 10% (5% x 2)
15. **(d)** All describe operating leases.
16. **(f)** None of these conditions apply to a capital lease.
17. **(d)** 4 / 5 = 80%
18. **(a)** Property is returned under an operating lease.
19. **(b)** 50,000 / 2.40183 = $20,817

    Present value minimum lease payments > or = 90% Full Market Value $20,817 x number of payments > or = 50,000 x 90%

    The answer is yes, because the minimum lease payment was determined based on the full market

    value of the truck. However, we might have chosen c, because we need to know the interest rate, compound method, and time period to determine the annuity factor.

20. **(e)** The lease is capital due to the bargain purchase option.

Short Essay Answers

1. No, there are two key differences between calculating the present value of a bond and calculating the present value of a note:

    a. Bonds are normally paid off in two payment streams. The principal, which is paid off at the end (lump sum), and the interest paid on the principal, which is normally paid out over the life of the note (annuity).

    b. The interest rate used to calculate the present value of the bond is not always the interest rate used to calculate the interest payments. The interest rate used to calculate the periodic interest payment on the bond is called the coupon rate or stated interest rate, and the interest rated used to calculate the present value of the bond is called the market rate. If total proceeds equal the face value of the bond, the bond is issued at par and the coupon rate equals the market rate. If the total proceeds are geater than face value, the bond is issued above par at a premium and the oupon rate is greater than the market rate. If total proceeds are less than face value, the bond is issued below par at a discount and the coupon rate is less than the market rate.

2. Discounts are contra liabilities at the time of issuance, if the coupon rate is less than the market rate. Contra liabilities normally have debit balances. The discount is the difference between the face value and the present value of principal plus interest. Upon amortization, interest expense equals the amount of the interest payment plus the discount amortized. The discount amortized increases and interest expense increases over the life of the loan.

    Premiums are adjunct liabilities (and normally have a credit balance) at the time of the issuance, if the coupon rate is greater than par. The premium is the difference between the face value and the present value of the principal plus interest. Upon amortization, interest expense is equal to the interest payment

    minus the amortized premium. The premium amortized increases over the life of the bond, while the interest expense decreases.

Chapter 8: Bonds Payable and Leases

3.

Coupon rate = market rate
Present value of principal + interest = face value.
Interest payment = (face value x coupon rate)

Cash	102,500	
Bond Payable		100,000
Interest Payable		2,500
Interest Expense	2,500	
Interest Payable	2,500	
Cash		5,000

4.

Cash	108,111		bond payable + premium
Bond Payable		100,000	face value
Premium		8,111	face value less
			(present value of principal (100,000 x 0.67556 +
			present value of interest (5,000 x 8.1109))
Interest Expense	4,324		(bond payable plus premium x 4%)
Premium	676		(interest owed less interest expense)
Cash		5,000	(face value x coupon rate)

5.

Cash	96,807		PV bond (92,640) + 5 months interest (4167)
Discount on Bond Payable	7,360		(face value less present value principal(100,000
			x .55840) + present value interest (5,000 x 7.36009))
Bond Payable		100,000	(face value)
Interest Payable		4,167	((100,000 x 5%) / 6 months x 5 months)
Interest Expense	1,391		(1 month interest (833) + discount amortized (558))
Interest Payable	4,167		(5 months of interest from above)
Discount on Bond Payable		558	((92,640 x 6%) - (100,000 x 5%))
Cash		5,000	(100,000 x 5%)

6.

Interest Expense	5,747		(95,788 x 6%)
Discount		747	(Interest owed less interest expense)
Cash		5,000	(100,000 x 5%)

To record interest payment.

Bond Payable	100,000		(face value)
Discount on Bond Payable		3,465	(100,000 - 96,535 or (95,788 + 747))
Cash		93,226	(Present value at (r = 7, n = 4))
Gain on Retirement		3,309	(100,000 - 96,691) (Discount on Bond Payable + present value)

Chapter 8: Bonds Payable and Leases

7. **a.** This is a capital lease because:
   90% of full market value = 90% x 75,000 or 67,500
   (3 x 31,226) or 93,678 = total lease payments
   93,678 > 67,500, so the minimum lease payments are > or = 90% of full market value

   b.
Leased Asset	75,000	
Capital Lease Obligation		75,000

   To record asset and corresponding liability on the books at time of signing.

   c.
Depreciation Expense	25,000		(75,000 / 3)
Amortization Depreciation		25,000	

   d.
Interest Expense	9,000		(75,000 x 12%)
Capital Lease Obligation	22,226		(31,226 - 9,000)
Cash		31,226	(payment)

   e.
Amortization Depreciation	75,000	
Leased Asset		75,000

Chapter

Alternative Revenue Recognition and Income Tax

9

Chapter 9: Alternative Revenue Recognition and Income Tax

Overview

This chapter will teach you how to record transactions that affect income statement accounts. First, we will examine in detail the alternative methods of revenue recognition that were described briefly in Chapter 2. We will then review the appropriate methods of computing income tax expenses, as well as the issues surrounding the calculation of income taxes payable and deferred income taxes. By the end of this chapter, you should be able to:

- understand three alternative methods of revenue recognition

- calculate revenue using the percentage-of-completion and completed contract methods of revenue recognition

- understand and compute deferred tax assets and deferred tax liabilities

- record income tax expense and income tax payable for a company with temporary and permanent tax differences

Chapter 9: Alternative Revenue Recognition and Income Tax

Concepts

Revenue Recognition: A Closer Look

In Chapter 2 we defined the revenue recognition principle as the basis for determining how to record transactions affecting income statement accounts. The **revenue recognition principle** states that revenue should be recognized and recorded when it is both 1) **realized** or **realizable** and 2) **earned**, which is generally at the **time of sale**. We defined each of these standards as follows:

1. a) **Realized:** Revenue is realized when goods or services are exchanged for cash or claims to cash.

   b) **Realizable:** Revenue is realizable when goods or services are saleable in an active market at readily determinable prices (and without significant additional cost) in exchange for cash or claims to cash.

2. **Earned:** Revenues are considered earned when the company has substantially completed everything that it must do to be entitled to the revenue.

Recognition of revenue at the time of sale provides a uniform test that can be applied to companies in a variety of industries. For some companies, however, it is more appropriate to recognize revenue before or after the sale. Under alternative methods, revenue can also be recognized during production, at the end of production, or on a cash basis. The determination of when to recognize revenue depends primarily on two factors:

1. Whether the company has substantially completed everything that it must do to be entitled to the revenue.

2. The certainty of the future cash inflows and outflows related to the project

The sections below take a closer look at the three alternative methods of recognizing revenue.

Revenue Recognition During Production

Recognition before the time of sale occurs primarily when a company has entered into a long-term contract to provide a particular service or product and it has completed such a

Chapter 9: Alternative Revenue Recognition and Income Tax

substantial portion of the product that it is entitled to some portion of the revenue. In addition, to the requirement that a substantial portion of production has been completed the receipt of cash flows must be certain.

Accountants commonly recognize revenue during production when accounting for long-term construction contracts. Suppose, for example, that a company has a three-year construction contract. Under the usual method, the company would not recognize any revenue at the end of each of the first two years. The company would then show a huge profit at the end of the third year. By recognizing revenue during production, on the other hand, the company can "smooth out" its earnings over each of the years that the services are being performed, even though the sale won't be complete until the end of the project.

The most common method of accounting for the recognition of revenue during production is the **percentage-of-completion method.** Under this method, revenue is recognized based on the percentage of the job completed. The percent of the job completed is measured based on the total expenses incurred during the period by using the following formula:

$$\frac{\text{total costs incurred during the period}}{\text{total anticipated costs to complete}} \times \text{total estimated revenues}$$

Let's illustrate this method with an example.

Contractors Unlimited agrees to construct a building for Rider Realty Corp. for $6,000,000. Contractors Unlimited estimates that the total cost of building will be $4,500,000, which will spread out according to this schedule: to be incurred as follows: Year 1, $1,500,000; Year 2, $2,500.000; Year 3, $500,000. Contractors Unlimited expects to earn a total profit of $1,500,000 on this project ($6,000,000 - $4,500,000). Using the formula above, Contractors Unlimited will recognize revenue and profit in Year 1, Year 2, and Year 3 as follows:

Year	Total Costs Incurred	Total Estimated Costs to Complete	Percentage Complete		Estimated Revenues		Revenue Recognized	Profit
1	1,500,000 /	4,500,000	= 33.33%	x	6,000,000	=	2,000,000	500,000
2	2,500,000 /	4,500,000	= 55.56%	x	6,000,000	=	3,333,333	833,333
3	500,000 /	4,500,000	= 11.11%	x	6,000,000	=	666,667	166,667
							6,000,000	1,500,000

While the percentage-of-completion method provides construction companies a way to smooth out their income, some companies still opt to recognize revenue at the time of sale (when the production is complete). The most common method of accounting for revenue recognition after production is complete is the **completed contract method.** This method is

Chapter 9: Alternative Revenue Recognition and Income Tax

also used when there is some uncertainty about the collection of revenues earned on the project. Under this method, revenue earned and expenses incurred are not recognized until the year that the contract is completed. Therefore, if Contractors Unlimited were using the completed contract method of accounting for the Rider Realty contract, the total revenues of $6,000,000 and total expenses of $4,500,000 would not be recognized until Year 3. As a result, the entire $500,000 profit on the project would not be reflected in the company's income until Year 3.

Revenue Recognition at the End of Production

In some instances, revenue recognition can occur after production is complete but before the time of sale. This type of recognition occurs when a company has substantially completed the product and is entitled to the revenue earned, but the actual sales transaction in which the revenue is realized has not taken place. In most instances, the revenue is still realizable, because there is a readily available market to purchase the product. These conditions can only occur when the selling price and the amount are certain. One common example is in the mining of certain minerals, such as copper. Once mined, a readily available market exists for copper at a standard price.

Revenue Recognition on a Cash Basis

Some companies recognize revenue on a cash basis – when the cash is actually received (which can be after the time of sale). This method is generally used only if it is uncertain at the time of sale whether the cash can be actually collected. The most common method of accounting for the recognition of revenue on a cash basis is the **installment sales method.** Under this method, revenue is recognized by a seller as portions of the sale price of a product are received. To properly reflect the profit on the sale in the income statement, expenses (most often the cost of goods sold) are recognized in the same proportion as the revenue.

Income Tax Expense

Income tax expense is the tax expense recognized during an accounting period. It is based on the net income reflected in the income statement. The formula for calculating income tax expense is as follows:

Chapter 9: Alternative Revenue Recognition and Income Tax

net income   x   corporate tax rate   =   current year
(for financial report purposes)   income tax expense

For example, a company with a net income before taxes of $60,000 and a tax rate of 40% would report an income tax expense of $24,000. The entry to record the current year income tax expense would be a debit to the expense account and a credit to the liability account:

Income Tax Expense	24,000	
Income Taxes Payable		24,000

The income tax actually paid is based in the income reported on a company's income tax return. In the example above, the total income taxes payable equal the income tax expense reported in the income statement. However, the income tax actually paid is almost always different from the income tax expense reported on the income statement. This discrepancy is the result of differences in accounting for financial reporting purposes (this report is also called "book income") and accounting for income tax purposes. There are two types of differences, permanent and temporary differences.

- **permanent differences:** Permanent differences arise when book income includes revenues or expenses that are never included in taxable income. The most common examples of permanent differences are interest revenues on municipal bonds and expenses incurred for premiums paid on the life insurance of a company's officers.

- **temporary differences:** There are two situations that can give rise to temporary differences:

    1. Revenues and expenses are included in book income now but will not be reflected in taxable income until later.

    2. Revenues and expenses are included in taxable income now but will not be reflected in book income until later.

    The most common types of temporary differences arise in accounting for depreciation expenses, long-term contracts, and bad debt expense.

In the next two sections, we will work through the accounting for income taxes when a company has permanent differences and temporary differences.

Chapter 9: Alternative Revenue Recognition and Income Tax

Income Taxes: Permanent Differences

Since permanent differences are irreversible, no additional accounting is necessary to report the differences in the financial statements. Net income is calculated for tax purposes; the income tax payable and the income tax expense are then recorded in the financial statements at the appropriate amount. Consider the following information for Rider Realty Corp.:

Net Income before taxes and adjustments	$75,000
Income tax rate	40%

Revenues and expenses not already included in net income:

Interest on municipal bonds	$6,000
Premiums paid on officers life insurance	$4,000

Net income for book and tax purposes is calculated as follows:

	Book Purposes	Tax Purposes
Net income before additional adjustments and taxes	75,000	75,000
Interest on municipal bonds	6,000	not included
Premiums paid on officers' life insurance	(4,000)	not included
Net Income Before Taxes	77,000	75,000
	40%	40%
Currnet Year Income Tax	30,800	**30,000**
Net Income After Taxes	46,200	45,000

Although the current year income tax for book purposes is $30,800, only $30,000 will be recorded as income tax payable and income tax expense because the tax effects of permanent differences are not recorded in the financial statements. The following entry is made to record the income tax liability:

Income Tax Expense	30,000	
Income Taxes Payable		30,000

When the taxes are paid, the liability is removed from the books as follows:

Income Tax Expense	30,000	
Cash		30,000

Chapter 9: Alternative Revenue Recognition and Income Tax

Temporary Differences and Deferred Income Taxes

The difference between the income tax expense and the income tax actually payable is the deferred tax asset or liability. Deferred taxes are recorded for temporary differences in book and tax income, because they will be reversed in future periods.

A **deferred tax asset** arises when book income is less than taxable income (the income tax expense is less than the income taxes payable). The reason for the deferred tax asset is that the company is paying more taxes now, because taxable income is greater than book income. The company will, therefore, end up paying less taxes later, when the temporary differences reverse themselves.

A **deferred tax liability** arises when book income is greater than taxable income (income tax expense is greater than income taxes payable). The reason for the deferred tax liability is that the company is paying less taxes now, because taxable income is less than book income. However, the company will end up paying more taxes later, when the temporary differences reverse themselves.

Deferred tax assets are presented in the current asset section of the balance sheet, and deferred tax liabilities are presented in the current liability section of the balance sheet. If a company has both deferred tax assets and deferred tax liabilities, they are presented *separately* in the financial statements. The following table lists the most common causes of temporary differences and the accounting treatments for book and tax purposes:

	COMMON METHOD USED FOR: BOOK PURPOSES	TAX PURPOSES	EXPLANATION	DEFERRED TAX OR LIABILITY?
Depreciation	Most often straight-line	MACRS	MACRS is required for income tax purposes. However, many companies use the straight-line method for book purposes. This creates a difference in the depreciation expense reconized in the income statement.	Deferred tax liability, may be a deferred tax asset in the first year of depreciation.
Accounts Receivable	Allowance Method	Direct Write-Off Method	The direct write-off method is required for income tax purposes. However, this method may be used for book purposes only if the total of the bad debt expense is immaterial. This creates a difference in bad debt expense recognized in the income.	Can be a deferred asset or liability; if bad debt expense is greater under the direct write-off method, then a liability's created; if the reverse is true, then an asset is created.
Long Term Contracts	Percentage-of-Completion	Completed Contract	The completed contract method is required for tax purposes, but the percentage of completion method is preferrred for book purposes because of the smoothing effect on income. This creates a timing difference of the recognition of the profit.	Always a deferred tax liability

Chapter 9: Alternative Revenue Recognition and Income Tax

To illustrate the accounting for deferred tax assets and liabilities, consider the following information for Conglomerates, Inc. as of 12/31/Year 1 (the company's first year of operations):

Net income before taxes and adjustments:	$140,000
Income tax rate:	40%

Additional information not already included in net income is given below.

1. Conglomerates, Inc, uses the allowance method for the recognition of bad debt expense. Total bad debt expense for the year is $9,000. Total write-offs during the year totaled $7,000.

2. Total revenues and expenses recognized on long-term contracts accounted for under the percentage-of-completion method were $100,000 and $80,000, respectively. The project began during this year and is not expected to be completed until Year 4.

3. The assets of Conglomerates, Inc. consist of only furniture and fixtures, which are depreciated on a straight-line basis over a period of 5 years for book purposes. For tax purposes, furniture and fixtures are in 7-year asset class. The following depreciation schedule shows the depreciation for each year under the straight-line method and MACRS:

Total Cost of all Furniture & Fixtures purchased   120,000

Year	Straight Line Depreciation	MACRS Percentages (for 7-Year Class)	MACRS Depreciation	Temporary Difference
1	24,000	14.3%	17,160	6,840
2	24,000	24.5%	29,400	(5,400)
3	24,000	17.5%	21,000	3,000
4	24,000	12.5%	15,000	9,000
5	24,000	8.9%	10,680	13,320
6		8.9%	10,680	(10,680)
7		8.9%	10,680	(10,680)
8		4.5%	5,400	(5,400)
	120,000	100.0%	120,000	0

Chapter 9: Alternative Revenue Recognition and Income Tax

Based on this information, we can calculate the income tax expense and income tax payable for Conglomerates, Inc., as shown below.

	Book Purposes	Tax Purposes	Deferred Tax Asset	Deferred Tax Liability
Net income before additional adjustments and taxes	140,000	140,000		
Bad Debt Expense	(9,000)	(7,000)	2,000	
Total Profit on construction contracts	20,000	0		20,000
Depreciation Expense	(24,000)	(17,160)	6,840	
Net Income Before Taxes	127,000	115,840	8,840	20,000
	40%	40%	40%	40%
Current Year Income Tax	50,800	46,336	3,536	8,000
Net Income After Taxes	76,200	69,504		

Since Conglomerates, Inc. has no permanent differences, income tax expense is calculated based on net income for book purposes. If there were permanent differences, the "net income before taxes" for book purposes would be adjusted before the income tax expense is calculated.

In this problem, the gross profit on construction contracts is considered a deferred tax liability, because Conglomerates, Inc. will have to pay taxes on an additional $20,000 in revenue when the contract is complete. However, the differences in bad debt expense and depreciation expense recognized for book and tax purposes are considered deferred tax assets. They are considered deferred tax assets because less expense is recognized for tax purposes due to the different accounting methods used. When the differences reverse themselves, more expense will be recognized, creating a lower net income for tax purposes and, therefore, lower income taxes payable. The following entry is made to record the current year's tax expense and liability:

Deferred Tax Asset	3,536	[(2,000 + 6,840) x 40%]
Income Tax Expense	50,800	
Income Taxes Payable		46,336
Deferred Tax Liability		8,000 (20,000 x 40%)

Chapter 9: Alternative Revenue Recognition and Income Tax

Key Terms

completed contract method: a common method of accounting for revenue recognition after production is complete. Under this method, revenue earned and expenses incurred are not recognized until the year the contract is completed.

deferred tax asset: a deferred tax asset arises when book income is less than taxable income (income tax expense is less than the income taxes payable).

deferred tax liability: a deferred tax liability arises when book income is greater than taxable income (income tax expense is greater than income taxes payable).

installment sales: a common method of accounting for the recognition of revenue on a cash basis. Under this method, revenue is recognized by a seller as portions of the sale price of a product are received.

percentage-of-completion method: a common method of accounting for the recognition of revenue during production. Under this method, revenue is recognized based on the percentage of the job completed.

permanent tax differences: permanent differences arise when book income includes revenues or expenses that are never included in taxable income. The most common examples of permanent differences are interest revenues on municipal bonds and expenses incurred for premiums paid on the life insurance of a company's officers.

temporary differences: temporary tax differences arise when book income includes revenue and expenses in one accounting period that will become a part of taxable income in another accounting period. The most common types of permanent differences arise in accounting for depreciation expenses, long-term contracts, and bad debt expenses.

Chapter 9: Alternative Revenue Recognition and Income Tax

Thrills, Chills and Drills

True or False

1. Revenues are considered realized when goods or services are exchanged for cash or claims to cash.

2. Revenues are considered realizable when goods or services are saleable in an active market at readily determinable prices.

3. Revenues are considered earned when the company has not substantially completed everything that it must do to be entitled to the revenue.

4. Companies can choose either the percentage-of-completion method or the completed contract method for tax purposes.

5. In order to calculate the percentage completed, a company computes the ratio of total anticipated costs to costs incurred during the period.

6. If a builder expected to make a profit of $500,000, and the costs by year are $1,000,000, $2,500,000, and $500,000, the builder must have charged the customer $4,000,000.

7. If total job costs to construct a building are $5,000,000 and the price of the building is $8,000,000, the profit per year for 5 years of work is $600,000.

8. If the total costs incurred during year one were $2,000,000, and the anticipated cost was $5,000,000, the percentage complete is 40%.

9. Say we have the same situation as in question 8, and we know the price of the building is $10,000,000. The amount of revenue recognized during year 1 would be $4,000,000.

10. For the situation in questions 8 and 9, the amount of profit recognized in year 1 would be $2,000,000.

11. Income tax expense is the tax expense recognized during the period and is based on the net income reflected in the income statement.

12. If Jones Enterprizes had $802,000 net income per the income statement, then the company would record the following transaction with a tax rate of 35%:

Income Tax Expense	$280,700	
Cash		$280,700

Chapter 9: Alternative Revenue Recognition and Income Tax

13. An example of a temporary timing difference is municipal bond interest.

14. Temporary tax differences are either: a) revenues and expenses included in book income now but not in taxable income, or b) revenues and expenses included in taxable income now but not in book income.

15. In order to calculate book income, interest on municipal bonds is excluded.

16. When recording the income tax liability, income tax based on the income statement is recorded.

17. When book depreciation is greater than tax depreciation, a deferred tax liability is recorded.

18. When depreciation for tax purposes is greater than depreciation for book purposes, a deferred tax asset is recorded.

19. Deferred tax assets and deferred tax liabilities are netted together when recorded.

20. The journal entry to record the current year's tax expense and liability is

Deferred Tax Liability	XXXX	
Income Taxes Payable	XXXX	
Deferred Tax Asset		XXX
Cash		XXX

Multiple Choice

1. Revenue can be recognized
    a) at the time of sale
    b) during production
    c) at the end of production
    d) on a cash basis
    e) all of the above

Chapter 9: Alternative Revenue Recognition and Income Tax

2. According to the revenue recognition principle, revenue should be recorded when
    a) goods or services are exchanged for cash or claims to cash
    b) goods or services are saleable in an active market at a readily determinable price in exchange for cash or claims to cash
    c) the company has substantially completed everything that it must do to be entitled to the revenue
    d) all of the above
    e) none of the above

3. Under the percentage-of-completion method, the percent of the job complete is measured:
    a) based on the total expenses incurred during the period
    b) using the formula: total costs incurred/total anticipated costs to complete
    c) by the amount of revenue collected
    d) none of the above

4. If the equipment being constructed is expected to cost $500,000, and, to date, the company has incurred $250,000 in expenses, what percent complete is the equipment?
    a) 25
    b) 50
    c) 75
    d) 100

For questions 5-10, refer to the following situation.

In order to expand their warehouse, Able Company solicited bids from contractors. Smith & Sons anticipated that the expansion would cost $250,000. Jones & Brothers expects the building to cost $500,000. The actual costs incurred at the end of year one are calculated to be $100,000.

5. What percent complete is the building if Jones & Brothers is doing the construction?
    a) 10
    b) 20
    c) 40
    d) 50

6. What percent is complete if Smith & Sons is doing the construction?
    a) 20
    b) 10
    c) 50
    d) 40

Chapter 9: Alternative Revenue Recognition and Income Tax

7. How much total profit would Smith recognize if the estimated revenue from the building was $600,000?

    a) 250
    b) 100
    c) 350
    d) 0

8. How much total profit would Jones recognize if the estimated revenue from the building was $600,000?

    a) 0
    b) 100
    c) 250
    d) 350

9. How much revenue would Smith recognize in Year 1 of construction?

    a) 120
    b) 140
    c) 240
    d) 200

10. How much revenue would Jones recognize in Year 1 of construction?

    a) 20
    b) 120
    c) 70
    d) 240

11. A company has on its income statement $100,000 in net income before taxes and a tax rate of 15%. The entry to record the current year income tax expense is

    a)
Income Tax Expense	$15,000	
Income tax payable		$15,000

    b)
Income Tax Payable	$15,000	
Cash		$15,000

    c)
Income Tax Payable	$15,000	
Cash		$15,000

    e) none

Chapter 9: Alternative Revenue Recognition and Income Tax

12. **Identify the false statement.**
    a) The income statement journal entry for income tax expense includes a debit to income tax expense, and a credit to cash.
    b) To record the actual income tax liability, the journal entry includes a debit to income tax expense, and a credit to income taxes payable.
    c) To remove the liability from the books, the journal entry includes a debit to income taxes payable, and a credit to cash
    d) All of the above.
    e) None of the above.

13. **If Charlie Company has net income for book purposes of $80,000, and net income for tax purposes of $90,000, the proper journal entry to record the income tax liability is what? Assume a tax rate of 40%.**

    a)
Income Tax Expense	$32,000	
Income Taxes Payable		$32,000

    b)
Income Tax Expense	$32,000	
Cash		$32,000

    c)
Income Tax Expense	$36,000	
Income Taxes Payable		$36,000

    d)
Income Tax Expense	$36,000	
Cash		$36,000

14. **A deferred tax asset**
    a) arises when book income is less than taxable income
    b) arises when income tax expense is less than income taxes payable
    c) is recorded for temporary differences
    d) none of the above
    e) all of the above

15. **A deferred tax liability**
    a) arises when book income is less than taxable income
    b) arises when income tax expense is greater than income taxes payable
    c) is recorded for permanent differences
    d) none of the above

Chapter 9: Alternative Revenue Recognition and Income Tax

For questions 16-20, refer to the following information.

Net income before taxes and adjustments	$150,000
Income tax rate	35%
Straight-line depreciation	$40,000
MACRS depreciation	$36,000

16. What is net income before taxes for book purposes?
    a) 100,000
    b) 114,000
    c) 110,000
    d) 150,000

17. What is net income before taxes for tax purposes?
    a) 100,000
    b) 114,000
    c) 110,000
    d) 150,000

18. What is the income statement income tax expense?
    a) 25,900
    b) 38,500
    c) 39,900
    d) 52,500

19. What is the amount of income taxes payable?
    a) 25,900
    b) 38,500
    c) 39,900
    d) 52,500

20. Calculate the deferred tax (asset or liability).
    a) asset   4,000
    b) liability 4,000
    c) asset   1,400
    d) liability 1,400

Chapter 9: Alternative Revenue Recognition and Income Tax

Short Essays

1. Jungle Jim Enterprises agreed to construct a building for Dream Limos Inc. for $5,400,500. Construction estimates for total cost per year are as follows: year 1: $1,000,500; year 2: $1,100,000; year 3: $1,200,000.

   a. What total profit does Jungle Jim anticipate from this project?

   b. What is the amount of revenue and profit that Jungle Jim will recognize in each year?

2. Rocking Robbins Child Care company had net income before taxes and adjustments of $125,000 for book purposes. Interest on municipal bonds of $32,000, and premiums paid on officers' life insurance of $50,000 are not included. Rocking Robbins is in the 40% tax bracket.

   a. What is net income before taxes?

   b. What is the current year income statement income tax?

   c. What is the current year income taxes payable?

   d. What are the journal entries to record the liability and the subsequent payment of taxes?

3. JR Construction company anticipates earning a profit of $2,000,000 on the construction of a bridge for DelValJer Company. The total costs for the project are $6,850,000 for the first two years and $2,050,000 for the last two years. Normally, the company recognizes its revenue and profit evenly over the construction period.

   a. What is the total cost of the project?

   b. What is the amount of revenue JR will recognize each year?

   c. What is the amount of profit JR will recognize each year?

   d. What are the percentages complete for each year?

Chapter 9: Alternative Revenue Recognition and Income Tax

4. Queen Limos had net income after taxes and adjustments of $132,000 for books and $90,000 for taxes. Included in book income were the proceeds from life insurance ($100,000), premiums for key man life insurance ($55,000), and municipal bond interest ($25,000). Income taxes were $88,000 according to the books.

   a. What is book net income before taxes and adjustments?

   b. What is net income for tax purposes?

   c. What is the income tax liability, if the tax rate is 40%?

   d. What is the journal entry to record the current year's tax expense and liability?

5. Harry Lu Builders had net income before taxes of $220,000 and a tax rate of 50%. The company uses the allowance method for the recognition of bad debt expense. Total write-offs during the year were $12,000. Total bad debt expense for the year was $15,000. The company depreciates on a straight-line basis for 10 years. For tax purposes, these assets are depreciated over a seven-year period. The depreciable assets cost $80,000.

   a. Calculate net income before taxes for book purposes.

   b. Calculate net income before taxes for tax purposes.

   c. Calculate income taxes for book purposes.

   d. Calculate income taxes for tax purposes.

   e. Calculate the deferred asset or liability.

   f. Make the journal entry to record the current year's tax expense and liability.

6. Wu Lee Inc. had total bad debt expense of $44,000. The company's depreciation expense for the equipment for book purposes was $15,000; for tax purposes, it was 19,000. Total write-offs for bad debts were $40,000. Net income before taxes and adjustments was $250,000. Wu Lee Inc. has a tax rate of 40%. The company uses the allowance method for the recognition of bad debt expense.

   a. What is net income before taxes?

   b. What is net income after taxes?

   c. What is the journal entry to record the current year's tax expense and liability?

7. What is the difference between permanent and temporary tax differences? Give an example of each.

Chapter 9: Alternative Revenue Recognition and Income Tax

Answers

True or False

1. True.
2. True.
3. **False.** Revenues are earned when a company has substantially completed everything it must do.
4. **False.** Companies have a choice for accounting purposes, but percentage-of-completion is preferred to smooth out income.
5. **False.** Costs incurred / Total anticipated costs.
6. **False.** Adding costs ($1,000,000 + $2,500,000 + $500,000) we get $4,000,000
   In order to make a profit of $500,000, the builder must charge $4,000,000 + $500,000 = $4,500,000.
7. **True.** The total profit is $8,000,000 - $5,000,000 = $3,000,000. The profit per year is $3,000,000 / 5 = $600,000 if earned equally over five years.
8. True.
9. True.
10. True.
11. True.
12. **False.** Income tax expense is debited and income taxes payable is credited.
13. **False.** This is an example of a permanent tax difference.
14. True.
15. **False.** Interest on municipal bonds is included in book income and excluded from taxable Income.
16. **False.** Income tax based on taxable income is recorded.
17. **False.** A deferred tax asset is recorded.
18. **False.** A deferred tax liability is recorded.
19. **False.** They are recorded separately.
20. **False.**

Deferred Tax Asset	XXXX	
Income Tax Expense	XXXX	
Deferred Tax Liability		XXX
Income Taxes Payable		XXX

Multiple Choice Answers

1. **(e)** All of the above.
2. **(d)** Revenues should be recorded in all of these instances.
3. **(b)** Percent complete equals costs incurred divided by total costs anticipated.
4. **(b)** 250 / 500 = 50%

Chapter 9: Alternative Revenue Recognition and Income Tax

5. **(b)** 1 / 5 = 20%
6. **(d)** 100 / 250 = 40%
7. **(c)** 600 - 250 = 350
8. **(b)** 600 - 500 = 100
9. **(c)** 40% x 600 = 240
10. **(b)** 20% x 600 = 120
11. **(a)** Record expense based on income statement (book) income.
12. **(a)** Income tax expense is debited & income tax payable is credited.
13. **(c)** The tax is not paid, so not b or d. Income tax liability is based on taxable income, so not a. Therefore, the correct entry is c.
14. **(e)**
15. **(b)**
16. **(c)** 150 - 40 = 110
17. **(b)** 150 - 36 = 114
18. **(b)** 110 x 35%
19. **(c)** 114 x 35%
20. **(a)** Book depreciation ($40,00) is greater than tax depreciaition ($36,000), therefore, creates asset $4,000.

Short Essay Answers

1. a.

Price to construct building	$5,400,500
Cost per year 1 1,000,500	
2 1,100,000	
3 1,200,000	
Total construction cost	3,300,500
Profit anticipated	$2,100,000

b.

	Year 1	Year 2	Year 3	Total
Percent	0.303135889	0.3332828	0.36358128	1
Revenue reconized	$1,637,085.37	1799894	1963520.68	$5,400,500.00
Profit recognized	$636,585.37	699,864	763,521	$2,100,000.00

2.

Rocking Robbins Child Care	Book	Tax
Net Income before Taxes & Adjustments	$125,000	$125,000
Municipal Bond Interest	32,000	0
Premiums on Officers' Life Insurance	-50,000	0
Net Income before Taxes	$107,000	$125,000
Taxes	42,800	50,000
Net Income after Taxes	$64,200	$75,000

Chapter 9: Alternative Revenue Recognition and Income Tax

Income Tax Expense	75,000	
Income Taxes Payable		75,000

Income Taxes Payable	75,000	
Cash		75,000

3.

Profit	2,000,000
Costs for first two years	6,850,000
Costs for last two years	2,050,000
Total cost to DelValJer	10,900,000
Cost for first two years	6,850,000
Recognized evenly	3,425,000
Cost for last two years	2,050,000
Recognized evenly	1,025,000

Profit	Year	Revenue	Costs	Percentage
769662.9	year 1	4194662.921	3,425,000	0.38483146
769662.9	year 2	4194662.921	3,425,000	0.38483146
2300337.1	year 3	1255337.079	1,025,000	0.11516854
2300337.1	year 4	1255337.079	1,025,000	0.11516854
2,000,000		10,900,000	8,900,000	1

4.

	Book	Tax
Income from Ops	$150,000	$150,000
Proceeds Life Insurance	100,000	0
Municipal Bond Interest	25,000	0
Less Key Man Insurance Premiums	-55,000	0
Income before Taxes and Adjustments	$220,000	$150,000
Tax rate 40%		
Income Tax	88,000	60,000
Income after Taxes and Adjustments	$132,000	$90,000

To record the liability

Income Tax Expense	$60,000	
Income Taxes Payable		$60,000

To pay the taxes

Income Taxes Payable	$60,000	
Cash		$60,000

Chapter 9: Alternative Revenue Recognition and Income Tax

5.

	Book	Tax	Asset	Liability
Net Income before adjustments and taxes	220,000	220,000		
Bad Debt Expense	-15,000	-12,000	3,000	
Depreciation Expense	-8,000	-11,440		3,440
Net Income before Taxes	197,000	196,560		
Tax rate 50%			(1,500)	(1,720)
Taxes	98,500	98,280		
Net Income after Taxes	98,500	98,280	1,500	1,720

Deferred Tax Asset	1,500	
Income Tax Expense	98,500	
Income Taxes Payable		98,280
Deferred Tax Liability		1,720

6.

	Book	Tax	Asset	Liability
Net Income before adjustments and taxes	250,000	250,000		
Bad Debt Expense	-44,000	-40,000	4,000	0
Depreciation Expense	-15,000	-19,000	0	4,000
Net Income before Taxes	191,000	191,000		
Taxes @ $0%	76,400	76,400	(1,600)	(1,600)
Net Income after Taxes	114,600	114,600	2,400	2,400

Deferred Tax Asset	2,400	
Income Tax Expense	76,400	
Income Taxes Payable		76,400
Deferred Tax Liability		2,400

7. Permanent tax differences arise when book income includes revenues or expenses that are never included in taxable income like interest earned on municipal bonds. Temporary tax differences arise when book income includes revenue and expense items in one accounting period that will become a part of taxable income in another accounting period. An example would be different methods of calculating depreciation for book and tax purposes.

Chapter

The Statement of Cash Flows

10

Chapter 10: The Statement of Cash Flows

Overview

The **statement of cash flows** reconciles the Cash account and presents a detailed picutre of the inflows and outflows of cash during a period. This documentation makes the statement of cash flows a valuable tool for anyone interested in analyzing a company's liquidity, solvency, or financial flexibility. The statement of cash flows is divided according to three different types of activity:

- cash flows from operating activities
- cash flows from investing activities
- cash flows from financing activities

The statement of cash flows is particularly complex because it integrates all three of the other financial statements we have covered:

- Net income from the income statement is shown in cash flows from operating activities.
- Dividends from the statement of retained earnings is shown in cash flows from financing activities.
- Investments, accounts payable, and other asset and liability accounts from the balance sheet are shown in all three sections.

Now that you understand the various balance sheet and income statement accounts, we are ready to integrate what you have learned and prepare a statement of cash flows. By the end of this chapter, you should be able to understand the components and prepare each section of the statement of cash flows. Remember: examinations in accounting frequently ask you to prepare a statement of cash flows, so be sure to work through this chapter carefully.

Chapter 10: The Statement of Cash Flows

Concepts

Cash flows from operating activities

Cash flows from operating activities include the cash effects of transactions involved in the determination of net income. To record cash flows from operating activities, follow these four steps:

Step 1: Start with net income.

The income statement presents the net income from the operations of a company. Therefore, the net income provides the starting point for describing how much cash is flowing into (or out of) a company.

Step 2: Add back depreciation and amortization.

All items presented in the income statement are not cash transactions. The most common non-cash expenses are the depreciation and amortization expenses on long-term assets (or liabilities in the case of leases and bonds) and bad debt expenses on accounts receivable. These non-cash expenses are recognized in the income statement over the life of the related assets, although the actual cash outlay occurs at the time of purchase. To arrive at an accurate statement of cash flows from operating activities, we must add back to income any non-cash expenses, including those related to depreciation and amortization.

Step 3: Adjust for the effects of gains and losses.

As you will see in our comprehensive example, the gains or losses on marketable securities, sales of equipment, and even the retirement of debt are reflected in the actual cash paid out or received. Therefore, the gains or losses that are recorded in the income statement are considered non-cash revenues; gains and losses must be subtracted or added back, respectively, to the net income.

Step 4: Make balance sheet adjustments.

The final step in arriving at cash flows from operating activities is to make adjustments to net income for the increases and decreases in current assets and current liabilities from the

Chapter 10: The Statement of Cash Flows

prior period. The adjustments are made based on the type of balance sheet account and the direction of the change. We'll now examine these adjustments.

Decrease cash for any increases in current asset accounts, including accounts receivable, inventory, and prepaid assets. The reason for this adjustment is that as assets increase, cash expenditures are being made that are not reflected in the income statement. For example, suppose that you purchase $10,000 of goods for resale in Year 1. These goods would not be reflected on the income statement, but would be recorded in the inventory as follows:

Inventory	10,000	
Cash		10,000

As the journal entry shows, there is still a cash expenditure. Therefore, the purchase must be subtracted from net income to adjust for a cash expenditure not already included in net income. For accounts receivable, the logic for the adjustment is slightly different. An increase in accounts receivable means that more sales were made during the period than cash was received. Therefore, more revenue is reflected in the income statement than actual cash inflows. As a result, net income must be adjusted to account for revenue recognized for which no cash was actually received.

Increase cash for any decrease in current asset accounts. The reason for this adjustment is that as assets decrease, less cash expenditures are being made than are reflected in the income statement. Using our inventory example from above, suppose that you actually sold the inventory in Year 2. You would record the following entry:

Cost of Goods Sold	10,000	
Inventory		10,000

Here, no cash expenditure was made. However, there is still $10,000 of expenses included in net income. Therefore, net income must be adjusted for an expense incurred for which no cash was paid out. On the revenue side, if accounts receivable decreases, then more cash was received than sales were made. This is because customers who made purchases on account in prior periods are making cash payments in the current period. As a result, the net income must be adjusted according to the amount of cash received for which revenue was recognized in prior periods.

Increase cash for any increases in current liability accounts, including accounts payable, wages payable, and other accrued expenses. The reason for this adjustment is that as your obligations increase, you have more cash to spend than is reflected in your income statement. For example, suppose that you purchase $5,000 in supplies on account in Year 1.

Chapter 10: The Statement of Cash Flows

You would record this $5,000 as an expense in your income statement:

| Supplies Expense | 5,000 | |
| Accounts Payable | | 5,000 |

In this transaction, no cash was paid out. However, the net income has been reduced by $5,000 to recognize the expense. To present cash flows from operating activities in Year 1, the increase in the liability of $5,000 must be added back into the net income to adjust for an expense incurred for which no cash was paid out.

Decrease cash for a decrease in current liability accounts. The reason for this adjustment is that as your obligations decrease, you have spent more cash than is reflected in your income statement. Using the example above for supplies purchased on account, suppose that in Year 2 you pay the supplier the $5,000. This transaction decreases your accounts payable as shown on the following entry.

| Accounts Payable | 5,000 | |
| Cash | | 5,000 |

In this transaction, the cash is paid out. However, the cash expenditure is not reflected in net income, because the expense was recognized in the prior period. To present cash flows from operating activities in Year 2, the decrease in the liability of $5,000 must be subtracted from net income to adjust for a cash outlay not already included in net income.

You can apply this four-step process to problems that provide you with both the balance sheet and the income statement. However, as you will see in the comprehensive example later in this chapter, exam problems may present transactions in the form of "additional information" — which will require you to modify your approach.

Cash flows from investing activities

Cash flows from investing activities includes the cash effects of transactions involving non-current assets on the balance sheet. The most common of these transactions are the purchases and sales of equipment, and available-for-sale and held-to-maturity marketable securities. These transactions are recorded in the statement of cash flows for the amount of the actual cash received or paid. Net income is adjusted in the operating section for these transactions only to the extent that there are gains, losses, discounts, or premiums. As the comprehensive example will illustrate, these items (gains, losses, discounts or premiums) have already been included in the actual cash received or paid.

Chapter 10: The Statement of Cash Flows

Cash flows from financing activities

Cash flows from financing activities includes the cash effects of transactions involving non-current liabilities and equity accounts. The most common transactions include the issuance of debt or equity, the repayment of debt, and the payment of dividends. These transactions are recorded in the statement of cash flows at the actual cash received. In a similar way to its adjustment with to the cash flows from investing activities, net income is adjusted in the operating section for these transactions only to the extent that there are gains, losses, discounts, or premiums. As the example will illustrate, these items are already reflected in the cash received or paid.

Preparing a statement of cash flows: A comprehensive example

The four steps that we have described for determining the cash flows from operating activities provide a general approach for preparing the operating section of a statement of cash flows and is useful if all the information you need to prepare the statement is given to you. However, problem sets and exam questions are usually not that straightforward. The gains and losses are instead frequently embedded within other questions. Furthermore, if you are not provided with an income statement, the amount of depreciation and amortization is not always readily apparent.

By combining the journal entry approach with a T-account summary, the most complex cash flow transactions can be simplified. T-accounts provide a simple way of summarizing the effects of the changes in the various balance sheet accounts on the statement of cash flows. Using the information on the next page for Just Toys Manufacturing, Inc., we will prepare a statement of cash flows for the year ending December 31, 1999.

Chapter 10: The Statement of Cash Flows

JUST TOYS MANUFACTURING COMPANY
Balance Sheet
As of December 31, 1998 and December 31, 1999

Assets	12/31/98	12/31/99	Liabilities & Shareholders' Equity	12/31/98	12/31/99
Current Assets			**Current Liabilities**		
Cash	14,000	19,000	Accounts Payable	27,000	45,000
Marketable Securities	10,000	0	Wages Payable	6,000	13,000
Accounts Receivable	50,000	30,000	Total Current Liabilities	33,000	58,000
Less: Allowance for Uncollectibles	(14,000)	(12,000)			
Inventory	11,000	35,000	**Non-Current Liabilities**		
Prepaid Insurance	6,000	3,000	Capital Lease Obligation		
Total Current Assets	77,000	75,000	Bonds Payable	100,000	50,000
			Discount on Bonds Payable	(8,000)	(7,000)
Non-Current Assets					
Long-Term Investments	20,000	140,000	Total Liabilities	125,000	101,000
Land	100,000	100,000	**Shareholders' Equity**		
Machinery & Equipment	300,000	276,000	Common Stock	100,000	125,000
Less: Accumulated Depreciation	(75,000)	(105,000)	Additional Paid-In Capital	121,000	141,000
Patent	22,000	11,000	Retained Earnings	98,000	130,000
Total Non-Current Assets	367,000	422,000	Total Shareholders' Equity	319,000	396,000
Total Assets	440,000	497,000	**Total Liabilities & Stockholders Equity**	444,000	497,000

Additional Information:

1. Net income for the year was $52,000.
2. Dividends totaling $20,000 were declared and paid.
3. Equipment having a net book value of $13,000 was sold during the year for $17,000. No other purchases or sales were made.
4. Bad debt expense for the year was $3,000.
5. Marketable securities were purchased during the year for trading purposes. The balance in the account was sold on 12/15/99 for $8,000.
6. Twenty-five thousand shares of common stock with a par value of $1 were issued at a market value of $45,000.

Step 1: Prepare an expanded cash T-account and T-accounts for all balance sheet accounts.

The statement of cash flows is a detailed reconciliation of the changes in the cash account. Therefore, the first step in preparing the statement is to set up a T-account showing the beginning balance in cash and to divide it into three sections, as the example on the next page shows. As we reconcile the changes in all of the other balance sheet accounts, we will make the appropriate adjustments to the cash account.

CHAPTER 10: THE STATEMENT OF CASH FLOWS

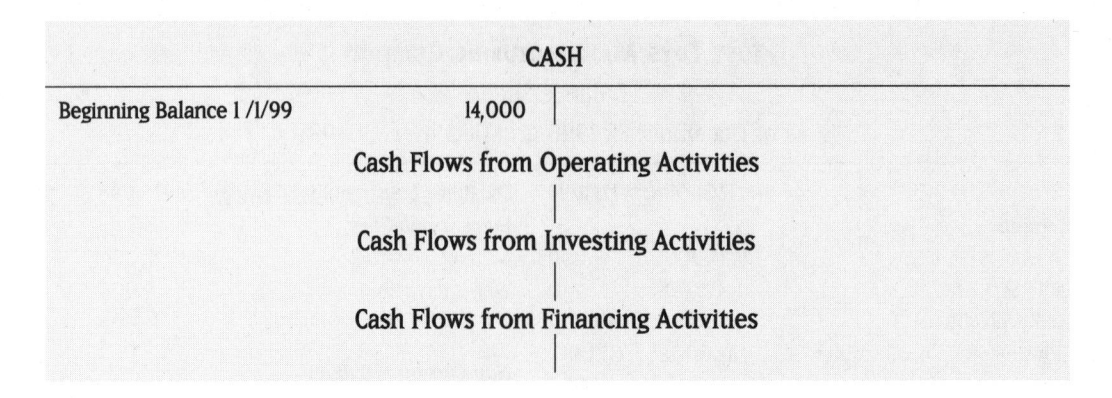

```
                         CASH
Beginning Balance 1/1/99      14,000
                Cash Flows from Operating Activities
                            |
                Cash Flows from Investing Activities
                            |
                Cash Flows from Financing Activities
                            |
```

After the Cash T-account is set up, prepare T-accounts for all balance sheet accounts that changed for the year by entering the beginning and ending balances similar to the posting process in Chapter 3. The objective of setting up the individual T-accounts is to reconcile the changes in the account with their effects on cash. Preparing the T-accounts prior to beginning a problem such as this is the most efficient way of ensuring that all balance sheet accounts that changed during the year have been reconciled. However, with this example, instead of presenting them in advance, we will set up the T-accounts as we address each account.

STEP 2: ADDRESS THE ADDITIONAL INFORMATION.

The additional information (separate from the main body of the balance sheet) usually presents the most complex transactions affecting the preparation of the statement of cash flows. After addressing the most difficult transactions, the remaining items can normally be reconciled by making balance sheet adjustments. Let's adjust our cash balance for the six items of additional information provided in our example.

1. **Net income for the year is $52,000.** The first step in determining the cash flows from operating activities is to record the net income for the year. Recall that net income represents an increase in a company's retained earnings for the year. Therefore, to record net income, retained earnings will be increased on the credit side. To balance the entry, cash flows from operating activities will be increased on the debit side. Based on this information, net income for the year would is posted to T-accounts as shown below.

CASH FLOWS FROM OPERATING ACTIVITES		RETAINED EARNINGS	
		98,000	Beg Bal
52,000		52,000	
		130,000	Ending Bal

2. **Dividends totaling $20,000 were declared and paid.** Note that by posting the net income of $52,000 to the retained earnings account, the change in the account is not fully

Chapter 10: The Statement of Cash Flows

explained ($98,000 + $52,000 = $150,000). An additional $20,000 debit adjustment is necessary to bring the account in line with the figure of $130,000 on the balance sheet. The second item of additional information states that dividends totaling $20,000 were declared and paid during the year. To record the dividends declared and paid, retained earnings is debited for $20,000. To balance the entry, cash flows from financing activities is credited for $20,000.

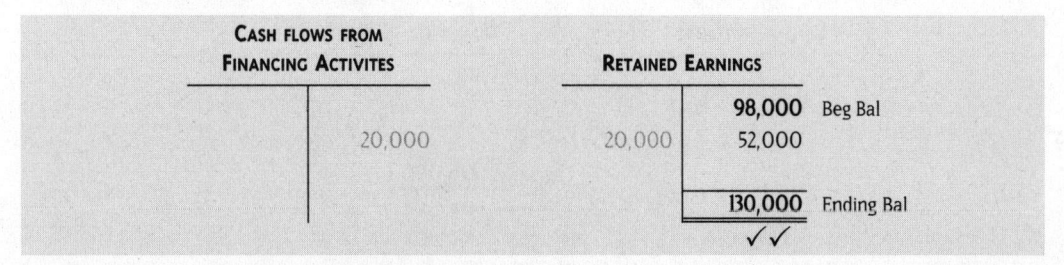

Cash Flows from Financing Activites		Retained Earnings	
	20,000	20,000	98,000 Beg Bal
			52,000
			130,000 Ending Bal ✓✓

Note that the retained earnings account now reconciles, meaning that the cash effects of the change in this account has been fully reflected in the statement of cash flows. A good method to indicate that the completion of the reconciliation of an account is to draw a double underline under the ending balance and/or two checkmarks.

3. **Equipment having a net book value of $13,000 was sold during the year for $17,000. No other purchases or sales were made.** This transaction is tricky because it affects three accounts: Machinery & Equipment, Accumulated Depreciation, and Cash (both operating and investing). If no additional purchases or sales were made, then the total decrease in Machinery & Equipment of $24,000 ($300,000 - $276,000) must be related to this sale. If the original cost of the equipment was $24,000 and the net book value was $13,000, then the accumulated depreciation at the time of sale must have been $11,000. Finally, if the net book value is $13,000 and the total cash received is $17,000, then Just Toys must have realized a gain on the sale of $4,000. Let's record the journal entry for this transaction to get a clearer picture of what happened.

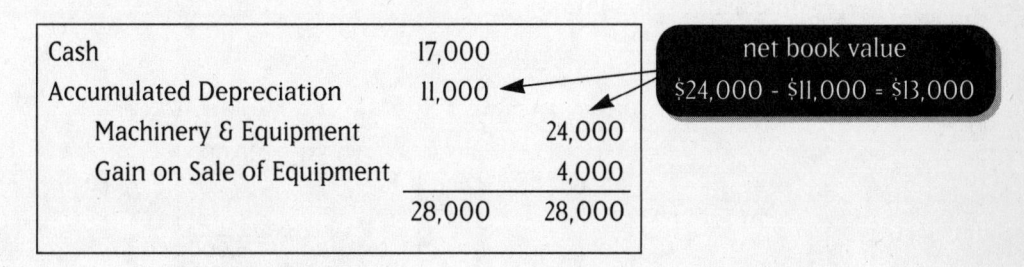

Cash	17,000	
Accumulated Depreciation	11,000	
Machinery & Equipment		24,000
Gain on Sale of Equipment		4,000
	28,000	28,000

net book value $24,000 - $11,000 = $13,000

The journal entry shows that the total effect of this transaction on cash flows is $17,000. This amount will be recorded directly in Cash Flows from Investing Activities. However, at the time of the transaction, a gain of $4,000 was recorded in the income statement. Since the cash has already been recorded in the investing section, this $4,000 must be

Chapter 10: The Statement of Cash Flows

deducted from net income in the operating section. (Note: If the sale had been at a loss and not a gain, the $4,000 would be added back to net income in the operating section.) To record the cash affects of this transaction in the two sections of the statement of cash flows, we reconcile the T-accounts affected in this transaction by posting the journal entries in the following manner:

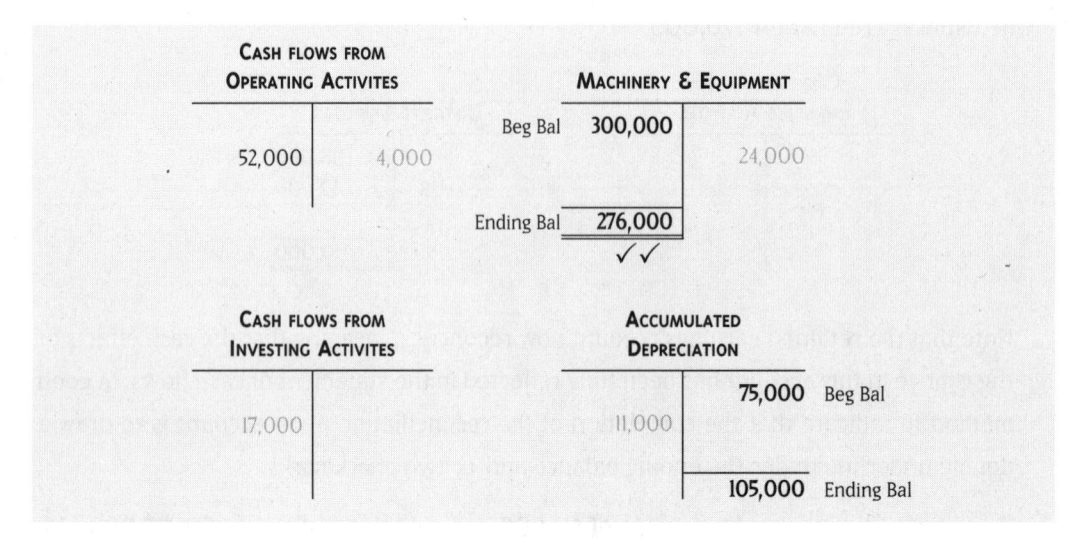

CASH FLOWS FROM OPERATING ACTIVITES		MACHINERY & EQUIPMENT	
		Beg Bal 300,000	
52,000	4,000		24,000
		Ending Bal 276,000 ✓✓	

CASH FLOWS FROM INVESTING ACTIVITES		ACCUMULATED DEPRECIATION	
			75,000 Beg Bal
17,000		11,000	
			105,000 Ending Bal

You should notice two things about the posting of this transaction. First, total debits ($17,000 + $11,000) equal total credits ($24,000 + $4,000). Second, the change in the Machinery & Equipment Account is fully explained. However, the Accumulated Depreciation account has not been completely reconciled. As we discussed in Chapter 6, the yearly depreciation expense increases the Accumulated Depreciation account. Since there were no additional equipment purchases and sales made during the year, then the $41,000 additional credit adjustment required in the Accumulated Depreciation account ($75,000 - $11,000 + X = $105,000) must be the depreciation expense for the year. We must add the depreciation expense back into net income in the operating section of the statement of cash flows:

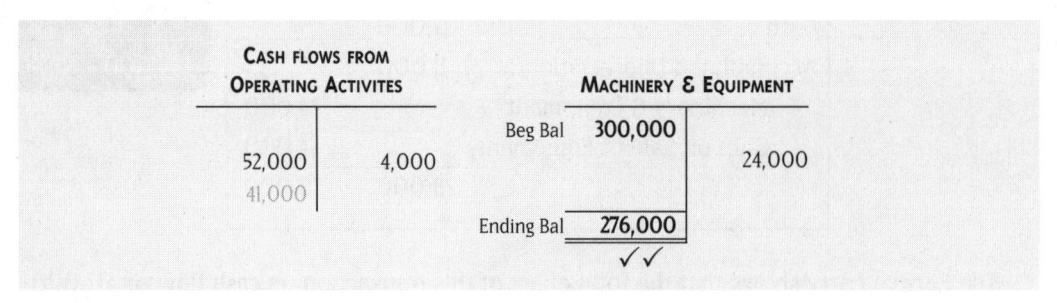

CASH FLOWS FROM OPERATING ACTIVITES		MACHINERY & EQUIPMENT	
		Beg Bal 300,000	
52,000	4,000		24,000
41,000			
		Ending Bal 276,000 ✓✓	

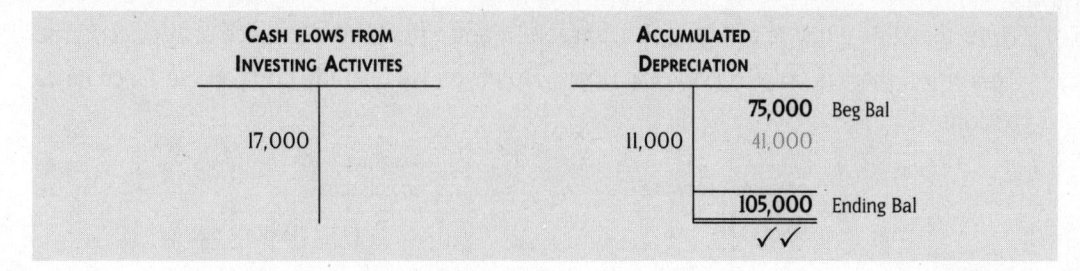

Chapter 10: The Statement of Cash Flows

CASH FLOWS FROM INVESTING ACTIVITES		ACCUMULATED DEPRECIATION	
			75,000 Beg Bal
17,000		11,000	41,000
			105,000 Ending Bal
			✓✓

BROWNIE POINTS

Sometimes depreciation expense will be given to you in a problem, and it is not necessary to deduce its amount in this manner. However, never assume that the net change in accumulated depreciation is only related to the depreciation expense of the current year. If depreciation expense is not given to you, always remember to check for sales made during the year and any related accumulated depreciation on the assets sold, as they will also affect the change in the account.

4. **Bad debt expense for the year was $3,000.** Bad debt expense is another type of non-cash expense recorded in the income statement; it is treated in the same manner as depreciation expense for cash flow purposes. You should recall from Chapter 4 that the allowance for uncollectibles account is increased by the total bad debt expense recognized for the year and decreased by any write-offs taken during the year. Therefore, to record bad debt expense, the allowance for uncollectibles account is increased on the credit side by $3,000. To balance the entry, bad debt expense is added back into the net income by debiting cash flows from operating activities:

CASH FLOWS FROM OPERATING ACTIVITES		ALLOWANCE FOR UNCOLLECTIBLES	
			14,000 Beg Bal
52,000	4,000		3,000
41,000			
3,000			12,000 Ending Bal

DIFFICULT TERRAIN

Posting the bad debt expense does not completely reconcile the allowance for uncollectibles account. Although the problem does not specifically state the reason, we can assume that the required debit adjustment relates to accounts written off during the year (in this case, in the amount of $5,000). We make the following journal entry to write off the accounts:

Accounts for Uncollectibles	5,000	
Accounts Receivable		5,000

Chapter 10: The Statement of Cash Flows

Note that this entry is a non-cash transaction and affects two balance sheet accounts. Therefore, there is no effect on cash flows. However, we post the entry to the T-accounts as follows:

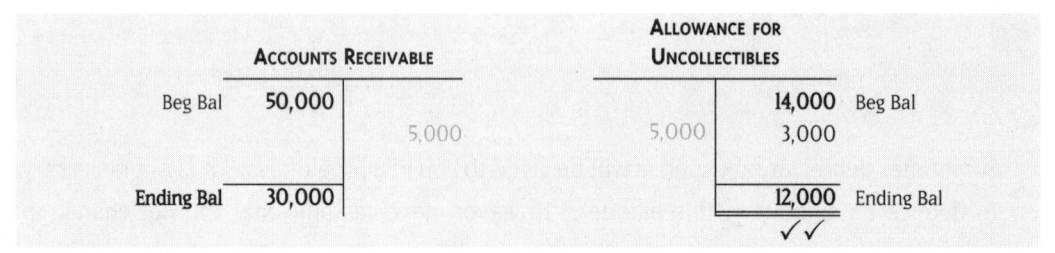

Accounts Receivable		Allowance for Uncollectibles	
Beg Bal 50,000			14,000 Beg Bal
	5,000	5,000	3,000
Ending Bal 30,000			12,000 Ending Bal

Making this entry is necessary to determine that the remaining decrease in accounts receivable is $15,000. In making balance sheet adjustments, cash from operating activities is increased for any dereases in current asset accounts. Since accounts receivable is a current asset account, we make the following entry to record the effects of the change in accounts receivable on cash flows from operating activities:

Cash Flows from Operating Activites		Accounts Receivable	
		Beg Bal 50,000	
52,000	4,000		5,000
41,000			15,000
3,000		Ending Bal 30,000	
15,000			

5. **Marketable securities were purchased as available-for-sale securities. The balance in the account at the beginning of the year was sold on 12/15/99 for $8,000.** The entry to record the sale of marketable securities on 12/15/99 is:

Cash	8,000	
Realized Loss on Available-For-Sale Securities	2,000	
Marketable Securities		10,000

As the journal entry shows, the total effect of this transaction on cash flows is $8,000. We record this amount directly in Cash Flows from Investing Activities. However, at the time of the transaction, a loss of $2,000 was recorded in the income statement. Since the cash has already been recorded in the investing section, this $2,000 must be added back into net income in the operating section. To record the cash affects of this transaction in the two sections of the statement of cash flows, we reconcile the T-accounts affected in this transaction in the following manner:

CHAPTER 10: THE STATEMENT OF CASH FLOWS

CASH FLOWS FROM OPERATING ACTIVITES		MARKETABLE SECURITIES
	Beg Bal	10,000
52,000 4,000		10,000
41,000		
3,000	Ending Bal	0
15,000		✓✓
2,000		

CASH FLOWS FROM
INVESTING ACTIVITES

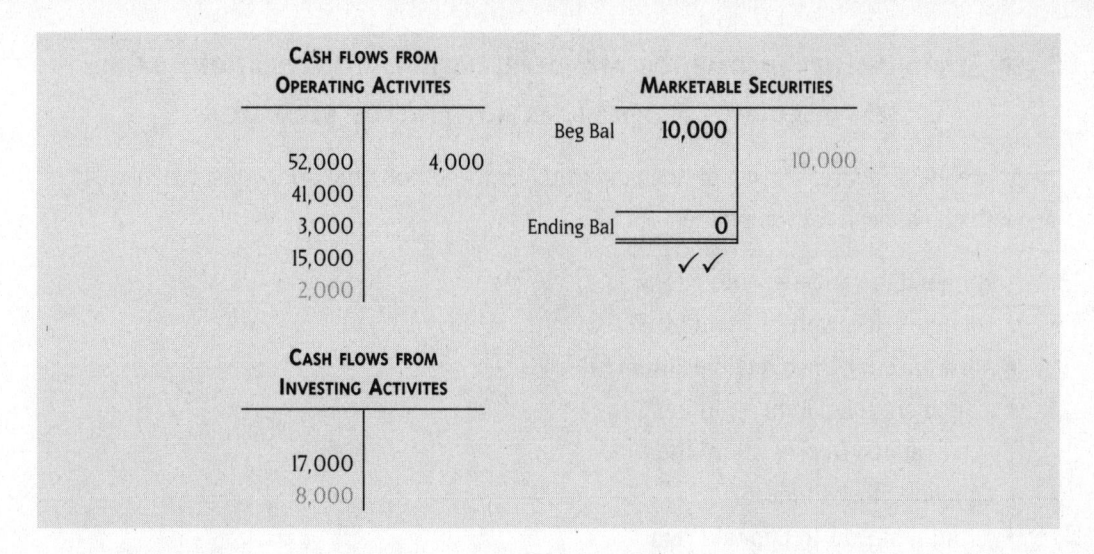

17,000
8,000

Note that after this transaction is posted, total debits ($8,000 + $2,000) equal total credits ($10,000). You should also note that the change in the marketable securities account is fully explained.

6. **25,000 shares of $1 par value common stock were issued at a market value of $45,000.**
   The issuance of stock represents a financing activity and will, therefore, be reflected in the financing section of the statement of cash flows. We record the following entry at the time the stock is issued:

Cash	45,000	(market value)
Common Stock	25,000	(par value)
Additional Paid – In Capital	20,000	(excess market over par)

   The journal entry shows that the total effect of this transaction on cash flows is $45,000. We record this amount directly in cash flows from financing activities:

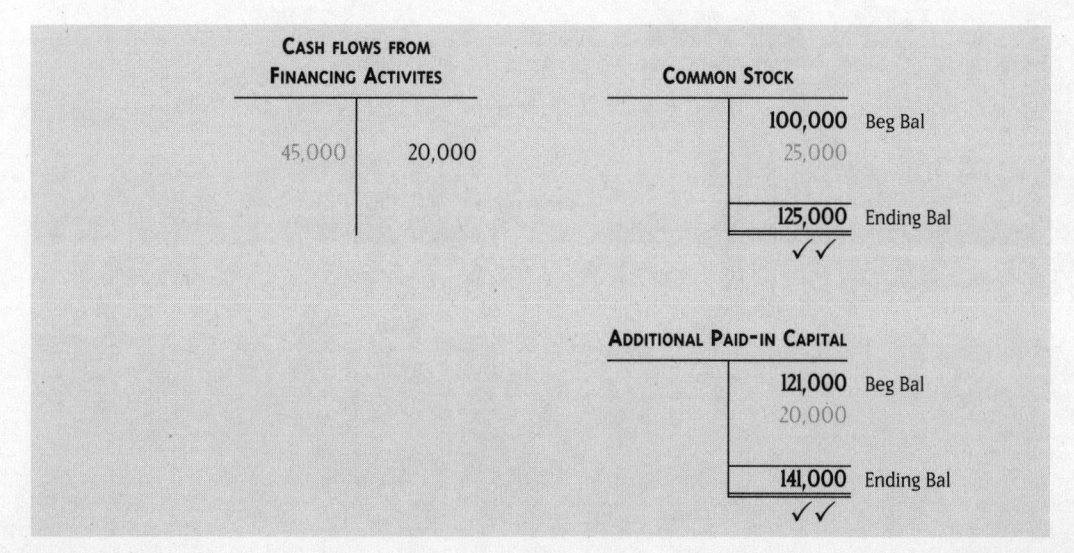

CASH FLOWS FROM FINANCING ACTIVITES		COMMON STOCK	
		100,000	Beg Bal
45,000 20,000		25,000	
		125,000	Ending Bal
		✓✓	

   ADDITIONAL PAID-IN CAPITAL

	121,000	Beg Bal
	20,000	
	141,000	Ending Bal
	✓✓	

CHAPTER 10: THE STATEMENT OF CASH FLOWS

STEP 3: ADJUST NET INCOME FOR ANY DEPRECIATION, AMORTIZATION, GAINS, LOSSES, DISCOUNTS OR PREMIUMS NOT ALREADY RECORDED.

After we have addressed all of the additional information, the following balance sheet accounts have been fully explained:

- Marketable Securities (item #5)
- Accounts Receivable (item #4)
- Allowance for Uncollectibles (item #4)
- Machinery & Equipment (item #3)
- Accumulated Depreciation (item #3)
- Common Stock (item #6)
- Additional Paid-In Capital (item #6)
- Retained Earnings (items #1 and #2)

Our next step is to examine the comparative balance sheet for any additional income statement adjustments that we must make to net income:

The patent account decreased, indicating amortization for the year of $11,000 for this intangible asset.

You should recall from Chapter 8 that total interest expense recognized differs from the actual cash paid out by the amount of discount or premium amortized during the period. Therefore, the decrease in the bond discount account represents amortization for the year of $1,000 and is the excess of interest expense recognized above the interest actually paid out.

We will make these non-cash adjustments to net income so that they are reflected in the operating section of the statement of cash flows:

CASH FLOWS FROM OPERATING ACTIVITES			PATENT	
52,000	4,000	Beg Bal	22,000	
41,000				11,000
3,000		Ending Bal	11,000	
15,000			✓✓	
2,000				
11,000				
1,000			BOND DISCOUNT	
		Beg Bal	8,000	
				1,000
		Ending Bal	7,000	
			✓✓	

Chapter 10: The Statement of Cash Flows

Step 4: Make any remaining balance sheet adjustments for current asset and liability accounts.

After we have made all the income statement adjustments, the final step toward the completion of the calculation of cash flows from operating activities is to make any remaining balance sheet adjustments for changes in current asset and current liability accounts. In this case, the remaining unreconciled current asset and current liability accounts are inventory, prepaid insurance, accounts payable, and wages payable. The operating section of the statement of cash flows should be adjusted to account for the changes in these accounts as shown below.

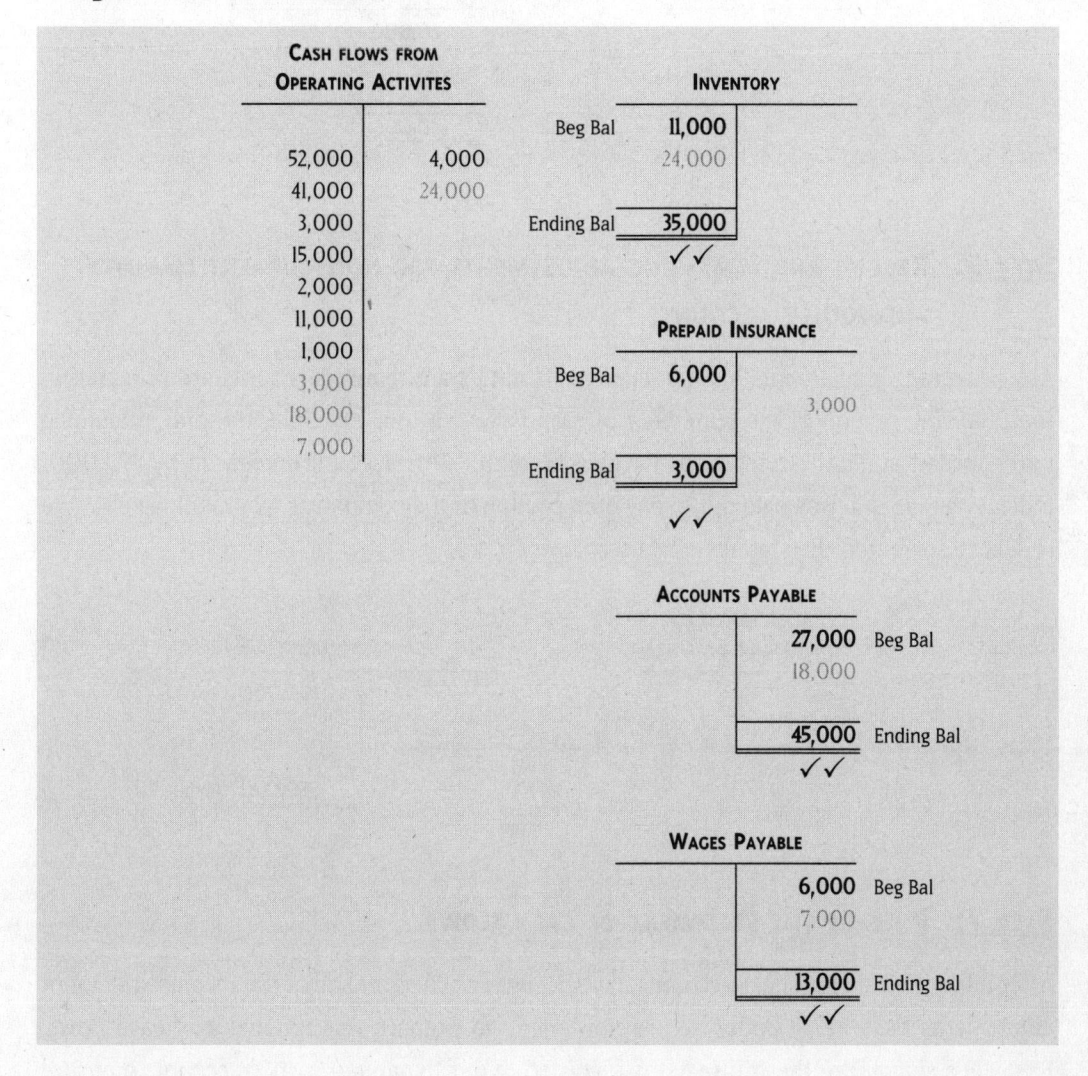

Cash Flows from Operating Activites		Inventory	
52,000	4,000	Beg Bal	11,000
41,000	24,000		24,000
3,000		Ending Bal	35,000
15,000			✓✓
2,000			
11,000		**Prepaid Insurance**	
1,000		Beg Bal	6,000
3,000			3,000
18,000			
7,000		Ending Bal	3,000
			✓✓

Accounts Payable

	27,000	Beg Bal
	18,000	
	45,000	Ending Bal
	✓✓	

Wages Payable

	6,000	Beg Bal
	7,000	
	13,000	Ending Bal
	✓✓	

Chapter 10: The Statement of Cash Flows

Step 5: Record any remaining adjustments for non-current asset accounts.

Any remaining adjustments for non-current assets are reflected in the investing section of the statement of cash flows. For Just Toys Manufacturing, the only remaining unreconciled account is the Long-Term Investments account. This account increased by $120,000, indicating that investments were purchased for cash during the year. We would reflect this event in the statement of cash flows as follows:

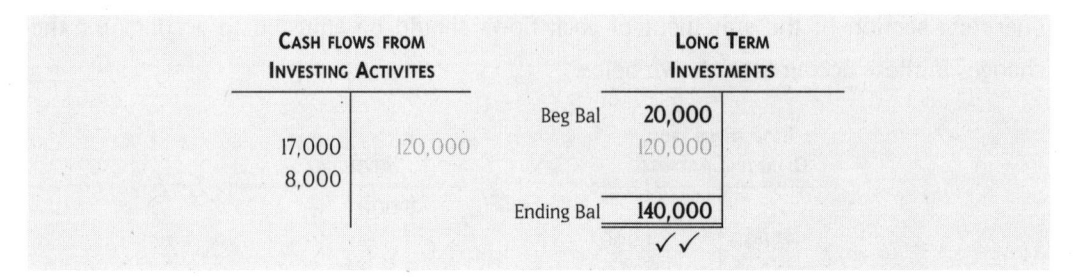

Cash Flows from Investing Activites		Long Term Investments	
		Beg Bal	20,000
17,000	120,000	120,000	
8,000			
		Ending Bal	140,000 ✓✓

Step 6: Record any remaining adjustments for non-current liability and equity accounts

Any remaining adjustments for non-current liabilities and equity accounts are reflected in the financing section of the statement of cash flows. In our example, the only remaining unreconciled account is the Bonds Payable account. This account decreased by $50,000, indicating that cash was paid out to pay off a portion of the company's outstanding debt. We reflect this event in the statement of cash flows:

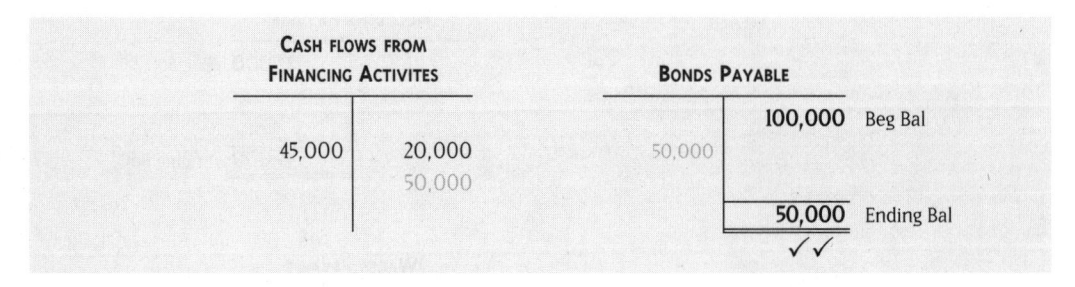

Cash Flows from Financing Activites		Bonds Payable	
			100,000 Beg Bal
45,000	20,000	50,000	
	50,000		
			50,000 Ending Bal ✓✓

Step 7: Prepare the statement of cash flows.

After all of the balance sheet accounts have been reconciled and all of the income statement adjustments have been made, we are now ready to prepare the statement of cash flows. First, let's summarize the transactions recorded in our expanded cash T-account to ensure that the account reconciles to the ending balance of $19,000:

CHAPTER 10: THE STATEMENT OF CASH FLOWS

CASH

Beginning Balance 1/1/99	14,000		

Cash Flows from Operating Activities

Net Income	52,000	4,000	Gain on sale of equipment
Depreciation expense	41,000	24,000	Increase in inventory
Bad debt expense	3,000		
Decrease in Accounts Receivable	15,000		
Loss on sale of Market Securities	2,000		
Amortization expense	11,000		
Decrease in Bond Discount	1,000		
Decrease in Prepaid Insurance	3,000		
Increase in Accounts Payable	18,000		
Increase in Wages Payable	7,000		
Total	125,000		

Cash Flows from Investing Activities

Sale of Equipment	17,000	120,000	Purchase of Long-Term Investments
Sale of Marketable Securities	8,000		
Total	(95,000)		

Cash Flows from Financing Activities

Issuance of common stock	45,000	20,000	Declaration and payment of dividends
		50,000	Repayment of bonds payable
Total	(25,000)		
Total change in cash	5,000		
Ending balance 12/31/99	19,000		

Using this T-account summary, we are ready to present the statement of cash flows for Just Toys Manufacturing, Inc.:

Chapter 10: The Statement of Cash Flows

Just Toys Manufacturing, Inc.
Statement of Cash Flows
For the year ended December 31, 1999

Operations	
Net Income	52,000
Add: Depreciation expense	41,000
Bad debt expense	3,000
Amortization expense	11,000
Gain on Sale of Equipment	(4,000)
Loss on sale of Market Securities	2,000
Decrease in Bond Discount	1,000
Decrease in Accounts Receivable	15,000
Increase in Inventory	(24,000)
Decrease in Prepaid Insurance	3,000
Increase in Accounts Payable	18,000
Increase in Wages Payable	7,000
Cash Flow from Operating Activities	125,000
Investing	
Purchase of Long-Term Investments	(120,000)
Sale of Equipment	17,000
Sale of Marketable Securities	8,000
Cash Flow from Investing Activities	(95,000)
Financing	
Issuance of Common Stock	45,000
Declaration and Payment of Dividends	(20,000)
Repayment of Bonds Payable	(50,000)
Cash Flow frrom Financing Activities	(25,000)
Net change in cash	5,000
Cash, beginning of year	14,000
Cash, end of year	19,000

Chapter 10: The Statement of Cash Flows

Key Terms

cash flows from financing activities: the cash effects of transactions involving non-current liabilities and equity accounts. The most common transactions include the issuance of debt or equity, the repayment of debt, and the payment of dividends.

cash flows from investing activities: the cash effects of transactions involving non-current assets on the balance sheet. The most common transactions include the purchase and sales of equipment, as well as available for sale and held-to-maturity marketable securities.

cash flows from operating activities: the cash effects of transactions and other events involved in the determination of net income.

statement of cash flows: a detailed summary of all of the cash inflows and outflows during a period.

Chapter 10: The Statement of Cash Flows

Thrills, Chills and Drills

True or False

1. Net income from the income statement is shown in cash flows from financing activities.

2. Depreciation and amortization are added back to cash flows.

3. Gains are added to cash flows.

4. The sale of an asset is recorded under income from operating activities only.

5. In order to record the sale of marketable securities, two separate entries must be made to two separate sections of the cash flows statement.

6. The issuance of common stock is a financing activity.

7. The decrease in bond discount will decrease the cash flows.

8. Company X had Sales on Credit of $457,000. They collected $470,000. The amount that will be put on the Statement of Cash Flows is $13,000.

9. Company Y had paid Interest of $48,000 with an Interest Expense of $42,000. The amount recorded in the Statement of Cash Flows under Financing Activities will be $48,000.

10. Jones, Inc prepaid Insurance for 12 months in December 1997. The cost was $6,500. The amount that should be added back to the Statement of Cash Flows for January 1998 is $500.

11. The statement of cash flows gives the financial user a picture of the company's liquidity.

12. The statement of cash flows uses only the information in the balance sheet and income statement.

13. The change in the Inventory account for Slim Pickings, Inc was an increase of $117,000. The Cost of Goods Sold was $223,000. The adjustment to Income in the Statement of Cash Flows is $117,000.

14. A statement of cash flows for a company shows the following.

Net Income	66,790
Net Cash from Operating Activities	4,710
Net Cash from Financing Activities	-46,000
Cash balance December 31, 1995	20,600

This shows that the company's Cash had a net decrease.

Chapter 10: The Statement of Cash Flows

15. All items on the income statement are cash items.

16. If the accounts receivable account increases, that means that there were less sales on credit than cash collected from clients.

17. The increase in liabilities is deducted from the statement of cash flows because it is a non-cash increase.

18. The income from operating activities includes the increase in the equipment account.

19. When Hopeful, Inc. sold Common Stock to help the company raise much needed funds, the bookkeeper correctly posted the amount to the Statement of Cash Flows from Investing Activities.

20. Bad debt expense causes an increase in the statement of cash flows from operating activities.

Multiple Choice

1. The statement of cash flows would report an increase in accounts receivable in which of the following manners?
    a) an addition to net income under cash flows from operating activities
    b) an addition to net income under cash flows from investing activities
    c) a subtraction from net income under cash flows from operating activities
    d) a subtraction from net income under cash flows from investing activities

2. The Duchess of Albert, Inc had Depreciation and Amortization expenses of $20,000 and $15,000 respectively. Which fact is correct concerning these two items?
    a) they increase the Cash Flow by $35,000
    b) they decrease the Cash Flow by $35,000
    c) they have an effect on the cash flow if assets are increased
    d) they have no effect on the cash flow

3. On January 1, 1998 Dupme, Inc prepaid $36,000 of rent for the 12 months ending December 31, 1998. For the month of January 1998, the bookkeeper correctly recorded this as
    a. Rent Expense $36,000 / Cash Outflow ($36,000)
    b. Rent Expense $3,000 / Cash Outflow ($36,000)
    c. Rent Expense $36,000 / Cash Outflow ($36,000)
    d. none of the above

Chapter 10: The Statement of Cash Flows

4. Operating activities are reflected in the company's balance sheet in
   a) current assets and liabilities
   b) income from operations
   c) a and b
   d) none of the above

5. Financing activities are reflected in the company's
   a) balance sheet
   b) income statement
   c) statement of stockholders' equity
   d) all of the above
   e) none of the above

6. Susie Homemaker, Inc. had Sales Revenues of $112,000 and an increase in Accounts Receivable of $ 12,000. What is the adjustment to Net Income in computing Cash Flows from Operating Activities?
   a) Cash Collected from Customers $112,000
   b) Cash Collected from Customers $100,000
   c) Cash Collected from Customers $ 12,000
   d) none of the above

7. In January 1998, Spellberg, Inc. had Cost of Goods Sold of $10,000, an increase in Inventory of $5,000, and a decrease in Accounts Payable of $ 2,000. What is the company's adjustment to net income in computing cash flows from operating activities?
   a) cash paid to suppliers ($17,000)
   b) cash paid to suppliers ($10,000)
   c) cash paid to supplier ($7,000)
   d) none of the above

8. A company's Wages expense for the period ended June 30, 1997 was $100,000. Wages Payable increased for the same period by $25,000. How much Cash was paid to employees for the period?
   a) 100,000
   b) 75,000
   c) 25,000
   d) 125,000

Chapter 10: The Statement of Cash Flows

9. In the situation given in question 8, what is the adjustment to Net Income for the Cash Flow from Operating Activities?
    a) 100,000
    b) 75,000
    c) 25,000
    d) 125,000

10. Tommy Lee Inc. makes an investment in Seawatch, a new TV show starring his wife, Pam. The T-accounts are as follows:

Cash Flows from Investing Activites		Long-Term Investments	
		Beg Bal 75,000	
25,000			
3,000		Ending Bal 285,000	

    The entry to reconcile the Investments account should contain which of the following?
    a) Long-Term Investments credited for $210,000
    b) Cash Flows from Investing Activities debited for $210,000
    c) both of the above
    d) none of the above

11. Dino Corporation has an account called Bonds Payable. The company issued the bonds to invest in a new factory. The company made a Cash payment of $80,000. This should be entered on the Statement of Cash Flows as
    a) $80,000 debit to Cash Flows from Investing Activities
    b) $80,000 credit to Cash Flows from Investing Activities
    c) $80,000 debit to Cash Flows from Financing Activities
    d) $80,000 credit to Cash Flows from Financing Activities

12. Soggy Socks, Inc., a laundry service, sold its GE dryer in the hopes of purchasing a new Maytag. They did not have all the money they needed to purchase the new dryer at this time and decided to put the proceeds from the sale of the old dryer into a certificate of deposit at the bank. The gain should be recorded as
    a. a credit to Cash Flows from Operating Activities
    b. a credit to Cash Flows from Financing Activities
    c. a credit to Cash Flows from Investing Activities
    d. none of the above

Chapter 10: The Statement of Cash Flows

13. Which of the following would be an adjustment to cash flows from investing activities?
    a) increase in accounts payable account
    b) loss on marketable securities
    c) sale of equipment
    d) repayment of bonds payable

14. A company's journal entry reads as follows

Cash	$45,000	
Realized Loss on AFS securities	5,000	
Marketable securities		$50,000

    The correct description of this entry when it comes to the Statement of Cash Flows is
    a) Cash Flow from Operating Activities is a debit for $5,000.
    b) Cash Flow from Operating Activities is a credit for $5,000.
    c) Cash Flow from Investing Activities is a credit for $5,000.
    d) Cash Flow from Financing Activities is a debit for $5,000.

15. Shelly Short Company purchased an insurance policy for $42,000 that covered the company's delivery vans for the 6-month period beginning January 15, 1998. The amount of Insurance Expense and Cash Outflow that should be reported in January is
    a) Insurance Expense $42,000/Cash Outflow of $42,000
    b) Insurance Expense $7,000/Cash Outflow of $42,000
    c) Insurance Expense $42,000/Cash Outflow of $7,000
    d) Insurance Expense $7,000/Cash Outflow of $7,000

16. The Handy Dandy Gentlemen's Club recognized a Uniform expense of $30,000 in June to pay for costumes for the exotic dancers. The balance in the company's Uniforms Payable account decreased by $10,000. The amount of cash paid by the company for the costumes was
    a) $30,000
    b) $40,000
    c) $10,000
    d) $20,000

17. Crosswords Weekly collected $400,000 from its customers from 1997. The balance in their Accounts Receivable increased by $120,000. What is the amount of the adjustment to the Statement of Cash Flows from Investing Activities?
    a) $400,000
    b) $120,000
    c) $280
    d) 0

CHAPTER 10: THE STATEMENT OF CASH FLOWS

18. Some Like It Rich sold Marketable Securities for $695,000 in 1997 that were purchased in 1992 for $195,000. How would this be recorded in the Statement of Cash Flows?
    a) ($695,000) Cash from Operating Activities
    b) ($195,000) Cash from Operating Activities
    c) $695,000 Cash from Operating Activities
    d) 195,000 Cash from Operating Activities

19. Which statements are true about the statement of cash flows?
    I. losses are subracted.
    II. non-cash transactions are added
    III. an increase in accounts receivable is subtracted
       a) I, II
       b) II, III
       c) I, III
       d) None of the above

20. The sale of equipment is recorded under
    I. operating activities
    II. investing activities
       a) I
       b) II
       c) both
       d) neither

True or False

1. The following information was recorded for Snappy Jacks in January 1997.

Sale of Equipment	$ 80,000
Decrease in Inventory	100,000
Bad Debt Expense	75,000
Depreciation	30,000
Amortization	5,000
Increase in Accounts Payable	20,000
Increase in Accounts Receivable	10,000
Net Earnings	300,000
Sale of Marketable Securities	400,000

    What was Snappy's Cash Flow from Operating Activities?

Chapter 10: The Statement of Cash Flows

2. From the list below, determine if the item appears on the statement of cash flows under operating, investing or financing activities and whether it is added or subtracted.

   a. Sale of plant assets

   b. Issuing of common stock

   c. Depreciation expense

   d. Payment of long-term debt

   e. Decrease in accounts receivable

   f. Dividends paid

   g. Purchase of long-term investment

   h. Sale of equipment

3. The following information was made available to Connie, the bookkeeper at Rock-A-Buy Limited, a retailer of stone sculpture. Help her set up the statement of cash flows for the year ended 12/31/97.

	12/31/97	12/31/96
Accounts Receivable	600,000	243,000
Accounts Payable	700,000	900,000
Inventory	1,000,250	600,100
Sale of Equipment	2,000,000	
Dividends Paid	60,000	
Depreciation	83,000	
Amortization	6,000	
Net Income	1,250,000	
Loss on Sale of Equipment	300,000	
Bonds Paid	400,000	
Cash Balance		300,000

Chapter 10: The Statement of Cash Flows

4. Use T-accounts to show the following adjustments.

   a. Sold Marketable Securities   120,000

   b. Increase in Accounts Receivable   30,000

   c. Issued Bonds   1,000,000

   d. Gain on Sale of Equipment   40,000

   e. Dividends Paid   6,000

   f. Issued Common Stock   600,000

   g. Increase in Wages Payable   20,000

   h. Decrease in Bond Discount   4,000

5. Wendy Watson, a retail grocer had Bad Debt Expense for the year of $25,000. The T-accounts are shown below.

Cash Flows from Operating Activites		Allowance for Uncollectible	
	10,000	Beg Bal	75,000
107,000			
86,000		Ending Bal	50,000

Accounts Receivable	

   Make the appropriate entries into the T-accounts.

CHAPTER 10: THE STATEMENT OF CASH FLOWS

6. Equipment with a Net Book Value of $437,000 was sold during the year for $450,000. No other purchases or sales were made.

Show the correct journal entry for the transaction and update the following T-accounts.

CASH FLOWS FROM OPERATING ACTIVITES		EQUIPMENT	
	20,000	Beg Bal 1,842,000	
35,000			
		Ending Bal 1,242,000	

CASH FLOWS FROM INVESTING ACTIVITES		ACCUMULATED DEPRECIATION - EQUIPMENT	
		Beg Bal	985,000
		Ending Bal	822,000

Chapter 10: The Statement of Cash Flows

7. Below is the cash flow statement for Robin International. The bookkeeper, Bud, had a problem and could not remember how the statement should look. Correct Bud's mistakes.

Robin International
Statement of Cash Flows
As of December 31, 1999

Operations

Net Income	400,000
Deduct: Depreciation Expense	(185,000)
Bad Debt Expense	(40,000)
Amortization Expense	(20,450)
Decrease in Bond Discount	(4,000)
Decrease in Accounts Receivable	100,000
Increase in Inventory	85,000
Decrease in Prepaid Insurance	10,000
Increase in Accounts Payable	50,000
Increase in Wages Payable	(45,000)
Gain on Sale	6,000
Cash Flow from Operations	356,550

Investing

Purchase of Long Term Investments	(200,000)
Sale of Equipment	95,000
Cash Flow from Investing Activiriesl	(105,000)

Financing

Issuance of Common Stock	65,000
Declaration and payment of dividends	(20,000)
Repayment of Bonds Payable	(50,000)
Sale of Marketable Securities	100,000
Gain on Sale of Marketable Securities	(45,000)
Cash Flow from Financing Activities	50,000
Net Change in Cash	251,550
Cash, Beginning of Year	(175,000)
Cash, End of Year	76,550

Chapter 10: The Statement of Cash Flows

Answers

True or False

1. **False.** Net income from the income statement is shown in cash flows from operating activities. Dividends from the statement of retained earnings is shown in cash flows from financing activities.
2. **True.** Depreciation & amortization are added back to the statement of cash flows.
3. **False.** Gains are non-cash revenues and are therefore subtracted from statement of cash flows.
4. **False.** The transaction must also be recorded in the income from investing activities.
5. **True.** The sale of marketable securities is recorded under income from operating activities and in income from investing activities.
6. **True.** The issuance of common stock is a financing activity because the sale of the stock finances the operations of the company by using the money to buy or upgrade equipment or purchase something needed by the company.
7. **False.** The decrease in the bond discount account will increase the cash flow statement because the transaction that decreased net income.
8. **False.** The cash flow from operating activities would be $457,000, the actual cash received.
9. **False.** The $6,000 change in Interest Payable would be recorded as a decrease under Operating Activities.
10. **True.** Expenses that do not affect cash, must be added back to net income in computing the statement of cash flows.
11. **True.** The statement of cash flows gives a financial user a way to analyze the company's liquidity, solvency and financial flexibility.
12. **False.** The statement of cash flows integrates the information from the balance sheet, the statement of retained earnings and the income statement.
13. **True** The amount of the adjustment to income in the statement of cash flows for inventory should be $117,000, as shown below.

Purchases	340,000
Cost of Goods Sold	-223,000
Change	117,000

14. **False.** The net change in the cash amount was $25,500 as shown below.

Net income from the income statement	66,790	
Net cash flow from operating activities	4,710	
Net cash flow from financing activities	-46,000	
Net increase in cash	25,500	Net Change
Cash balance December 31, 1997	20,600	
Cash balance December 31, 1998	46,100	

15. **False.** The items on the income statement are both cash and non-cash items.

Chapter 10: The Statement of Cash Flows

16. **False.** If the accounts receivable account increases, that means that there were more sales on credit than cash collected from clients.

17. **True.** The statement of cash flows income is increased when a liability increases to account for an expense incurred but not yet paid.

18. **False.** The increase in the equipment account is an adjustment to income from investment activities.

19. **False.** The change in common stock is shown in the section of statement of cash flows for financing activities.

20. **True.** The bad debt expense must be added back to net income because it was deducted from book income.

Multiple Choice Answers

1. **(c)** Accounts receivable is a current asset and therefore accountable under operating activities. The account is a subtraction from net income because no cash has been received as of yet.

2. **(d)** Depreciation and amortization are non-cash items and therefore have no effect on the cash flow.

3. **(b)** The cash outflow would be less the whole amount but the expense would only be for January.

4. **(a)** Operating activities are drawn from the income from operations on the income statement and current assets & liabilities on the balance sheet.

5. **(d)** All.

6. **(b)** Net income would increase by the cash collected from the customers. This would indicate a cash inflow that is not included in the net income on the income statement.

7. **(a)** The correct answer is shown in the table below.

Cost of Goods Sold	-10,000
Increase in Inventory	-5,000
Decrease in Accounts Payable	-2,000
	17,000

8. **(b)**

WAGES EXPENSE	WAGES PAYABLE	CASH
100,000	25,000	
	100,000	75,000
75,000		
	50,000	

9. **(c)** The $25,000 increase in the liability (wages payable) would be added back to the net income because it is the amount of an expense not yet paid which was deducted from the book income.

10. **(d)** Because the long-term investments account has increased, the entry would have to be a debt to long-term investments, so a is not correct. B is not correct because it would be a cash outlay of $210,000 and should be a credit to the cash flow statement.

11. **(d)** Not a or b, because this is a financing activity. Not c, because this is not an increase in cash flows. The answer is d because the decrease in Bonds Payable means that payment was made and therefore a cash outflow.

Chapter 10: The Statement of Cash Flows

12. **(a)** Not b or c, because a gain on sale of equipment is an operating activity. The answer is a, because gains on the sale of equipment are subtracted from cash flows, since they are a non-cash transaction from operating activities.

13. **(c)** Not a, because an increase in accounts payable is an adjustment of operating activities. Not b, because gains and losses are adjustments to operating activities. Not d, because repayment of bonds is an adjustment to financing activities. The answer is c, because the sale of equipment is an investing activity.

14. **(a)** Not b, because the loss is added back. Not c or d, because gains and losses are operating activities. The correct choice is a, because losses, non-cash transactions are added back to net income.

15. **(b)** Not a, because the insurance should be expensed when used not when purchased. Not c, because the cash flow was $42,000. Not d, because the expense is correct but the cash outflow should be the whole $42,000. Therefore, the correct choice is b.

16. **(b)** The correct answer is b - the $30,000 for the period plus the $10,000 owed from the previous period and paid in the current period. Not a, because that represents uniform expense only. Not c, because the decrease in uniform payable of $10,000 only accounts for the cash paid on the costumes owed from the previous paid period. Not d, because the amounts are added not subtracted.

17. **(d)** The adjustment of accounts receivable would be from operating activities, not investing activities.

18. **(b)** Not a or c, the proceeds would be an increase in cash flows from investing activities. Not d, because it is a gain, not a loss. The answer is b - a gain is subtracted from cash flows because it is a non-cash transaction added to net income.

19. **(b)** II & III are both true so the answer is b. Not a, because losses are added, gains are subtracted. Not c, because I is not true.

20. **(c)** The gain or loss will be recorded under cash flows from operating activities and the proceeds from sale will recorded under cash flows from investing activities.

Short Essay Answers

1.

SNAPPY JACKS
Statement of Cash Flows
For the period ended January 31, 1997

Operations	
Net Income	300,000
Increase in Inventory	(100,000)
Add: Bad Debt Expense	75,000
Depreciation Expense	30,000
Amortization Expense	5,000
Increase in Accounts Payable	20,000
Increase in Accounts Receivable	(10,000)
Cash Flows from Operating Activities	320,000

Chapter 10: The Statement of Cash Flows

2.

		Section of Cash Flow Statement	Add/ Subtract
a.	Sale of Plant Assets	Investing	Add
b.	Issuing of Stock	Finance	Add
c.	Depreciation Expense	Operating	Add
d.	Payment of Long Term Debt	Financing	Subtract
e.	Decrease in Accounts Receivable	Operating	Add
f.	Dividends Paid	Finance	Subtract
g.	Purchase of Long Term Investment	Investing	Subtract
h.	Sale of Equipment	Investing	Add

3.

ROCK-A-BUY
Statement of Cash Flows
For the year ended 12/31/97

Operations
Net Income	1,250,000
Add: Depreciation Expense	83,000
Amortization Expense	6,000
Loss on Sale of Equipment	300,000
Increase in Accounts Receivable	(357,000)
Decrease in Accounts Payable	(200,000)
Increase in Inventory	(400,150)
Cash Flows from Operating Activities	681,850

Investing
Sale of Equipment	2,000,000
Cash Flows from Investing Activities	2,000,000

Financing
Dividends Paid	(60,000)
Bonds Repaid	(400,000)
Cash Flows from Financing Activities	(460,000)
Net change in cash	2,221,850
Cash Balance at 12/31/97	300,000
Cash Balance at 12/31/97	2,521,850

Chapter 10: The Statement of Cash Flows

4.

Cash Flows from Operating Activities		Marketable Securities		Accounts Receivable	
	30,000				
	40,000		120,000	30,000	
20,000					
4,000					

Cash Flows from Investing Activities		Bonds Payable		Gain on Sale	
			1,000,000		40,000
120,000					

		Retained Earnings		Common Stock	
		6,000			600,000

Cash Flows from Financing Activities		Wages Payable		Bonds Discounts	
600,000			20,000	4,000	
1,000,000					
	6,000				

5.

Cash flows from Operating Activites		Allowance for Uncollectible	
		Beg Bal	75,000
	10,000		25,000
107,000		50,000	
86,000		Ending Bal	50,000
25,000			

Accounts Receivable	
	50,000

Chapter 10: The Statement of Cash Flows

6.

Cash flows from Operating Activites		Equipment	
		Beg Bal 1,842,000	
35,000	20,000		600,000
		Ending Bal 1,242,000	
	13,000		

Cash flows from Investing Activites		Equipment	
13,000		Beg Bal	985,000
450,000			
		163,000	
		Ending Bal	822,000

Journal entry:

Cash	450,000	
Accumulated Depreciation	163,000	
Equipment		600,000
Gain on Sale		13,000

Chapter 10: The Statement of Cash Flows

7.

Robin International
Statement of Cash Flows
For the year period ended January 31, 1999

Operations		
Net Income	400,000	
Add: Depreciation Expense	**185,000**	Expenses, such as depreciation, etc non-cash
Bad Debt Expense	**40,000**	transactions are added back not subtracted
Amortization Expense	**20,450**	
Decrease in Bond Discount	**4,000**	Decrease in Bond Discount (Non Cash should be added back
Increase in Accounts Receivable	100,000	
Increase in Inventory	**(85,000)**	Increases in assets accounts should be subtracted not added
Decrease in Prepaid Insurance	10,000	
Increase in Acounts Payable	50,000	
Increase in Wages Payable	**45,000**	Increases in Liabilities should be added back not subtracted
Gain on Sale	**(6,000)**	Gains are subtracted; Losses are added
Cash Flows from Operating Activities	763,450	
Investing		
Purchase of Long-Term Investments	(200,000)	
Sale of Equipment	95,000	
Sale of Marketable Securities	**100,000**	Sale of Marketable Securities is an investing activity not a financing activity
Cash Flow from Investing Activities	(5,000)	
Financing		
Issuance of Common Stock	65,000	
Declaration and payment of dividends	(20,000)	
Repaymemt of Bonds Payable	(50,000)	
Gain on Sale of Marketable	(45,000)	
Cash Flow from Financing Activities	(50,000)	
Net Change in Cash	758,450	

ABOUT THE AUTHOR

Stacy S. Brown graduated Magna Cum Laude from the Wharton School of Business at the University of Pennsylvania, earning a Bachelor of Science in Economics with a concentration in accounting. She is currently employed by Coopers & Lybrand, LLP, an international professional services firm, and provides auditing services to a variety of financial services clients, including mutual funds and investment advisers. She recently completed the exam requirement for obtaining her certification as a Public Accountant and participates in a variety of community and professional activities, including her sorority.

LOOKING TO PUT YOUR KNOWLEDGE OF ACCOUNTING TO GOOD USE? VISIT VAULT REPORTS ON THE WEB

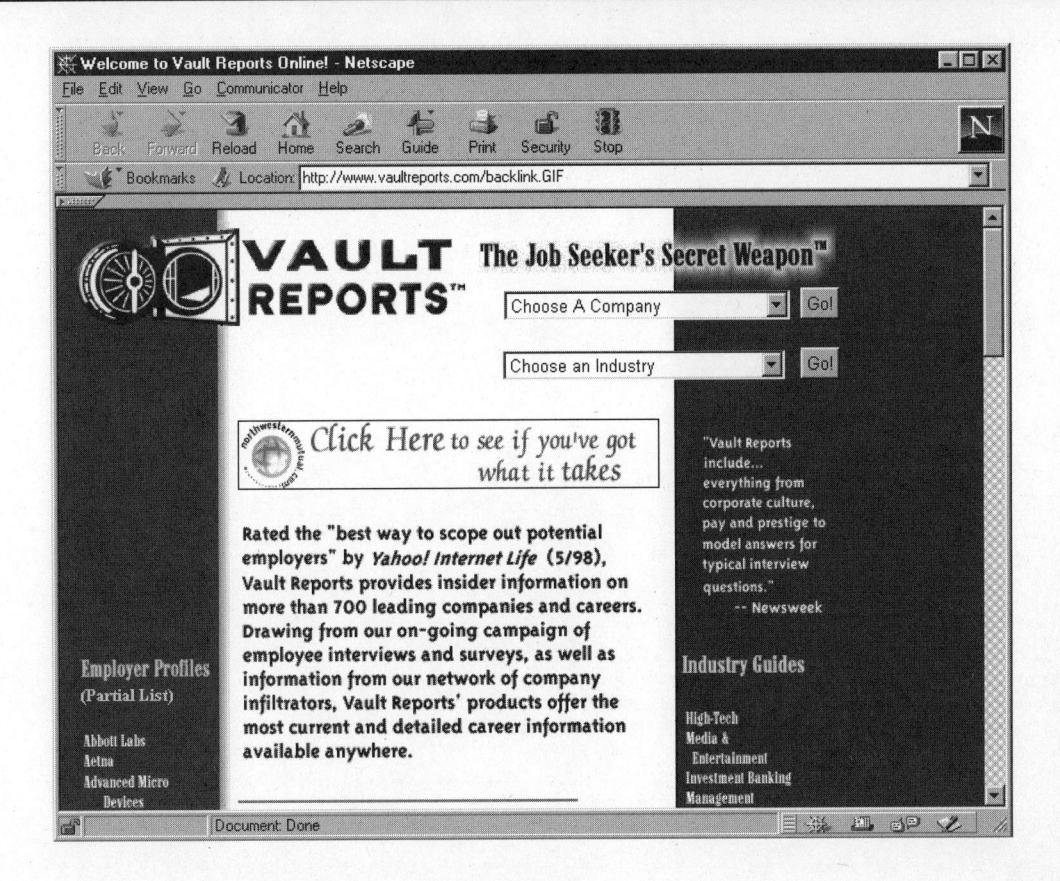

- **EMPLOYER PROFILES**
- **INDUSTRY GUIDES**
- **FREE CAREER NEWSLETTER**
- **EXPERT CAREER ADVICE**
- **CELEBRITY INTERVIEWS AND PROFILES**

www.vaultreports.com

VAULT REPORTS™

NEW EMPLOYER GUIDES BY VAULT REPORTS

VAULT REPORTS™

The first career guides of their kind, **The Job Vault** and Vault Reports' Guides to **High Tech, Law Firms, Media and Entertainment, Management Consulting, Investment Banking,** and **MBA Employers** offer detailed evaluations of America's leading employers. Enriched with responses from thousands of insider surveys and interviews, these guides tell it like it is — the good and the bad — about the companies everyone is talking about. Each guide also includes a complete industry overview. The guides were created by the team that brought you the best-selling **America's Top Internships** and **The Internship Bible**.

The guides review major employers with entries that include:

The Scoop: the juicy details on each company's past, present, and future.

Getting Hired: insider advice on what it takes to get that job offer.

Our Survey Says: thousands of employees speak their mind on company culture, satisfaction, pay, prestige, and more.

As featured in Newsweek & The Wall Street Journal

THE JOB VAULT™

The Job Vault, published by Houghton Mifflin, reviews more than 600 of America's top employers, from the American Broadcasting Company (ABC) to Zeneca, an English pharmaceuticals company with U.S. headquarters in Delaware. The book is also loaded with scores of sidebars offering career advice and inspirational stories of celebs and CEOs.

624pp. • $20.00

GUIDE TO MEDIA AND ENTERTAINMENT™ ('99 Edition)

Reviews America's top employers in the media and entertainment industry, including AOL, Blockbuster, CNN, Dreamworks, Gannett, National Public Radio, Time Warner, and many more! Includes information on the industry's job opportunities, career paths, hiring procedures, culture, pay, and commonly asked interview questions.

225pp. • $35.00

GUIDE TO INVESTMENT BANKING™ ('99 Edition)

Reviews America's top employers in the investment banking industry, including Bankers Trust, Goldman Sachs, JP Morgan, Morgan Stanley, and many more! Includes information on the industry's job opportunities, career paths, hiring procedures, culture, pay, and commonly asked interview questions.

225pp. • $35.00

GUIDE TO HIGH TECH™ ('99 Edition)

Reviews America's top employers in the high tech industry, including Broderbund, Cisco Systems, Hewlett-Packard, Intel, Microsoft, Sun Microsystems, and many more! Includes information on the industry's job opportunities, career paths, hiring procedures, culture, pay, and commonly asked interview questions.

225pp. • $35.00

GUIDE TO MANAGEMENT CONSULTING™ ('99 Edition)

Reviews America's top employers in the management consulting industry, including Andersen Consulting, Boston Consulting, McKinsey, Price Waterhouse, and many more! Includes information on the industry's job opportunities, career paths, hiring procedures, culture, pay, and commonly asked interview questions.

225pp. • $35.00

GUIDE TO MBA EMPLOYERS™ ('99 Edition)

Reviews America's top employers for MBAs, including Fortune 500 corporations, management consulting firms, investment banks, venture capital and LBO firms, commercial banks, and hedge funds. Includes information on the industry's job opportunities, career paths, hiring procedures, culture, pay, and commonly asked interview questions.

300pp. • $35.00

"Don't Interview Naked!"

VAULT REPORTS™

EMPLOYER PROFILES

Detailed, opinionated, and savvy, Vault Reports™ Employer Profiles are 50-to 60-page profiles of America's top employers. Based on Vault Reports' exclusive surveys and interviews with over 100,000 employees and recruiters since 1992, Vault Reports™ Employer Profiles provide the hard-to-get company information that no recruiting brochure would dare reveal. Don't interview without them!™

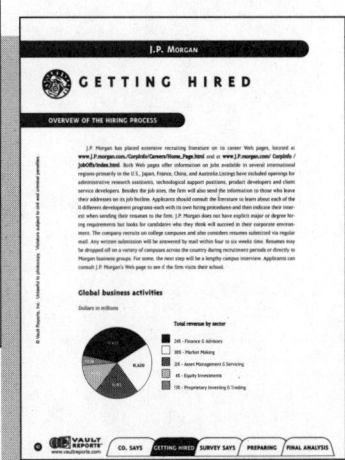

Each Vault Reports™ Employer Profile provides:

- Loads of charts, graphics, and eye-pleasing icons
- Detailed accounts of a company's history and current activities
- Results of our exclusive surveys of company culture and lifestyle
- Intensive preparation for finessing the interview
- Secrets on each company's curveball interview questions
- Insider information on company pay and perks

"The Best Way to Scope Out Potential Employers"
— Yahoo Internet Life

Vault Reports™ Employer Profiles are available for major companies, including:

American Express	Gemini
American Management Systems	General Mills
Andersen Worldwide	Goldman Sachs
Arthur D. Little	Hewlett Packard
AT Kearney	Intel
Bain	JP Morgan
Bankers Trust	KPMG Peat Marwick
Bear Stearns	Lehman Brothers
Booz Allen & Hamilton	McKinsey & Co.
Boston Consulting Group	Mercer
Chase	Merrill Lynch
Citicorp/Citibank	Microsoft
Coopers & Lybrand	Monitor
Credit Suisse First Boston	Morgan Stanley
Deloitte & Touche	Price Waterhouse
Deutsche Morgan Grenfell	Procter & Gamble
Donaldson Lufkin & Jenrette	Salomon Smith Barney
Enron	Walt Disney
Ernst & Young	.... 100s more!
Fidelity	

MANY MORE TITLES AVAILABLE.
VISIT OUR WEB SITE FOR THE MOST CURRENT LIST!

"This place is electric. You come to work and everyone is buzzing with a 'we-kick-butt' attitude, from the mail room guys to the president's office."
— Intel employee, Intel Vault Report

"Goldman Sachs is a golden gig any way you look at it: golden pay, golden prestige, and unfortunately, golden handcuffs."
— Goldman associate, Goldman Vault Report

Per Employer Profile: $25

Call 1-888-JOB-VAULT or visit www.vaultreports.com

Founded by Stanford and Wharton alums, Vault Reports is a New York City-based publishing company dedicated to creating powerful tools for job seekers.

TURBO CHARGE YOUR JOB SEARCH!
VAULT REPORTS RESUME DISTRIBUTION

HAVE YOUR RESUME SENT TO HUNDREDS OF TOP EMPLOYERS THIS WEEK!

Vault Reports Resume Distribution is a painless way for you to get your resume on the desk of hundreds of top employers — virtually overnight. We print your resume and cover letter on bond paper, address it to the appropriate hiring contact, and mail or fax it to the companies that meet your criteria. Our database includes over 10,000 of the nation's top employers with a track record of hiring large numbers of employees. The selection of companies is based on Vault Reports research and includes the best companies in the nation (including companies that don't advertise their job openings).

THE ADVANTAGES OF VAULT REPORTS RESUME DISTRIBUTION INCLUDE:

- Targets your industry and geographical preferences.
- A hassle-free way of reaching 100s of top companies.
- Continuously updated database with accurate contact information.
- Cover letters customized to include contact name, address, and greeting.
- Laser-printed resume and customized cover letter addressed to the hiring manager.

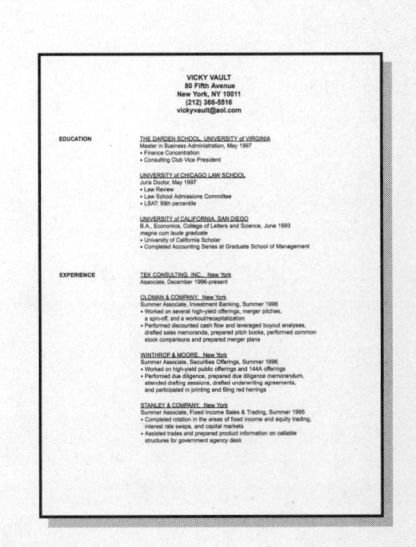

VAULT REPORTS™

To receive a free information packet on Resume Distribution, call 1-888-JOB-VAULT ext. 300 or visit www.vaultreports.com